The Illusions of Entrepreneurship

Scott A. Shane

The Illusions of Entrepreneurship

The Costly Myths That Entrepreneurs, Investors, and Policy Makers Live By

Yale University Press/New Haven & London

Designed by Mary Valencia. Set in Century Old Style type by Technologies 'N Typography.

Printed in the United States of America.

Library of Congress Cataloging-in-Publication Data

Shane, Scott Andrew, 1964–
    The illusions of entrepreneurship : the costly myths that entrepreneurs, investors, and policy makers live by / Scott A. Shane.
        p.   cm.
    Includes bibliographical references and index.
    ISBN 978-0-300-11331-0 (cloth : alk. paper)
    1. Entrepreneurship.   2. New business enterprises.   3. Success in business.
I. Title.
    HB615.S478 2007
    658.1′1—dc22   2007027402

A catalogue record for this book is available from the British Library.

The paper in this book meets the guidelines for permanence and durability of the Committee on Production Guidelines for Book Longevity of the Council on Library Resources.

10 9 8 7 6 5 4 3 2

To Lynne, Ryan, and Hannah

Contents

Acknowledgments

I decided to write this book after having a series of conversations with would-be entrepreneurs, students, government officials, and representatives of major foundations that support economic development activity. While each of these conversations was focused on a different topic, and each had a different purpose, they all had a common theme. The people I spoke with consistently expressed very inaccurate perceptions of what entrepreneurship in America really looks like. Whether they were referring to the number of people who start businesses, how new businesses are typically financed, who starts companies, or the economic impact of start-ups, my counterparts made statement after statement that was factually incorrect.

As a professor, I find it difficult to let incorrect information pass unchallenged, so I asked, "Where did you learn that?" The answers were varied: "in a book," "in a white paper," "in an article," "on the Web." It seemed that no matter where people looked for information about entrepreneurship, much of what they were getting was incorrect. It was then that I realized that I needed to write a book that accurately describes what entrepreneurship, as undertaken by the typical entrepreneur, looks like.

Writing this book turned out to be more difficult than I expected. Not only were there many incorrect statements floating around the Web and in articles in the mainstream press, but many ideas academics had about entrepreneurship turned out to be inconsistent with the facts. In fact, several of my own beliefs turned out to be wrong when I took a careful look at the data.

The result was that my efforts to come up with the answers presented in this book required me to look through many more data sources, articles, and books than I had originally thought necessary. But the effort was worth it. From the process, I learned a lot about entrepreneurship myself, as well as discovering the work of several obscure academic and government researchers who had figured out the right answers to many of the questions about entrepreneurship that most of us have wrong.

I am indebted to the authors of the surveys, research projects, and books and articles that gathered and summarized the answers I present here. While many people were valuable sources for the answers contained in this book, several stand out: Zoltan Acs, Tim Bates, David Blanchflower, Andrew Burke, Arnie Cooper, Marc Cowling, Robert Fairlie, Douglas Holtz-Eakin, Paul Reynolds, and Mark Taylor. The research projects these people conducted, and the books and articles they wrote were crucial to my effort to provide the information about the reality of entrepreneurship.

Writing this book also required me to gain access to sources of data with which I was unfamiliar. I would like to thank several people who helped me to gain access to and analyze these data, in particular Jon Eckhardt, Rob Fairlie, Brian Headd, Ying Lowery, and Paul Reynolds.

My work on this book was helped immensely because I had the great fortune of serving as the principal investigator on the Kauffman Firm Survey, a national probability sample of businesses founded in the United States in 2004. In addition to having access to the data from this survey, I had the opportunity to work with Alyse Freilich of the Kauffman Foundation and with Janice Ballou, Dave DesRoches, and Frank Potter of Mathematica Policy Research, Inc. I learned a great deal about researching entrepreneurship by working with them.

Over the years, a number of my colleagues have taught me a great deal about the topics discussed in this book. Howard Aldrich, Per Davidsson, Frederic Delmar, Jon Eckhardt, Bill Gartner, Dave Hsu, and Nicos Nicolaou stand out as particularly important. My colleagues at Case Western Reserve University, particularly Sue Helper and Jim Rebitzer, generously gave their time to discuss many of the ideas in this book with me. This book would not have been possible without their help.

Nicos Nicolaou, Frederic Delmar, Bill Gartner, and Dave Hsu read and commented on the entire draft of the book. Their comments were invaluable in helping me to refine my arguments. My editor, Michael O'Malley, went over the manuscript with a surgeon's precision. His insightful comments helped me to clarify key points in the book.

Lastly, I would like to thank my wife Lynne, daughter Hannah, and son Ryan, each of whom helped me as I worked on this book, Hannah and Ryan by being excellent playmates when I needed breaks from writing, and Lynne by encouraging and supporting my efforts to create this book.

Introduction

Entrepreneurship is one of the most popular topics of our time. If you enter the word *entrepreneur* into the Google search engine, you will get more than 76,500,000 hits. This is far more than the 43,800,000 you will get if you search another popular keyword—*sex*. Clearly there is a lot of information out there about entrepreneurship. Yet, here I am, adding another book to the mix. Why?

The reason is that we are surrounded by myths about entrepreneurship. When I say myths, you probably know what I mean: there's the story about the penniless high-school dropout who comes to America with $10 in his pocket and starts a construction company that makes him a multimillionaire, or there's the one about the engineers who invent an Internet phone, get some venture capital, and build a billion-dollar company.

Most people like these myths. Some of them appeal to our love of the heroic, like the Horatio Alger stories that describe people who overcome great odds to become successful. Others appeal to our sense of voyeurism, giving us a window on a life that seems exciting and exotic. And because we like hearing these myths, we tell them and retell them, and write them down in articles and books. When people write books and articles recounting these myths, other people buy them, leading to a self-perpetuating cycle of more authors writing down similar myths.

The result of all this telling and retelling is that myths about entrepreneurship pervade all kinds of media, from television to radio to newspapers to the World Wide Web. Millions of Web pages, tens of thousands of books, and hundreds of thousands of articles about entrepreneurship tell the stories of the meteoric growth of start-up companies. Television and the radio profiles describe entrepreneurs, the businesses they start, and the impact they have, all in ways consistent with our myths.

This book is different. Rather than offering the myths that most people believe, this book looks at data on entrepreneurship. And not just any data. Good data. Data that come from studies of representative samples of the population, conducted by academic and government researchers at places like the University of Chicago and the University of Michigan, the Census Bureau and the Bureau of Labor Statistics, places that have a reputation for gathering facts carefully and precisely to ensure their accuracy.[1]

In this book I use these data to challenge the myths about entrepreneurship and describe the phenomenon as it really occurs. In these pages I will paint a picture of the typical entrepreneur in America, what he does and how he does it, and will describe what the typical start-up looks like and what impact that business has on the U.S. economy. (I use "he" to refer to entrepreneurs because the typical entrepreneur is male.) This book may not make you feel as good as those myth books about entrepreneurship, but it will be more helpful.

What Is Entrepreneurship?

People define entrepreneurship in different ways. To some people entrepreneurship means to act in a way that is innovative, creative, and oriented toward growth or opportunity. For instance, to some authors, there are corporate entrepreneurs, people who pursue new business opportunities within established corporations, like managers at Intel Capital, the semiconductor firm's internal venture capital arm; social entrepreneurs, people who found new nonprofit organizations, religions, or social movements, like L. Ron Hubbard; and people who just act "entrepreneurially," like my four-year-old daughter who realizes that getting a cookie depends on creative and innovative thinking to overcome the obstacles imposed by mommy and daddy.

I use much simpler definitions of *entrepreneur* and *entrepreneurship* in this book, the ones most closely aligned with common sense. *Entrepreneurship* is, as noted in the Merriam-Webster Online Dictionary, "the activity of organizing, managing, and assuming the risks of a business or enterprise."[2] An *entrepreneur* is a person who engages in these activities.

This definition isn't far off of other popular definitions of the word. For instance, Wikipedia defines entrepreneurship as "the practice of starting new organizations, particularly new businesses, generally in response to identified opportunities."[3] So when you think about entrepreneurs while reading this book, think of people who found new businesses, not people who found new religions, social movements, or corporate ventures, or people who are just acting creatively. Those might be interesting people to know more about, but they aren't the topic of this book.

Our Image of Entrepreneurship

Our myths tell us that "entrepreneurs are . . . a rare breed,"[4] "a kind of genius who is born, not made,"[5] which gives us a very inaccurate image of what the typical entrepreneur is like. Some people think that the typical entrepreneur is a jet-setting, Silicon Valley–residing engineer who, along with a couple of his buddies, has raised millions of dollars of venture capital to start a new company to make a patent-protected gizmo. This company will, of course, employ thousands of people, go public in four years, and generate huge gobs of money for its founders and investors.

The reality couldn't be more different. First, entrepreneurship is as a very common vocation, much more common than our myths suggest.[6] Take a look at the numbers:

- 11.1 percent of U.S. households have a self-employed head.[7]
- 11.3 percent of households own a business.[8]
- Business owners compose 13 percent of the nonagricultural labor force.[9]
- In 2005, approximately 13 percent of people in the United States between the ages of 18 and 74 were in the process of starting a business.[10]

In fact, each year in the United States, more people start a business than get married or have children.[11] And as much as 40 percent of the U.S. population will be self-employed for some part of their work life![12]

Just as entrepreneurship is much more common than most of us think, the typical entrepreneur is very different from our stereotypical image. The typical American entrepreneur is a married white man in his forties who attended but did not complete college. He lives in a place like Des Moines or Tampa, where he was born and has lived much of his life. His new business is a low-tech endeavor, like a construction company or an auto repair shop, in an industry where he has worked for years. The business that the typical entrepreneur has started is a sole proprietorship financed with $25,000 of his savings and maybe a bank loan that he guarantees personally. The typical entrepreneur has no plans to employ lots of people or to make lots of money. He just wants to earn a living and support his family. In short, the typical entrepreneur is your neighbor—he's the entrepreneur next door.

So What If People Believe the Myths?

Does it matter if your image of the typical entrepreneur is incorrect and that most of what you read about entrepreneurship is a myth? That depends. If you approach what you read about entrepreneurship in the same way you think about a good novel—as a work of fiction—then it doesn't matter. But many people think of these myths as nonfiction. They take as gospel an inaccurate and romanticized view of who entrepreneurs are, what they do, and the impact they have. And they act on their beliefs. When people act on fiction thinking it is reality, they often get hurt and also harm those around them.

One of the ways that believing myths about entrepreneurship can hurt you and people close to you is through your assessment of the odds of success. If you are thinking of starting a new business, then you should have the information you need to weigh the probabilities correctly. That way you can make an informed decision about your true odds of success. You don't want to base your decision on mistaken beliefs.

This is true of any risky decision. Think about having surgery. If you have cancer and your doctor tells you that you need surgery, you want to know what the odds are that surgery will get rid of the cancer and return you to good health. You don't want a doctor telling you, "Oh, you'll be fine; the surgery is nothing" when it has a 10 percent success rate.

Likewise, when you start a business, you need to know what the odds are for your success. Although it might make you feel all warm and fuzzy inside to read that most entrepreneurs are financially successful, this information won't help you make an informed decision. To make an informed decision about starting a new business, you need to know that the typical start-up ceases operations within five years, and that the entrepreneur who manages to keep his new business alive for ten years actually earns less money than he would have earned by working for someone else (although a small number of entrepreneurs earn much more than they would have earned working for others; see chapter 6). After all, you might have to decide whether it is wise to take out a second mortgage on your house or to quit a good job in order to start a company.

Very few people who are thinking of becoming entrepreneurs or who are financing them are looking to fail. Most people who start or finance new businesses aim to succeed, which brings us to the next reason why you need to understand the reality of entrepreneurship—so you can increase the odds that the company that you start or invest in will be successful.

Studies have shown that successful entrepreneurs do a lot of things differently from failed entrepreneurs. Knowing what these things are will help you succeed. But knowing what makes some entrepreneurs successful isn't easy. You can't just ask other entrepreneurs as the typical one is a failed entrepreneur. What he does *lowers* a new business's chance of success. To figure out what you should do; you need to look hard to find the information about what makes a start-up successful.

Myths about entrepreneurship make finding this information difficult for two reasons. First, the myths imply that many things that actually matter for success really don't matter. For instance, the myths about entrepreneurship tell you that how much money you start with, or the industry in which your business operates, or the legal form of your business, or how many employees you have when you start, or what strategy you adopt don't matter for success. But as it turns out, they matter a lot. Believing the myths might keep you from doing the things that you need to do to succeed.

Second, the myths tell you that many things that actually don't matter will make a difference in terms of the success of a start-up. For instance, the myths about entrepreneurship maintain that having persistence, being self-confident, and being a leader will make you a successful entrepreneur. But there's no good evidence that new businesses founded by people with these characteristics perform any better than other start-ups. Believing these myths might focus your attention on the very things that you shouldn't spend your time on.

Regardless of whether you are planning to start a business or finance one, it's important for you to know the reality of entrepreneurship. In fact, you need to know the reality just to be an informed citizen. The myths about entrepreneurship are so strong that, as citizens, we have fashioned our public policies around them. Much of American society believes that start-ups are a magic bullet that will transform depressed economic regions, create a lot of jobs, generate innovation, and conduct all sorts of other economic wizardry. And so, as a society, we encourage these activities through policies that providing transfer payments, loans, subsidies, regulatory exemptions, and tax benefits to people who start businesses. Any businesses.

Unfortunately, the truth is that entrepreneurship is not a panacea. Start-ups create far fewer jobs and generate a lot less economic growth than most people think. Moreover, only a small sliver of new businesses, the ones with the very highest potential for success, create the new jobs and the economic growth. So if you are a policy maker tasked with coming up with an economic development policy—or just a concerned citizen being asked to vote for that policy—you need to know what the typical start-up can and can't do for us. Making policy decisions on the basis of myths about the impact of start-ups leads to a lot of wasted resources and bad incentives.

Who Should Read This Book?

If you're a policy maker interested in encouraging more people to become entrepreneurs, or you're thinking of becoming an entrepreneur yourself, or you're just an interested citizen who thinks that start-ups are a good thing, you need to know the facts about entrepreneurship. Knowing the facts and correcting the myths will help you to make informed decisions about starting companies, financing them, encouraging their formation, and a host of other important issues. The information in this book will help you to get the facts right and disabuse you of many of the myths about entrepreneurship.

What Questions Does This Book Address?

No book can correct every myth about entrepreneurship, and this book is no exception. In this book I am going to address the myths that have emerged as answers to the questions about entrepreneurship that people ask most often. Things like:

- Are we living in a more entrepreneurial era than in the past?
- What makes some places more entrepreneurial than others?

- What industries are popular for start-ups?
- Why do people start businesses?
- What characteristics does the typical entrepreneur have?
- What does the typical new business look like?
- How do entrepreneurs finance the typical start-up?
- How well does the typical start-up perform?
- How many jobs do start-ups create?

Be prepared for the answers to these questions. If you are like most people, you will probably be surprised by them. The popular wisdom on many of these questions is dead wrong.

For Instance?

I want to get you to keep reading, so let me tell you a few things about entrepreneurship that might surprise you:

- America is becoming less entrepreneurial; a smaller proportion of the population starts businesses today than did so in 1910.
- The United States isn't a very entrepreneurial country; Peruvians are three-and-a-half times as likely as Americans to start their own businesses.
- Entrepreneurs are more likely to start businesses in less attractive, run-of-the-mill industries, like construction or retail trade, than they are to start businesses in more attractive, glitzy technology-based industries.
- The most common reason why people start businesses is to avoid working for others.
- People who change jobs often, who are unemployed, and who make less money are more likely than other people to start their own businesses.
- The typical start-up isn't innovative, has no plans to grow, has one employee, and generates less than $100,000 in revenue.
- Only one-third of people who start businesses manage to get a new business "up and running" within seven years.
- The typical start-up is capitalized with $25,000, taken primarily from the founder's savings.
- The typical entrepreneur works more hours but earns less money than he would have earned had he worked for someone else.

• Start-ups create fewer jobs than most people think; only 1 percent of people work in companies less than two years old, while 60 percent work in companies more than ten years old.

These are just a few of the realities of entrepreneurship. If as a would-be entrepreneur or start-up investor you're intrigued, read on; forewarned is forearmed.

1

America: Land of Entrepreneurship in an Entrepreneurial Era?

Suppose you're a policy maker interested in encouraging more people to become entrepreneurs, or you're thinking of becoming an entrepreneur yourself, or you're just an interested citizen who thinks start-ups are a good thing. You might want to understand some basic facts about entrepreneurship in America. Things like: Do Americans start a lot of companies? Are more people starting companies than used to? Why do some places have more start-ups than others? The answers to these questions will tell you where and when new companies are created and what factors affect their formation.

You soon realize that finding answers to these questions is pretty easy. Policy makers and entrepreneurs, investors and interested observers—they know the answers, and they're willing to tell you. They say that the world of big companies is over. More and more people are becoming entrepreneurs every year because people, fed up with a lack of job security and with a desire to do their own thing, are fleeing from the corporate world and starting businesses in ever-increasing numbers. In fact, your spin around the World Wide Web and your look in your local bookstore quickly tells you that:

- "Over the past decade or so, the emergence of a new entrepreneurial economy in America has begun. There has been significant growth in entrepreneurial start-ups and small businesses now are the engine of this economy."[1]

• "Observers comparing the U.S. economy to the economies of other countries often note that Americans seem much more willing to become entrepreneurs."[2]

• "We are in the midst of the largest entrepreneurial surge this country has ever seen."[3]

Everyone seems to be giving the same answer, and so it seems it must be true. But a little voice inside is nagging you, asking where's the data that backs up these views? If everyone has the same answers, then surely you should be able to find the data to support them.

Unfortunately, the policy makers and the pundits, the entrepreneurs and the experts don't give you the data. In fact, everyone's so convinced that these experts are right that no one has bothered to check the data to see if their answers are correct. If you dug a little deeper and found the data, you'd be surprised. The commonly accepted answers to these questions turn out to be incorrect. The received wisdom about trends in business formation, about how entrepreneurial America is, and about what leads places to have a lot of start-ups is wrong.

Let's take a closer look.

The Number of Entrepreneurs Isn't Growing

The proportion of the U.S. population that is starting businesses isn't growing; in fact, it might be shrinking. The data show that the rate of entrepreneurship in this country has been flat or declining over the past twenty years. For example, the Survey of Consumer Finances, a survey administered every three years by the Federal Reserve's Board of Governors to a representative sample of American households, measures a snapshot of the finances of American households at a moment in time. The results show that the proportion of America households owning a business declined from 14.2 percent in 1983 to 11.5 percent in 2004.[4]

But since so many people believe that this is the most entrepreneurial era in American history, you need to be really sure of the data before you give up the idea. Besides, business ownership might not be the right measure of entrepreneurial activity because it includes business owners who started their companies quite a while ago rather than just those people who are starting new businesses now.

Here is another measure: since the mid-1990s, Paul Reynolds, a business demographer and sociologist at Florida International University, has examined the number of people who are starting new businesses in the United States every year. Using data collected from a representative sample of people between the ages of 18 and 70, Reynolds measures something that he calls "total entrepreneurial activity," which combines the number people who are in the process of starting a business every year with people who own and manage a business started in the previous three-and-a-half years. Professor Reynolds's total entrepreneurial activity measure shows that entrepreneurial activity in this country was essentially constant from 1998 through 2006.[5]

Unfortunately, Reynolds' data don't go back much further (he gathered data in a couple of other years but he used slightly different methods to gather them), so his measures can't be used to give us a long-term estimate of trends in new business formation in the United States. But we can look at other data to try to tease out the longer-term patterns.

The U.S. Small Business Administration (SBA) provides one source of data on this question. The SBA measures the number of new "employer firms" created every year. (An employer firm is a business that has at least one employee.) To use the SBA data on the number of new employer firms created every year to measure the rate of new business formation annually, we need to normalize it by dividing it by the U.S. population, which grows every year. Figure 1.1 shows the birth of new employer firms measured on a per capita basis. It reveals that the per capita rate of new employer business formation in the United States declined from 1990 to 1992, then rose until the mid-1990s, subsequently declined until 2002, and has since increased from the lows of that year.

But new employer businesses are only a small fraction (roughly 25 percent) of the new businesses founded in the United States because three-quarters of all new businesses have no employees. Therefore, we might want to look at another measure of entrepreneurship—self-employment—to confirm that start-up rates are not increasing over time. The Bureau of Labor Statistics and the Census Bureau measure how much of the labor force is self-employed every year through their Current Population Survey. This survey asks people to identify their status in the workforce as "out of the workforce," "wage employed," "unemployed," or "self-employed."

The statistical agencies actually measure two types of self-employment: unincorporated self-employment and incorporated self-employment. The former being people who are self-employed and who

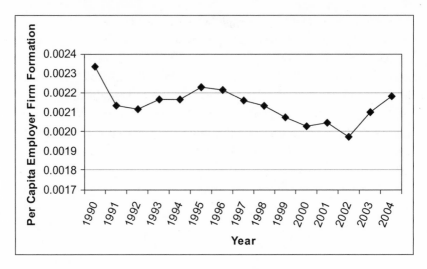

Figure 1.1. Per Capita Number of Employer Businesses Founded in the United States Annually, 1990–2004
Source: Adapted from data from the U.S. Bureau of the Census and the U.S. Small Business Administration, accessed at www.sba.gov/advo/research/data.html and www.census.gov/population/www/index.html.

do not report that they run a corporation, the latter being self-employed owners of a corporation. Neither measure suggests that the rate of entrepreneurship is increasing in the United States. The rate of unincorporated self-employment was basically unchanged during the 1980s and first half of the 1990s and has been declining ever since (see figure 1.2).[6]

However, these data do not take into account the 3 percent of the work force composed of self-employed people who run incorporated businesses and so might undercount enterpreneurs.[7] To get an accurate picture of the self-employed, we also need to look at data on this group of people. When we put together the data on incorporated and unincorporated self-employed, the trend in self-employment appears to be flat: incorporated self-employment is on a slight upward trend, but that trend is largely offset by the downward trend in the unincorporated self-employed (see figure 1.3).

The Bureau of Labor Statistics has been gathering self-employment data annually using a similar methodology for the past couple of decades. Therefore, we can produce nice figures tracking the rate of self-

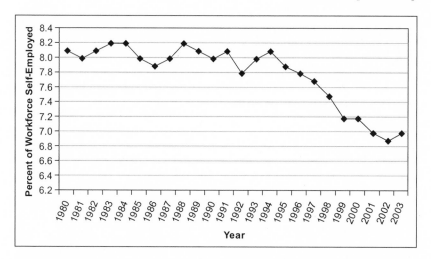

Figure 1.2. The Unincorporated Self-Employment Rate in the United States, over Time

Source: Adapted from the Office of Advocacy, U.S. Small Business Administration, *The Small Business Economy* (Washington, D.C.: U.S. Government Printing Office, 2004).

employment annually over the 1980s and 1990s. This trend, however, is not new. If we go back to 1948, the first year for which we have annual data on the unincorporated nonagricultural self-employment rate, we can see that it was then 12 percent of the labor force, much higher than it is today. In fact, the nonagricultural self-employment rate in 2004 was 58 percent of what it was in 1948.[8] Moreover, we can look at census data on self-employment going back to 1910. Economists who have looked at this historical data (which is less reliable than the data collected from 1948 to today) have found that the self-employment rate in the United States was much higher in 1910 than it was in 2004.[9] In short, the rate of self-employment in the United States has been declining for many decades.

This declining rate is not unique to the United States. The story is the same in other Organization for Economic Cooperation and Development (OECD) countries (Australia, Austria, Belgium, Canada, Czech Republic, Denmark, Finland, France, Germany, Greece, Hungary, Iceland, Ireland, Italy, Japan, Korea, Luxembourg, Mexico, Netherlands, New Zealand, Norway, Poland, Portugal, Slovak Republic, Spain, Sweden, Switzerland, Turkey, United Kingdom, and the United States). The

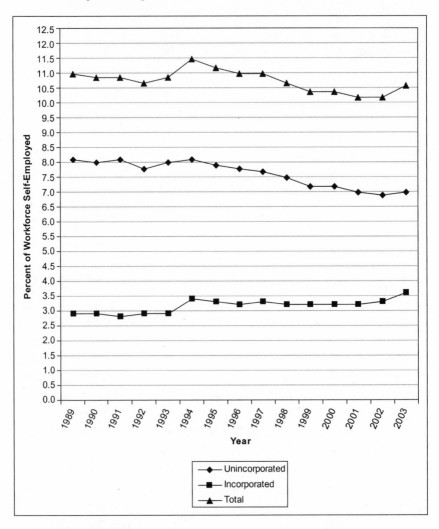

Figure 1.3. Incorporated, Unincorporated, and Total Self-Employment, over Time
   Source: Adapted from S. Hipple, "Self-Employment in the United States: An Update,"
Monthly Labor Review, July 2004, 13–23.

trends in self-employment rates from 1955 to 2002 go in a downward direction in all of the OECD countries except Portugal, New Zealand, and
the United Kingdom.[10]

   A last bit of data looks at different cohorts of people—people who
graduated from school in the same year—to see how their rate of self-

employment changes over time. These cohort studies show virtually no movement in self-employment rates. For example, one careful study examined the National Graduates Survey in Canada. This survey polled a representative sample of college graduates in Canada who finished school in 1982, 1986, 1990, and 1995. The data indicate that the different cohorts all have the same likelihood of being self-employed at two and five years after graduation, despite the economic, political, and social changes that occurred in Canada between 1982 and 2000.[11]

So what's the message here? Regardless of whether you measure entrepreneurship as people who are starting a business, new employer firms, or incorporated and unincorporated self-employment, there has been no trend toward increasing entrepreneurship in the United States (or most other developed nations) over the past twenty years. Contrary to the opinions of many people, we have not entered a more entrepreneurial era of history.

The United States Is Less Entrepreneurial Than You Think

Everyone says that the United States is one of the most entrepreneurial countries in the world—a place where a larger portion of the population starts or owns his own business than in virtually any other country in the world. Do the data agree?

They don't. For all the talk about how often Americans start businesses, we do it a lot less often than people in other countries. Measured by the rate at which people go to work for themselves, Turks are four times as likely as Americans to start their own businesses. Measured by the percentage of the working-age population in the process of starting a business or owning and operating a new business founded in the past three-and-a-half years, Peruvians are three-and-a-half times as likely as Americans to become entrepreneurs.[12] In fact, whether we measure entrepreneurship by the percentage of the population that is self-employed or as the percentage of the population that is in the process of starting a new business, the United States is nowhere near the top group of nations. Don't believe me? Take a look at the data in table 1.1, which shows that the United States is close to the bottom of the pack of OECD countries on the rate of self-employment in both 1992 and 2002.

Table 1.1 Self-Employment Rate in OECD Countries

Country	2002	1992
Turkey	30.0	29.7
Mexico	29.2	32.9
Korea	28.1	26.7
Portugal	24.5	26.5
Italy	23.6	23.8
Poland	22.6	30.0
New Zealand	18.9	19.1
Spain	17.8	19.7
Ireland	17.0	21.2
Iceland	16.5	17.8
Belgium	14.5	14.1
Australia	13.5	14.6
Finland	12.3	13.8
United Kingdom	11.2	12.9
Netherlands	10.8	9.5
Japan	10.8	13.5
Austria	10.5	10.2
Germany	9.9	8.2
Sweden	9.7	8.8
Canada	9.7	9.2
France	8.8	12.3
Denmark	8.0	9.0
United States	7.2	8.6
Norway	6.8	9.0
Luxembourg	6.1	8.4

Source: OECD Labour Force Statistics. http://www1.oecd
.org/scripts/cde/members/LFSDATAAuthenticate.asp (accessed
on October 2, 2006).

The United States is also in the bottom third of countries when measured by the number of young businesses per capita, the proportion of the population that owns and manages a business that has been in operation for at least three-and-a-half years (see table 1.2). Moreover, the United States is right in the middle of the countries when it comes to new business formation per capita, the proportion of the population that owns and manages a business that has been in operation for at least three months.

Clearly, the myth is wrong. Americans aren't among the most likely in the world to start businesses. Far from it.

Table 1.2 New and Young Business Ownership by Percent of Population

Country	New and Young Businesses	New Businesses	Young Businesses
Thailand	27.20	13.10	14.10
China	22.60	9.40	13.20
New Zealand	20.80	10.00	10.80
Greece	12.10	1.60	10.50
Brazil	18.30	8.20	10.10
Switzerland	13.40	3.70	9.70
Australia	14.30	4.70	9.60
Jamaica	16.20	6.70	9.50
Venezuela	16.10	7.50	8.60
Finland	10.50	1.90	8.60
Ireland	12.80	4.70	8.10
Spain	11.10	3.40	7.70
Canada	11.00	3.60	7.40
Norway	12.50	5.20	7.30
Iceland	10.00	2.70	7.30
Italy	8.70	2.30	6.40
Sweden	8.80	2.50	6.30
Slovenia	7.70	1.40	6.30
Netherlands	7.60	1.90	5.70
Belgium	6.80	1.20	5.60
Japan	6.50	1.10	5.40
United Kingdom	8.00	2.90	5.10
Argentina	8.90	3.90	5.00
Latvia	7.80	2.80	5.00
United States	9.90	5.20	4.70
Singapore	8.40	3.70	4.70
Denmark	6.80	2.40	4.40
Germany	6.90	2.70	4.20
Chile	9.10	5.30	3.80
Austria	6.20	2.40	3.80
Croatia	6.20	2.50	3.70
France	3.00	0.70	2.30
Hungary	2.80	0.80	2.00
Mexico	3.30	1.40	1.90
South Africa	3.00	1.70	1.30

Source: Adapted from the Global Entrepreneurship Monitor, Global 2005 Executive Report, (Accessed http://www.gemconsortium.org/category_list.asp?cid=179 October 2, 2006).

Why Do Some Countries Have More Start-Ups Than Others?

The data clearly show that new business formation is much more common in some countries than in others. For example, at any given point in time, only about 3 percent of the working-age population in Japan is starting a business, while in Thailand almost three times as many people (20 percent of the working-age population) are starting a business.[13]

Moreover, this isn't a one-year aberration. As we saw earlier for the United States, a country's rate of new business formation tends to change very little from year to year. That is, places that have a lot of people starting companies in one year tend to have a lot of people starting companies in the next year, whereas countries with few people starting companies at one point in time tend to have few people starting companies at other points in time.[14]

Why is starting a company more common in some countries than in others? People have offered a lot of explanations. Some explanations focus on taxes, regulations, access to capital, legal systems, and property rights;[15] others revolve around culture or attitudes. The French, for instance, are believed to be too interested in drinking wine and arguing about politics to start companies, while the Japanese are all just "salary men," too buttoned down to start their own businesses.

Although these things might matter, they aren't the primary explanation for why some countries have so many start-ups and others do not. If you leave all of the armchair experts' explanations aside and look at the data, you may be surprised. The key factor that explains the rate at which people start businesses is a country's wealth. But the direction of this relationship isn't the way people might expect: the wealthier a country is (the higher its per capita gross domestic product), the *lower* is its rate of self-employment, and the smaller the percentage of its working-age population that is in the process of starting a business or has recently started a business at a given point in time.[16] In fact, data from the Global Entrepreneurship Monitor, a survey of new business formation by people between the ages of 18 and 68 in 44 countries from 2000 to 2004 indicates that developing countries have a much higher rate of new business creation than developed countries. For example, the percentage of the working-age population in Peru, Uganda, Ecuador and Venezuela starting businesses is more than twice that of the United States.[17]

What's going on here? Why do richer countries have fewer people starting businesses than poorer ones? Economists have examined this question, and they have an answer. As countries become wealthier, the average wage paid to workers goes up. These wage increases encourage business owners to use machines to replace work that used to be done by hand. Capital (the machinery) is subject to greater economies of scale—the reduction in the cost of production that comes from generating things in higher volume—than labor. As a result, the increased use of capital leads companies to grow in size. For these companies to get bigger, people have to quit working for themselves and go to work for other people instead. This shift from self-employment to wage employment that occurs as countries get richer drives down the percentage of the population that is starting companies at any point in time.[18]

Moreover, when countries get wealthier and real wages (wages net of the effects of inflation) rise, the opportunity cost of running your own business goes up because the amount of money that you could have earned working for someone else increases. This increased opportunity cost leads more people to go to work for others than was the case when real wages were lower. As a result, the proportion of the population starting companies decreases.[19]

Finally, as countries get richer, they change where economic value is created; first from agriculture to manufacturing, and then from manufacturing to services. As the source of economic value shifts toward activities where self-employment is less common, like manufacturing, from activities where self-employment is more common, like agriculture, the proportion of people running their own businesses drops.[20] In fact, the shift from a primarily agricultural economy to a more manufacturing-based one leads to a large reduction in the proportion of the population that works for itself because farmers usually run their own businesses, whereas manufacturing workers do not.[21]

The data show that as countries reduce their reliance on agriculture as a source of economic value, the proportion of their population engaged in entrepreneurship—whether measured by self-employment or by starting a business at a point in time—goes down. For example, in the United States, the decline in the importance of agriculture to the overall economy led to a decline in the unincorporated self-employment rates from 12 percent in 1948 to 7.5 percent in 2003.[22]

The relation between value-added in agriculture and the proportion

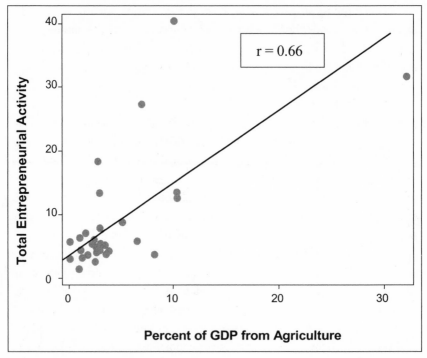

Figure 1.4. The Correlation across Countries between the Percentage of Value-Added in Agriculture and Total Entrepreneurial Activity in 2004
   Source: Calculated from data from the Global Entrepreneurship Monitor and the World Development Report.

of the population engaged in agriculture means that countries that are more reliant on agriculture tend to have more people running their own businesses than those that are less reliant on agriculture. The correlation between the percentage of a country's gross domestic product that comes from agriculture (as measured by the World Bank) and the country's total entrepreneurial activity (TEA) as measured by the Global Entrepreneurship Monitor can be seen in figure 1.4. The vertical axis shows a country's TEA (the numerator in this proportion is composed of people who are in the process of starting a business, as well as people who are owner-operators of a business founded in the past three-and-a-half years; the denominator is the working-age population.) The horizontal axis shows the percentage of the country's economic activity (value-added) generated by agriculture. The line through the graph shows the fitted values for the correlation. (A correlation is a measure of how similar two things are to each other; a correlation of 1.0 means that the patterns are exactly the same.) The correlation between the two sets of values is 0.66, a pretty strong relationship.[23]

If you reflect on what this means, it seems to contradict what you read in the newspaper. The United States is a middling nation in terms of its level of new business creation, put to shame by entrepreneurial powerhouses like Turkey and Peru. And, we know why these powerhouses create so many more new companies than we do: they are poorer and more reliant on agriculture.

Differences in Start-Up Rates within Countries

Not only are there differences in start-up rates between countries, but within one country rates of firm formation and self-employment often vary between regions.[24] For example, self-employment rates in the north of Great Britain are 25 percent lower than the national average, while those in the southwest average 28 percent higher than the national average.[25] In Canada, self-employment rates are lower in the Atlantic provinces than in the rest of the country.[26] These patterns are also present in the United States, where more of the population is self-employed in the West of the United States than in the Northeast, Midwest, or South (see figure 1.5).[27] (Similar though less pronounced patterns are also seen when you look at the number of new employer firms created per capita.)[28]

Of course regional variation in the rates at which people start businesses shouldn't be surprising to you if you've read anything about this topic. It is commonly understood that entrepreneurs create new businesses at a higher rate in some parts of the country than in others. Many articles, books, and Web blogs mention Silicon Valley; Route 128; the Research Triangle; Austin, Texas; Seattle, Washington; and other "entrepreneurial" parts of the United States. There's only one problem with the information we have: these places aren't the ones with the high start-up rates.

Don't believe me? Take a look at the data on the different states. What state do you think had the most people going to work for themselves in 2005? If you guessed California, home to Silicon Valley, you'd be

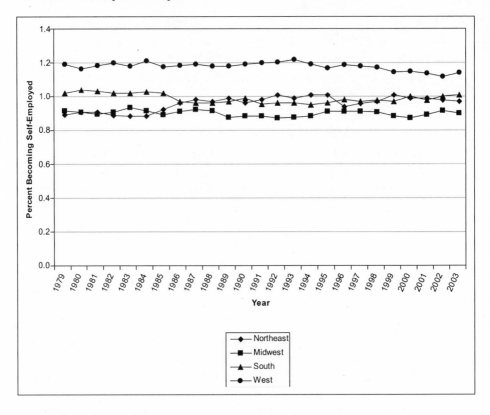

Figure 1.5. Percent of the U.S. Population Becoming Self-employed, by Region
Source: Adapted from R. Fairlie, "Self-Employed Business Ownership Rates in the United States, 1979–2003," *Report for the U.S. Small Business Administration,* Contract Number SBA-HQ04-M0248, 2004.

wrong. If you guessed Massachusetts, home to the Route 128 phenomenon, you'd be wrong again. How about Washington, home to Seattle and the Microsoft millionaires? Strike three. The answer is Vermont. In 2005, Vermont had the most people transitioning into self-employment of any state, with that transition occurring at a pace more than three times the rate of transition into self-employment in Delaware, the state with the lowest rate of transition to self-employment in that year.[29]

This is not just an artifact of looking at self-employment. The data are similar in studies that have looked at the per capita number of new employer businesses founded in different states in different years. In fact, one of these studies showed that California—home of Silicon Valley—and Massachusetts—home of Route 128—were *below the national average* in rates of new firm formation![30]

But states are large geographic areas, and there's a lot of difference between, say, San Jose and Sacramento California, and between Boston and Worcester, Massachusetts. If we want to figure out which places have a high percentage of people starting companies, we might want to look at differences between metropolitan areas.

Measuring the data at the level of metropolitan areas tells a similar story. The metro areas that mark Silicon Valley—San Francisco and San Jose—aren't among the top places for new business start-ups, according data from the Census Bureau's Longitudinal Enterprise and Establishment Microdata file, the government's best data source on the per capita number of new businesses created every year in different metro areas. In fact, these two metro areas aren't anywhere close to the number one metro area in terms of per capita firm formation; that honor goes to Laramie, Wyoming. San Francisco comes in at number 121 out of 394, with about 40 percent the per capita business formation rate of Laramie.[31]

And who is ahead of San Francisco on this list? Some not-very-often-thought-of centers of entrepreneurship, including Bozeman, Montana; Farmington, New Mexico; Rock Springs, Wyoming; Rapid City, South Dakota; Pikesville, Kentucky; Laredo, Texas; Brunswick, Georgia; Newark, New Jersey; Anchorage, Alaska; and Enid, Oklahoma.[32]

San Jose, California, that epicenter of technology start-ups, appears even lower on the ranking of start-ups per capita, coming in at 165 on the list. And who's ahead of San Jose? Some additional not-very-often-thought-of centers of entrepreneurship, including Yankton, South Dakota; Anniston, Alabama; and Corinth, Mississippi.[33]

What's going on here? Why does the place that many people think of as being the center of entrepreneurship in the United States, if not the world—Silicon Valley—have such a small percentage of its residents starting their own businesses? The answer becomes clear if we think about what start-ups look like in a place where a lot of people start them, in comparison to the high-growth technology start-ups that are found in places like Silicon Valley.

Think about what a place with a perfect score on the measure of firm formation per capita would look like. Everyone would be starting his or her own business. All of the businesses would be very tiny. They would have only the entrepreneur working in them, and none of them would grow. Why? Because if everyone is an entrepreneur, there is no one available for hire.

Now, admittedly, no place gets a perfect score on the measure of firm formation per capita. Far from it. But high-growth companies will have a harder time finding employees in a place with a higher rate of firm formation per capita than in a place with a lower rate of firm formation per capita. Places like Silicon Valley—with several very high-growth companies—don't have that high a rate of new business formation. The insatiable appetite for employees at companies like Google and Yahoo means that a smaller portion of the population is going into business for themselves in Silicon Valley than in Laramie, which has relatively few companies looking to hire a large number of people. As a result, in places like Laramie more of the population start new businesses than in places like Silicon Valley.

What Explains the Differences in Entrepreneurship across Regions?

The places where high-growth, high-tech companies are found aren't the places with the highest rate of firm formation, but that still doesn't tell us why some regions, states, and metropolitan areas have more of their populations starting businesses than others. What makes starting businesses a more common vocation in some places than in others?

Some factors are quite intuitive and not very interesting. Places with a greater population, faster population growth, greater population mobility, and greater population density have a higher proportion of people who start businesses.[34] Moreover, places with more educated people also have a greater percentage of the population starting businesses than other places because having more education increases the odds that a person will start a business.[35] Other factors are the same as those discussed earlier, for example, being a place that is poorer and more dependent on agriculture. There is little point in repeating those explanations here. So I'm going to focus on one factor that is not intuitive: unemployment.

Unemployment and New Firm Formation

Although you will never hear a policy maker say it, the pattern is pretty clear. If a place wants more of its population to start businesses, it needs to have more of its population out of work. (I can hear the election slogan now: "I will work to make Pleasantville a more entrepreneurial place. If you elect me, I will ensure that the unemployment rate will rise, so that more people will start their own companies.") Many studies have shown that in places with *more* unemployment, and in time periods when unemployment is *increasing,* people are more likely to go into business for themselves than at other times and in other places.[36]

This makes sense because unemployed people are more likely than people with jobs to start their own businesses. Why? Because they have less to lose by becoming entrepreneurs, something economists call a lower opportunity cost on their time. After all, it's less costly to start a company if your alternative is watching daytime television than it would be if you were to leave your job, and thus lose your paycheck, to work for yourself.

The Limits of Industrial Structure

Some places have more people starting companies than others because of their industrial composition. Most people start businesses in the industries in which they are currently working (that is, construction workers tend to start construction firms, doctors tend to start medical practices, and so on). And most entrepreneurs start businesses where they are living and working rather than in other places. Put together, these two patterns mean that the start-ups in an area tend to be similar to the companies that are currently in operation there.

For reasons that will become clearer after you read chapter 2 (which discusses the industries in which entrepreneurs tend to found new companies), different regions, states, provinces, metropolitan areas, and cities differ significantly in their industrial composition. For instance, some metropolitan areas, like Cedar Rapids, Iowa, rely more on agriculture, while other metropolitan areas, like Akron, Ohio, rely more on manufacturing, while still others, like New York City, rely more on services. And within those broad categories, the industrial composition of each place is different. For instance, the Peoria, Illinois, metropolitan area has very different types of manufacturing companies from those in Orange County, California.

Start-ups are not equally common in all sectors of the economy. They are much more common in services than in manufacturing. Moreover, within manufacturing, people employed in some types of businesses, say, metal goods making, are less likely than people employed in other types of businesses, for example, food manufacturing, to start new businesses. The same is true within services. Start-ups are more common in some types of services, like personal care services, than in other types of services, like professional services.

The tendency of people to start companies in industries in which they are already working, the different likelihood of start-ups forming in different industries, and the different industrial composition of different places combine to make the likelihood that residents of different regions, states, and cities will start companies at very different rates. For example, places like Detroit, Michigan, that have a lot of vehicle production, tend to have less new firm formation than places like Atlanta, Georgia, which have a lot of business services.[37]

What About Capital Availability?

Many observers have argued that places where capital is more abundant have more firm formation. For example, many experts say that more people start companies in places like Boston, Massachusetts, than in places like Topeka, Kansas, because there is more capital available in Boston. The greater number of venture capitalists and business angels (individuals who invest their own money in start-ups founded by people who are not their friends or relatives) in Boston, the argument goes, means there is more money available for start-ups, making firm formation easier. In fact, research has demonstrated a positive correlation between the amount of capital in a state or metropolitan area and the rate of new firm formation.[38] That is, places with more money available have more new firms forming than other places.

But does this correlation mean that capital availability *causes* the higher level of new firm formation in a region, state, or metro area? Actually, it seems more likely that the causality goes the other direction. That is, the correlation captures the tendency of capital to flow to places with more firm formation rather than the tendency of people in places with more capital to start more businesses.

Why might this be so? Consider the following thought experiment. Suppose that the place where you lived suddenly became awash in capital because all of the banks in town discovered they had more cash than they had previously thought. Would this greater availability of capital affect the rate at which people in town started companies? It is unlikely that the banks would send people around knocking on doors offering money to anyone willing to start a company. Moreover, even if they did, many of those people wouldn't have an interest in starting a business nor would they have any idea what kind of business to start should they have access to the necessary financing.

Now it's possible that entrepreneurs living elsewhere might hear that there is "gold in them thar hills" and move to town. But that's not too likely. It's not easy to know what kind of business to start or whom to hire or what suppliers to use in a town that's new to you, not to mention that most people don't like to move to a strange place just to start a company. In short, it's hard to see how having "easy money" in a place would *cause* a lot of people to start companies.

Now think about a place that has a lot of people interested in starting businesses but is short of capital. The entrepreneurs would go around knocking on the doors of banks and start-up investors. The investors and bankers would tell them that they are sorry, but it's a poor town, and they don't have the money to lend or invest. A few of the entrepreneurs might give up, but many of them will call or e-mail friends and relatives living elsewhere and tell them about the great businesses that they are trying to start. At the same time, the bankers and investors tell bankers and investors elsewhere about the overabundance of opportunities in their area. Some people—maybe the bankers and investors or maybe the friends and relatives of the entrepreneurs—will decide that there really are some opportunities worth pursuing and move a little money into town to invest in the start-ups there. This isn't very hard to do. In this day and age, capital can be moved from place to place by hitting a computer key. As a result, needed capital moves fairly easily to places where more businesses are being formed from places where fewer companies are being created. In short, it seems that the story of capital moving to places where new businesses are being started is more plausible than the story of people starting more companies in places where capital is abundant.

Surprisingly, we don't have much research on this question. Most people, it seems, just want to believe that providing more capital to entrepreneurs in an area will increase start-up rates, and they are willing to believe that the correlation between capital availability and firm formation rates mean that capital availability *causes* firm formation rates to rise.

One pair of enterprising professors, Steven Kreft, at the Kelley School of Business at Indiana University, and Russell Sobel, in the economics department at West Virginia University, did examine the causality of the relation between capital availability and new firm formation. They looked across states at whether changes in capital availability at one point in time led to changes in new firm formation at another point in time, or whether changes in new firm formation led to capital availability, while holding everything else about the places constant. Kreft and Sobel admittedly studied a very particular kind of capital—venture capital—which very few firms can get, so their results might not hold for other forms of capital. But for venture capital, they found that having more new firm formation leads a state to *receive* more venture capital but having more venture capital does not lead a state to *create* more start-ups.[39]

Busted Myths and Key Realities

1. America isn't becoming a more entrepreneurial place; the rate at which start-ups are created in this country is actually declining over time.

2. The United States isn't one of the most entrepreneurial countries in the world.

3. People are more likely to start companies in poorer and more agricultural places than in places that are richer and more reliant on manufacturing.

4. People in places with high rates of unemployment are more likely to start businesses than people in places with low rates of unemployment.

5. The industrial structure in an area, such as the balance between services and manufacturing, and the types of industries represented affect how much new firm formation occurs.

6. Capital availability doesn't increase the number of start-ups in an area; rather, having more start-ups appears to attract capital.

In Conclusion

So what's the message of this chapter? It's pretty straightforward, even if it doesn't match what you previously thought. Despite what many pundits say, America isn't becoming a more entrepreneurial place. The proportion of the U.S. population that goes into business for itself has not increased over the past twenty years, and it is much lower now than it was ninety years ago.

Contrary to popular wisdom, the United States isn't one of the most entrepreneurial countries in the world. That honor is reserved for developing countries like Peru and Uganda. People are more likely to start companies in poorer and more agricultural places than in places that are richer and more reliant on manufacturing.

Within countries, different regions, states, metro areas, and cities have very different rates of new firm formation. Although people talk all the time about what factors account for these differences, the factors discussed aren't the ones that jump out of the data. One of the most important factors—the rate of unemployment—doesn't get much air time, perhaps because the data show that unemployment reduces the opportunity cost of starting a business, thus making people in places with high rates of unemployment *more likely* to start businesses than people in places with low rates of unemployment. In addition, several aspects of the industrial structure in an area, such as the balance between services and manufacturing and the types of industries represented, affect how much new firm formation occurs. Finally, despite the fervent beliefs of many people, capital availability doesn't increase the number of start-ups in an area. Rather, having more start-ups appears to attract capital. In short, the data show that the patterns of new firm formation across time and place aren't what most people think they are.

2

What Are Today's Entrepreneurial Industries?

Reading newspapers or popular magazines might lead you to think that most entrepreneurs start sexy new companies in high-growth, technology-intensive, industries. It turns out, though, that those are just the kinds of start-ups that reporters like to write about. Most new businesses are in pretty mundane, run-of-the-mill industries, like construction or retail trade. In fact, every year only about 7 percent of new companies in the United States are started in industries that the government defines as high technology,[1] and only about 3 percent of business founders consider their new businesses to be "technologically sophisticated."[2]

Why am I pointing out that we have a misconception about the industries in which start-ups tend to be formed because of media bias? Because to understand entrepreneurship in America, you need to understand the industries in which most entrepreneurs start their companies, and why they tend to start businesses in those industries. In fact, the data on the industry distribution of start-ups tell a very interesting story.

In What Industries Do Entrepreneurs Start Businesses?

The typical entrepreneur today starts a service business. In fact, in the United States and other developed countries, very few entrepreneurs start businesses that make things any more; in the United States, start-ups in service industries outnumber start-ups in manufacturing by a factor of roughly 8 to 1.[3] In fact, between 35 to 40 percent of all new businesses started each year are in professional services, construction or retail alone, and fewer than 6 percent are found in manufacturing (see table 2.1).[4]

Table 2.1 Distribution of New Businesses by Industry for Different Samples

NAICS Code[a]	Industry Title	Percent of EIUS[b] New Firms (2004)	Percent of EIUS[b] Start-Ups (2004)	Percent of New Employer Firms (2003)
11	Agriculture, forestry, fishing and hunting	2.0	2.7	0.4
21–12	Mining and utilities	0.9	0.3	0.3
23	Construction	10.0	6.6	14.2
31–33	Manufacturing	3.5	4.1	3.3
42	Wholesale trade	1.5	2.2	4.7
44–45	Retail trade	18.6	19.2	12.5
48–49	Transportation and warehousing	2.4	1.7	3.3
51	Information	4.2	5.1	1.5
52–53	Finance, insurance and real estate	8.4	8.0	9.3
54	Professional, scientific and technical services	12.0	9.3	13.1
56	Administrative and support and waste management	2.1	0.9	5.9
61	Educational services	4.8	2.6	1.2
62	Healthcare and social assistance	2.9	4.3	7.9
71	Arts, entertainment and recreation	3.2	6.9	2.0
72	Accommodation and food services	10.9	14.1	8.7
81	Other services	0.3	0.4	9.2
Various	All other	12.4	11.6	2.5

Source: Adapted from data contained in P. Reynolds, *Entrepreneurship in the Unoted States* (Miami: Florida International University, 2005) and data provided by the Office of Advocacy, U.S. Small Business Administration, http://www.sba.gov/advo/research/dyn_us03.pdf (accessed March 24, 2007).

[a]NAICS = North American Classification System
[b]EIUS = Entrepreneurship in the United States
[c]This figure is not provided in the data but is estimated as the residual remaining, given all of the other figures.

Within these broad industry categories, entrepreneurial activity varies substantially. Take, for example, the variation in self-employment rates within the "other services" category. In 2003, 48.8 percent of barber shops, 43.1 percent of personal and household goods repair shops, 41.8 percent of nail salons and other personal care services, and 33.5 percent

Table 2.2 Birth Rate of Establishments with Fewer than 500 Employees in 2003

NAICS Title	NAICS[a] CODE	Establishments with Fewer than 500 Employees in 2002	New Establishments with Fewer than 500 Employees in 2003	Rate of Birth of New Small Establishments in the Industry in 2003
Paper mfg	322	3,509	173	0.05
Plastics and rubber products mfg	326	11,858	603	0.05
Machinery mfg	333	23,931	1,244	0.05
Fabricated metal product mfg	332	54,881	2,952	0.05
Religious/grantmaking/ civic/professional and similar org	813	280,511	16,140	0.06
Printing and related support activities	323	33,393	1,967	0.06
Electrical equipment, appliance, and component mfg	335	5,068	303	0.06
Utilities	221	8,257	507	0.06
Petroleum and coal products mfg	324	1,209	82	0.07
Building material and garden equipment and supplies dealers	444	72,768	4,940	0.07
Nonmetallic mineral product mfg	327	12,223	844	0.07
Chemical mfg	325	8,982	633	0.07
Furniture and related product mfg	337	19,734	1,521	0.08
Mining (except oil and gas)	212	4,672	362	0.08
Transportation equipment mfg	336	9,225	726	0.08
Computer and electronic product mfg	334	12,630	995	0.08
Management of companies and enterprises	551	21,842	1,729	0.08
Wood product mfg	321	14,497	1,156	0.08
Nursing and residential care facilities	623	44,714	3,619	0.08
Textile product mills	314	6,381	517	0.08
Textile mills	313	3,119	253	0.08
Museums, historical sites, and similar institutions	712	5,783	477	0.08
Miscellaneous mfg	339	25,978	2,188	0.08
Wholesale trade, durable goods	421	224,839	19,047	0.08
Primary metal mfg	331	4,691	409	0.09

Table 2.2 Birth Rate of Establishments with Fewer than 500 Employees in 2003
(continued)

NAICS Title	NAICS[a] CODE	Establishments with Fewer than 500 Employees in 2002	New Establishments with Fewer than 500 Employees in 2003	Rate of Birth of New Small Establishments in the Industry in 2003
Ambulatory health care services	621	416,958	37,434	0.09
Oil and gas extraction	211	6,000	546	0.09
Motor vehicle and parts dealers	441	96,922	9,003	0.09
Social assistance	624	116,692	10,990	0.09
Publishing industries	511	23,733	2,255	0.10
Leather and allied product mfg	316	1,344	128	0.10
Wholesale trade, nondurable goods	422	120,488	11,576	0.10
Health and personal care stores	446	43,960	4,302	0.10
Rental and leasing services	532	33,273	3,279	0.10
Food mfg	311	19,898	1,971	0.10
Insurance carriers and related activities	524	124,500	12,418	0.10
Gasoline stations	447	77,420	7,790	0.10
Repair and maintenance	811	201,961	20,708	0.10
Credit intermediation and related activities	522	90,045	9,354	0.10
Furniture and home furnishings stores	442	51,394	5,385	0.10
Support activities for mining	213	7,340	771	0.11
Forestry and logging	113	10,662	1,125	0.11
Sporting goods, hobby, book, and music stores	451	43,146	4,579	0.11
Accommodation	721	45,536	4,847	0.11
Waste management and remediation services	562	13,215	1,421	0.11
Heavy construction	234	33,117	3,748	0.11
Miscellaneous store retailers	453	101,342	11,527	0.11
Clothing and clothing accessories stores	448	69,771	8,098	0.12
Hospitals	622	2,666	315	0.12
Warehousing and storage	493	5,215	632	0.12
Water transportation	483	1,302	159	0.12
Educational services	611	60,553	7,427	0.12
Nonstore retailers	454	33,679	4,189	0.12

Table 2.2 Birth Rate of Establishments with Fewer than 500 Employees in 2003
(continued)

NAICS Title	NAICS[a] CODE	Establishments with Fewer than 500 Employees in 2002	New Establishments with Fewer than 500 Employees in 2003	Rate of Birth of New Small Establishments in the Industry in 2003
Support activities for transportation	488	26,045	3,248	0.12
Personal and laundry services	812	160,667	20,636	0.13
Transit and ground passenger transportation	485	13,464	1,732	0.13
Professional, scientific, and technical services	541	617,971	81,939	0.13
Beverage and tobacco product mfg	312	2,354	318	0.14
Agriculture and forestry support activities	115	9,451	1,278	0.14
Air transportation	481	2,874	403	0.14
Foodservices and drinking places	722	360,317	51,041	0.14
Amusement, gambling, and recreation industries	713	48,762	6,913	0.14
Motion picture and sound recording industries	512	15,476	2,222	0.14
Electronics and appliance stores	443	33,060	4,755	0.14
Special trade contractors	235	368,032	53,105	0.14
Real estate	531	202,732	29,333	0.14
Food and beverage stores	445	108,972	16,031	0.15
Broadcasting and telecommunications	513	16,992	2,518	0.15
Truck transportation	484	85,988	13,165	0.15
Scenic and sightseeing transportation	487	1,700	261	0.15
Administrative and support services	561	230,664	35,878	0.16
General merchandise stores	452	9,171	1,488	0.16
Building, developing, and general contracting	233	184,428	30,272	0.16
Securities intermediation and related activities	523	41,263	6,902	0.17
Pipeline transportation	486	245	41	0.17

Table 2.2 Birth Rate of Establishments with Fewer than 500 Employees in 2003
(continued)

NAICS Title	NAICS[a] CODE	Establishments with Fewer than 500 Employees in 2002	New Establishments with Fewer than 500 Employees in 2003	Rate of Birth of New Small Establishments in the Industry in 2003
Information services and data processing services	514	14,998	2,558	0.17
Lessors of intangible assets, except copyrighted works	533	1,607	281	0.17
Performing arts, spectator sports, and related industries	711	27,615	4,916	0.18
Fishing, hunting, and trapping	114	1,547	284	0.18
Apparel mfg	315	11,129	2,052	0.18
Couriers and messengers	492	7,350	1,360	0.19
Funds, trusts, and other financial vehicles	525	2,060	477	0.23

Source: Adapted from data contained in Office of Advocacy, U.S. Small Business Administration, www.sba.gov/advo/research/dyn_us_98_03n4.txt (accessed on March 24, 2007).
[a]NAICS North American Classification System.

of beauty salons were run by someone working for him or herself even though the average self-employment rate in "other services" was only 15.7 percent. Similarly, despite an overall self-employment rate of 13.7 percent, in "professional and business services," the self-employment rates were 39.4 percent for health care practitioners, 36.9 percent for specialized design service providers, 29.4 percent for landscapers, and 29.4 percent for child day care providers.[5]

The variation in start-up rates across industries is the same if we look at the number of new employer firms per existing firm. For example, the start-up rate in paper manufacturing is less than one-third of the start-up rate in building, developing, and general contracting (see table 2.2).

Moreover, these patterns are pretty stable. The industry distribution in new business formation rates changes very little over time and is pretty similar across industrialized countries.[6] In sum, in many countries across many years, most new businesses are started in mundane, run-of-the-mill service industries, like accounting and construction.

Why Are Some Industries So Popular among Entrepreneurs?

These patterns beg the question: why are some industries so much more popular among entrepreneurs than others? Are there secrets here to learn? Is the reason that some industries are more popular than others because they are better suited for new companies?

You might be surprised to learn that the industries in which people are most likely to start businesses are not the best industries for start-ups; if anything, they are the worst. For instance, you might think that entrepreneurs would start businesses in industries that face fewer competitors. Logic would suggest that they should focus on industries where it is possible to create some kind of barrier to competition, like a patent or a trade secret, or a special relationship with customers or suppliers. After all, less competitive industries tend to have fatter profit margins, so starting in these industries would increase the amount of money entrepreneurs could make.

But, rather than starting firms in industries with very few existing firms, most entrepreneurs start firms in industries where there are *a lot of firms* already in operation. The industry distribution of new companies mirrors the distribution of existing businesses (see figure 2.1).[7]

Moreover, most entrepreneurs don't start businesses in the most financially attractive industries. Using data provided by the Office of Advocacy of the U.S. Small Business Administration and the Internal Revenue Service, we can calculate the correlation between the rate of new firm formation in an industry and its average profit margin, income per establishment, and revenues. Whether we look at the 19 major sectors of the economy (2-digit North American Classification System [NAICS] codes) or the 73 major industries (3-digit NAICS codes), these data show that there is no significant positive correlation between the income per establishment, or profit margins, and the rate of new firm formation in an industry. Instead there is a weak *negative* correlation between revenues per firm and the rate of entry into the industry. That is, there is no evidence that entrepreneurs select industries in which profits, profit margins, or revenues are higher.

But this doesn't means that entrepreneurs select industries randomly. The data show that entrepreneurs systematically chose certain industries over others when starting new businesses. Unfortunately, they

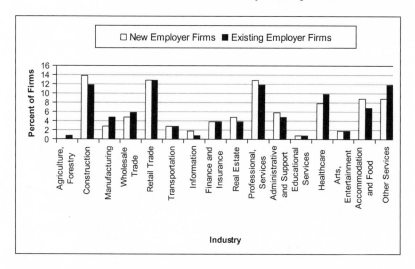

Figure 2.1. Industry Distribution of New and Existing Employer Firms
  Source: Adapted from www.census.gov/epcd/nonemployer/2002adv/us/US000.HTM
and www.sba.gov/advo/research/data.html#us.

tend to choose industries in which they are *most likely to fail.* Data from
the U.S. Small Business Administration reveal that the correlation between the start-up rate and the failure rate across industries at the 3-digit
level is approximately 0.77. That is, the industries that have the highest
firm failure rates are also the ones that have the highest firm start-up
rates.[8]

What's going on here? Are the entrepreneurs we idolize just plain
stupid? Why do they choose to start businesses in industries where they
are likely to fail? Why don't they choose to start new businesses in more
profitable industries? There appear to be two answers. First, many entrepreneurs start businesses in industries where they have worked before
and therefore understand. On average, these industries tend to be the
ones that employ the most people and are the most competitive. As a result, many entrepreneurs end up starting their new firms in industries
that aren't the most attractive ones for start-ups. Second, many entrepreneurs start businesses in industries where starting a new company is
easy, and businesses in industries in which it is easy to get started are
more failure prone than other industries.

The data show that many entrepreneurs start businesses in the industries in which they currently are working; that is, barbers tend to

open barber shops, chefs tend to open restaurants, taxi drivers tend to start taxi services, and so on. In fact, one study estimated that almost half (45 percent) of entrepreneurs start businesses in the industry in which they were previously employed. This relation between prior work experience and the industry in which entrepreneurs start companies means that there are more start-ups in industries that employ more people. Because a lot of people are employed in industries like construction and retail trade, a lot of people become entrepreneurs in these industries.[9]

Still, more than half (55 percent) of entrepreneurs start businesses in industries other than those in which they had previously been working. For these entrepreneurs, the ease of getting a business started explains why certain industries are favored over others. The data show that entrepreneurs are more likely to start businesses in industries that demand less capital, where the average size of firms—in terms of both number of employees and the amount of assets—is lower, and where products are not differentiated from each other.[10]

Busted Myths and Key Realities

7. Most new businesses are not started in glitzy, high-tech industries but rather in a few subsectors of pretty mundane, run-of-the-mill industries.

8. Most entrepreneurs don't select the most profitable industries but instead pick industries with the highest firm failure rates.

9. Entrepreneurs don't select industries because they are good for start-ups but rather because they know these industries and because it is easy to start businesses in them.

In Conclusion

So what's the message of this chapter? Most new businesses are started in a few unglamorous subsectors of mainstream industries. Entrepreneurs favor these industries not because they are profitable or good for start-ups but because these are the industries that entrepreneurs know and because it is easy to start businesses in them.

If you think about this pattern for a little while, it's kind of depressing. All of these people are starting businesses—between 10 and 13 percent of people in the United States between the ages of 18 and 74 every year[11]—and the typical person isn't picking an industry that's good for start-ups. Rather, he is setting himself up for failure by starting a business in an industry where it is likely to go under. Yet nobody cautions these would-be entrepreneurs.

When people appear to be making bad choices in picking spouses, their friends and family advise them against marriage so they don't end up as a divorce statistic. But every year more people start businesses than get married. Where are their friends and family at times like this? Why don't they tell the entrepreneurs not to start these businesses and thus keep them from ending up as a business failure statistic? Since more people start businesses than get married every year, shouldn't we give our friends and family at least as much feedback on the quality of their business decisions as we give them on their marriage choices?

3

Who Becomes an Entrepreneur?

If you asked the average American to describe an entrepreneur, what would she say? She would probably describe Bill Gates or Steve Jobs or Larry Ellison or some highly successful founder of a technology start-up who has taken his company public and built a financial empire. After all, conventional wisdom tells us that entrepreneurs are very special people. They are heroes who stand alone and overcome great odds to build companies through superhuman efforts.

The description of an entrepreneur offered by the average American might resemble the one provided by the Office of Public Affairs at the Federal Reserve Bank of Dallas: "Everyone loves a hero—a person whose values we revere, whose accomplishments we respect. We admire and appreciate people who venture forth to try something new and end up benefiting a host of other people. These qualities describe the essence of entrepreneurship. An entrepreneur is one who asserts, 'There is a better way, and I will find it.' Being entrepreneurial means charging down a new path, staying alert to opportunity and taking risks to seize the opportunity. It means having energy, vision, optimism and daring to try something new."[1]

Wow! If this is what entrepreneurs are like, then you must concede that they are pretty special people and probably not very much like you or me. But before you get too discouraged by thinking that you are nothing like the heroic creatures just described, let me point out that the Federal Reserve Bank of Dallas is recounting a myth. Real entrepreneurs don't look at all like this description.

The typical entrepreneur looks a lot less like Bill Gates and a lot more like the guy who lives across the street from you or sits next to you at church:

- He is a white man in his forties.
- He is married with a working spouse.
- He attended college but might not have graduated.
- He was born in the United States and has lived here his whole life.
- He has spent much of his life in the town where he started his business.
- He is just trying to make a living, not trying to build a high-growth business.
- He worked previously in the industry in which he started his company, something like construction or insurance or retail.
- He has no special psychological characteristics.[2]

People have the wrong image about what the typical entrepreneur looks like because he's too boring for anyone to write about. It's hard to find a description of him on television or in the newspaper. After all, who wants to read a *People* magazine article about the life of their plumber, see pictures of his $150,000 house, or hear what he ate for dinner last night? It's much more interesting to read about Larry Ellison's yacht, Bill Gates's foundation, or Sergei Brin's airplane. Thus only a handful of super-successful entrepreneurs get described in the media, giving us a distorted view of what entrepreneurs are like.

The Mind of the Entrepreneur

Perhaps nothing about entrepreneurs gets more attention in the popular press and in general discussion than their psychology. According to many sources, entrepreneurs have a special psychological makeup. They have different personalities and a different way of thinking than the rest of us. They are more passionate, creative, innovative, risk taking, driven, and optimistic than you or me.[3]

The conventional wisdom about the unique psychology and mind-set of entrepreneurs is so ingrained in us that if you can go online, through the Google search engine you can find dozens of Web sites that will administer a test to determine if you have the right psychological makeup to be an entrepreneur. Even the Small Business Administration offers one such test on its Web page.[4]

Save your time and money. These tests do little to predict whether you have the "right stuff" to be an entrepreneur. Of the large number of psychological characteristics that researchers have examined in carefully conducted studies, very few differentiate entrepreneurs from the rest of us.[5] (These psychological characteristics also don't do much to distinguish successful entrepreneurs from failed ones—there is more about that in chapter 7).

Those studies that do show differences between entrepreneurs and the rest of the population reveal that most differences are attributable to basic demographic factors like age, race, and gender and that the differences in psychological characteristics are very small in comparison to these factors.[6] The psychological factors—like risk tolerance, social confidence, anxiety-acceptance, novelty focus, role-expectation, and recognition-seeking—that people associate with being an entrepreneur are only the slightest bit different among entrepreneurs and nonentrepreneurs and have nowhere near the effect of being white or male, which almost double the odds that someone is an entrepreneur. Put another way, risk-tolerant, anxiety-accepting, socially confident, novelty-focused, role-expectation, and recognition-seeking older black women are so much less likely to be entrepreneurs than risk-intolerant, anxiety-avoiding, socially unconfident, nonnovelty-focused, role-expectation, and recognition-avoiding, middle-aged white men that we might be better off just focusing on demographic factors in trying to explain who is an entrepreneur and who isn't.

If entrepreneurs don't have a different psychological makeup from the rest of us, then why do our myths focus so much on the psychology of entrepreneurs? Psychologists explain that this is just the result of our tendency to engage in the fundamental attribution error. We tend to think that people behave in predictable ways, as a result of stable personality traits, and that personality and other psychological characteristics explain more than they do. And we think that people's actions—like starting businesses–depend more on their psychology than they actually do and less on forces beyond their control, like being born black or female.[7]

Why Do People Start Businesses?

You might think that entrepreneurs are primarily motivated by the desire to make money, or for the thrill of starting businesses, or to support their families, or to become well known. After all, that is the conventional wisdom. Take, for example, the following description, again provided by the Office of Public Affairs of the Federal Reserve Bank of Dallas: "Entrepreneurs can be found everywhere, doing just about everything. . . . Some wish to become rich and famous. Others wish to make themselves, their families or their communities better off. And some seek pure adventure—to challenge the limits of their capability."[8]

The real reason that most people start businesses, however, has nothing to do with wanting to make money, to become famous, to better their own communities, to seek adventure, or even to improve the world. Most people start businesses simply because they just don't like working for someone else.[9]

Are Entrepreneurs Really "Superior" People?

Descriptions of entrepreneurs are invariably positive. Entrepreneurs typically are seen as wiser, more insightful, more creative, more innovative, more persistent, more honorable, more optimistic, more resourceful, and more achievement oriented than the rest of us. The myth of entrepreneurship associates "good" characteristics with entrepreneurs and more modest characteristics with the rest of us, so we think entrepreneurs are "better than average" people. But are these myths accurate?

To answer this question, consider the following thought experiment: Suppose you have two friends, Joe and Tom. They are very similar. Both are 40-year-old white men who live in $140,000 houses in the same neighborhood. They went to the same college and got degrees in the same subject. They have spent their careers in the same industry and most recently worked at the same company. But last year Joe earned about 12 percent less than Tom. Of course, that was before Joe was laid off from his job. Now he has been unemployed for several months. Earlier in his career, before his last job, Joe changed jobs more often than Tom. He also has a bit of a checkered past, having once dealt drugs as a teenager. Tom, in contrast, has a squeaky clean record.

Which of your friends do you think is more likely to start a business next year? If you answered Joe, you'd be right. Four things about him make him more likely than Tom to go into business for himself:

- He's changed jobs often.
- He was laid off from his job and is now unemployed.

- He made less money in his last job.
- He was a drug dealer in his youth.

Studies show that people who work part-time or change jobs more often are more likely to go into business for themselves than people who work full-time or change jobs infrequently.[10] They also show that unemployed people are more than *twice as likely* as those who have jobs to start their own businesses.[11] In fact, the longer people are unemployed, the more likely they are to go into business for themselves.[12] Furthermore, studies show that the less money that people earn, the more likely they are to start their own businesses.[13] Finally, people who dealt drugs as teenagers are between 11 and 21 percent more likely than other people to start their own businesses in adulthood. And their higher rate of self-employment isn't the result of wealth accumulated dealing drugs, greater likelihood of having a criminal record, or lower wages.[14]

How do these data compare to the myths we hear so often? The reality is that entrepreneurs are more likely than the rest of us to have several characteristics that might be considered "undesirable." The myth of entrepreneurial superiority is not correct.

Is Entrepreneurship a Young Person's Game?

Another myth about entrepreneurship is that it is a young person's game. Take a look at the media. Newspapers and television shows are full of discussions of twenty-something entrepreneurs who are building new businesses. A Web search on the term *young entrepreneur* turns up more Web sites than a search on the words *old entrepreneur* or the phrase *middle-aged entrepreneur.*

Many Web sites and blogs explain that entrepreneurship is more appropriate for young people than their older counterparts. Take just one example: "Entrepreneurs are, by and large, risk-takers, and college students are especially prone to take risks because they are generally unencumbered by family obligations and mortgages."[15] Even academic studies give this impression, reporting things like: "New firm creation tends to be a young man's game. . . . Younger individuals are more likely to start a new firm than older ones."[16] Given the way entrepreneurship is portrayed, it wouldn't be surprising if you thought that young people were the age group most likely to start new businesses.

In contrast to this myth, middle-aged people are actually more likely

Table 3.1 Proportion of Entrepreneurs by Age Category

Age Group	Self-Employed	Business Owners
18–24	3.1%	1.0%
25–34	12.8%	8.0%
35–44	26.0%	24.0%
45–64	45.6%	53.0%
65+	9.5%	10.0%

Source: Small Business Administration, *The Small Business Economy: A Report to the President* (Washington, D.C.: U.S. Government Printing Office, 2005).

to be entrepreneurs. According to preliminary data for the Kauffman Firm Survey (for which I served as the principal investigator), only 2.4 percent of the founders of a national probability sample of new businesses started in the United States in 2004 were less than 24 years old at the time that they started their new businesses.[17] The most common age range for the founders was 35 to 44. In fact, most studies show that people aged 25 to 34 are either less likely or no more likely than people between the ages of 35 and 44 to start a business.[18]

Moreover, entrepreneurs don't just start businesses, they also run them once they have been started. Take Michael Dell, the poster child for young entrepreneurs because he started his business in a University of Texas dorm room. Should we no longer think of him as an entrepreneur once his business was up and running? Or should we think of Michael Dell and anyone else who started a business as being an entrepreneur as long as he or she runs that business? Looked at this way, the average entrepreneur tends to pretty old. The highest rate of self-employment and business ownership is actually found among people between the ages of 45 and 64 (see table 3.1).

What's the message here? Entrepreneurship is definitely not a young person's game.

Is It Only Education in the School of Hard Knocks That Helps People to Start Businesses?

Mark Zuckerberg, the founder of Facebook; Steve Jobs, founder of Apple Computer; Michael Dell, founder of Dell Computer; Bill Gates, founder of Microsoft; and Larry Ellison, founder of Oracle, all dropped out of college. Yet these people are the image of entrepreneurs to many of us. This

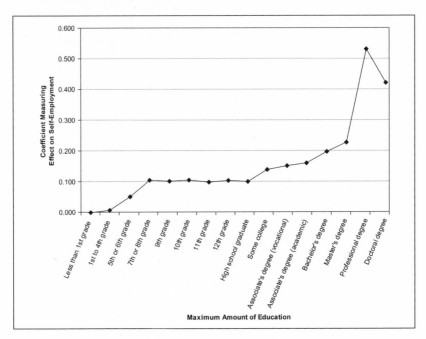

Figure 3.1. Effect of Education on Self-Employment, Controlling for Other Factors

   Source: Adapted from D. Blanchflower, "Self-Employment: More May Not Be Better," *Swedish Economic Policy Review* 11, no. 2 (2004): 15–74.

image has spawned a myth that going to school doesn't make people more likely to start businesses, that if anything, it keeps people from becoming entrepreneurs. If you read the blogs on the Web, you will quickly come to the same conclusion: going to college isn't very helpful if you want to be an entrepreneur. Education is expensive, time consuming, and not particularly relevant to the real world of starting a business. But what do the data say?

   To answer this question, we can't just look at the raw data. Many things that influence whether people become entrepreneurs also affect whether or not they get an education. For example, people who work in construction are more likely than people in many industries to start their own businesses, yet they are less likely than people who work in many other industries to get a college degree.[19] If we look only at the relation between people's education and their likelihood of starting businesses, we can't tell if they are driven to become entrepreneurs by their education or other things, like the industry in which they work. To understand how education affects the odds that a person will start a business, we need to control for the effects of other factors.

If we do that, we find that, including professional school, getting more education *increases* the likelihood that a person will start his own business.[20] This pattern is demonstrated in figure 3.1, which shows the effect of education on the likelihood that a person works for himself, controlling for the effects of other explanatory factors (e.g., race, age, gender, wealth, industry). As the data indicate, only after graduating from professional school does additional schooling reduce the likelihood that a person will start his own business.

The message here is quite simple: contrary to the myth, going to school actually *increases* the odds that you'll become an entrepreneur. But once you have a graduate degree, further education does not increase your chances of becoming an entrepreneur. Therefore, if you want to become an entrepreneur, go to school—just don't go on to get a PhD. With that much education you are likely to become a nerdy professor like me, who studies entrepreneurship instead of doing it.

Does It Matter What You Study?

Entrepreneurship education is booming in business schools. More than 2,000 universities and colleges around the country now offer courses in the area, many granting both majors and minors in the subject. You can even pay $8,200 for a four-week course on the topic at Dartmouth College.[21] In their promotional efforts, all these schools are telling you that their courses will help you get a leg up on starting your own business. But is it true? Does majoring in entrepreneurship make a difference in being able to start your own company?

There are no studies that survey a representative sample of the population to look at whether entrepreneurship majors are more likely than other majors to start their own businesses, so we can't fully address this question. But we can look at the effect of majoring in business as compared to other subjects. Business majors are more likely than many other majors to start their own businesses, which might not surprise you. But the majors of other people who tend to start their own businesses might. People who study health-related topics (things like medicine, nursing, and pharmacy) and those who study law, architecture, and agriculture are more likely than people majoring in other fields to start their own companies.[22] It seems that people who start their own businesses study not just the information contained in an entrepreneurship major: they also tend to study things that correspond to occupations in which a lot of people run their own businesses.

The Importance of Experience

The media is full of stories about people who founded their companies shortly after they graduated college. The image these stories give is that working for someone else doesn't really increase, and may even decrease, the chances that you will start your own business.

Again, this is the myth, not the reality. In contrast to the stories pervading the media, the data show that work experience increases a person's chances of starting his own business.[23] It seems that a lot of the information that makes people more comfortable taking the entrepreneurial plunge—understanding how to manage other people, figuring out how to satisfy customers, learning to keep financial records, and so on—is not unique to the start-up setting and can be learned by working for others.

So maybe working for someone else will increase the odds that you will start your own business some day.[24] But does it matter what you do when you work for someone else? The data show that the answer is an unequivocal "yes."[25] People who work in occupations that are found primarily in the business world are more likely to start their own businesses than people who work in occupations that are found primarily in government, education, health care, or other nonbusiness sectors.[26] In particular, people who have more management experience—experience supervising others—are more likely than other people to start their own businesses.[27]

Finally, as we saw in the previous chapter, people who work in jobs that are found primarily in industries that have a high rate of new firm formation, for example, in construction or professional services, are more likely than other people to start their own businesses. In fact, the difference in the odds for people with different occupations is huge. As the data in table 3.2 show, the odds are as much 5,000 times higher that a person in one occupation will start a business than a person in another occupation.

The differences shown in table 3.2 are for the occupations in which

Table 3.2 Percent of Self-Employed Workers, by Occupation, 1983–2002

Occupation	Percent Self-Employed
Horticultural specialty farmers	100.00
Farmers, except horticultural	98.59
Health diagnosing practitioners	90.00
Family child care providers	89.11
Podiatrists	81.99
Dentists	81.54
Auctioneers	75.13
Fishers	73.79
Managers, horticultural specialty farms	72.98
Authors	71.46
Barbers	67.89
Paperhangers	67.30
Optometrists	64.09
Captains and other officers, fishing vessels	60.84
Managers, farms, except horticultural	59.14
Veterinarians	54.41
Painters, sculptors, craft artists, and artist print makers	53.13
Hunters and trappers	49.92
Management analysts	46.87
Supervisors, personal service occupations	46.07
Business and promotion agents	45.81
Dressmakers	45.47
Shoe repairers	45.43
Supervisors, forestry and logging workers	45.25
Supervisors; brickmasons, stonemasons, and tile setters	45.21
Musicians and composers	44.77
Street and door-to-door sales workers	44.31
Real estate sales occupations	44.14
Physicians	42.73
Camera, watch, and musical instrument repairers	41.63
Hairdressers and cosmetologists	40.87
Tile setters, hard and soft	40.80
Supervisors; painters, paperhangers, and plasterers	40.73
Carpet installers	40.28
Photographers	39.97
Lawyers	39.33
Upholsterers	38.79
Artists, performers, and related workers	38.62
Painters, construction and maintenance	38.23
Timber cutting and logging occupations	37.22
Child care workers	37.01
Miscellaneous hand-working occupations	35.73
Inspectors, agricultural products	33.44
Funeral directors	33.14
Supervisors, related agricultural occupations	33.12
Precious stones and metals workers	32.81
Furniture and wood finishers	31.65
Architects	31.45
Supervisors, not elsewhere classified	31.41

Table 3.2 Percent of Self-Employed Workers, by Occupation, 1983–2002 (continued)

Occupation	Percent Self-Employed
Purchasing agents and buyers, farm products	31.29
Supervisors and proprietors, sales occupations	31.23
Cabinetmakers and bench carpenters	30.83
News vendors	30.68
Insurance sales occupations	30.15
Brickmasons and stonemasons	30.00
Psychologists	29.82
Carpenters	29.33
Designers	28.01
Managers and administrators	28.00
Miscellaneous precision apparel and fabric workers	27.95
Small engine repairers	27.05
Postmasters and mail superintendents	26.25
Managers, food serving and lodging establishments	26.06
Actors and directors	26.04
Miscellaneous woodworking machine operators	25.23
Automobile body and related repairers	25.13
Guides	25.06
Engravers, metal	24.98
Dancers	23.72
Securities and financial services sales occupations	23.61
Stenographers	23.57
Taxi cab drivers and chauffeurs	23.44
Roofers	22.74
Teachers, n.e.c.[a]	22.73
Hand painters, coating, and decorating occupations	22.43
Drywall installers	22.11
Animal caretakers, except farm	21.71
Dental laboratory and medical appliance technicians	21.62
Automobile mechanics	20.81
Marine engineers	20.54
Athletes	19.32
Personal service occupations, n.e.c.[a]	18.93
Drillers, earth	18.51
Groundskeepers and gardeners, except farm	18.30
Plumbers, pipefitters, and steamfitters	17.96
Miscellaneous precision woodworkers	17.55
Adjusters and calibrators	17.26
Agricultural and food scientists	17.25
Excavating and loading machine operators	17.09
Locksmiths and safe repairers	16.33
Ship captains and mates, except fishing boats	16.28
Supervisors, electricians and power transmission installers	16.04
Announcers	15.85
Grader, dozer, and scraper operators	15.25
Demonstrators, promoters and models, sales	15.20
Shaping and joining machine operators	14.87
Heating, air-conditioning, and refrigeration mechanics	14.65

Table 3.2 Percent of Self-Employed Workers, by Occupation, 1983–2002
(continued)

Occupation	Percent Self-Employed
Forestry workers, except logging	14.54
Pest control occupations	14.51
Pharmacists	14.10
Bookkeepers, accounting, and auditing clerks	13.91
Tailors	13.83
Social scientists, n.e.c.[a]	13.69
Buyers, wholesale and retail trade except farm products	13.65
Supervisors; plumbers, pipefitters, and steamfitters	13.51
Sales representatives, mining, manufacturing, and wholesale	13.17
Hand engraving and printing occupations	13.11
Construction trades, n.e.c.[a]	13.10
Concrete and terrazzo finishers	12.92
Glaziers	12.89
Specified mechanics and repairers, n.e.c.[a]	12.89
Supervisors, carpenters and related workers	12.78
Hand cutting and trimming occupations	12.72
Sales support occupations, n.e.c.[a]	12.47
Electronic repairers, communications and industrial equipment	12.21
Optical goods worker	11.91
Managers, service organizations, n.e.c[a]	11.82
Sales workers, motor vehicles and boats	11.77
Surveyors and mapping scientists	11.68
Farm equipment mechanics	11.58
Laundering and dry-cleaning machine operators	11.50
Geologists and geodesists	11.46
Economists	11.41
Plasterers	11.17
Household appliance and power tool repairers	11.04
Therapists, n.e.c.[a]	10.82
Accountants and auditors	10.65
Sales occupations, other business services	10.39
Truck drivers, heavy	10.30
Other financial officers	10.23
Physical therapists	9.88
Hand molders and shapers, except jewelers	9.85
Technical writers	9.85
Driver-sales workers	9.78
Editors and reporters	9.48
Launderers and ironers	9.21
Hand molding, casting, and forming occupations	8.97
Advertising and related sales occupations	8.88
Bakers	8.87
Electricians	8.77
Food batchmakers	8.56
Housekeepers and butlers	8.54
Transportation ticket and reservation agents	8.44
Broadcast equipment operators	8.34
Sales workers, furniture and home furnishings	8.27

Table 3.2 Percent of Self-Employed Workers, by Occupation, 1983–2002
(continued)

Occupation	Percent Self-Employed
Insulation workers	8.26
Supervisors, farm workers	8.25
Public relations specialists	8.23
Sales workers, other commodities	8.17
Sales counter clerks	7.93
Maids and housemen	7.79
Bus, truck, and stationary engine mechanics	7.50
Child care workers, private household	7.43
Sheet metal workers	7.40
Occupational therapists	7.33
Wood lathe, routing, and planing machine operators	7.21
Engineers, n.e.c.[a]	7.20
Teachers, postsecondary, n.e.c.[a]	7.07
Speech therapists	7.05
Photographic process machine operators	6.92
Private household cleaners and servants	6.90
Messengers	6.88
Patternmakers, lay-out workers, and cutters	6.78
Knitting, looping, taping, and weaving machine operators	6.59
Nursery workers	6.58
Supervisors, material moving equipment operators	6.45
Washing, cleaning, and pickling machine operators	6.32
Clergy	6.21
Early childhood teacher's assistants	6.17
Civil engineers	6.14
Heavy equipment mechanics	5.96
Construction laborers	5.92
Sales workers, parts	5.89
Forestry and conservation scientists	5.85
Computer systems analysts and scientists	5.83
Information clerks, n.e.c.[a]	5.80
Vehicle washers and equipment cleaners.	5.80
Operating engineers	5.76
Administrators, education and related fields	5.65
Bartenders	5.61
Janitors and cleaners	5.61
Welders and cutters	5.45
Printing press operators	5.34
Technicians, n.e.c.[a]	5.33
Drafting occupations	5.30
Dietitians	5.20
Typesetters and compositors	5.19
Sales workers; radio, TV, h-fi, and appliances	5.14
Tool and die makers	5.13
Miscellaneous electrical and electronic equipment repairers	5.12
Managers, medicine and health	5.04
Helpers, surveyor	5.02
Construction inspectors	4.85

Table 3.2 Percent of Self-Employed Workers, by Occupation, 1983–2002 (continued)

Occupation	Percent Self-Employed
Painting and paint spraying machine operators	4.84
Miscellaneous precision workers, n.e.c.[a]	4.70
Medical scientists	4.50
Sales engineers	4.49
Airplane pilots and navigators	4.49
Miscellaneous material moving equipment operators	4.46
Personnel, training, and labor relations specialists	4.28
Sheet metal duct installers	4.26
Helpers, mechanics and repairers	4.19
Textile cutting machine operators	4.19
Sales workers, apparel	4.16
Grinding, abrading, buffing, and polishing machine operators	4.10
Data processing equipment repairers	4.05
Mining machine operators	4.05
Truck drivers, light	4.04
Office machine repairers	3.99
Sales workers, hardware and building supplies	3.97
Legal assistants	3.91
Farm workers	3.90
Bill and account collectors	3.86
Production helpers	3.81
Computer programmers	3.77
Metal plating machine operators	3.69
Not specified mechanics and repairers	3.66
Butchers and meat cutters	3.65
Physicists and astronomers	3.60
Garage and service station related occupation	3.53
Miscellaneous plant and system operators	3.46
Miscellaneous textile machine operators	3.46
Pressing machine operators	3.46
Typists	3.44
Supervisors, cleaning and building service workers	3.36
Cooks	3.27
Physicians' assistants	3.21
Actuaries	3.16
Sales workers, shoes	3.16
Industrial machinery repairers	3.13
Supervisors, production occupations	3.01
Secretaries	2.98
General office clerks	2.96
Proofreaders	2.88
Insurance adjusters, examiners, and investigators	2.87
Paving, surfacing, and tamping equipment operators	2.86
Parking lot attendants	2.79
Chemists, except biochemists	2.74
Ushers	2.71
Textile sewing machine operators	2.70
Drillers, oil well	2.70

Table 3.2 Percent of Self-Employed Workers, by Occupation, 1983–2002 (continued)

Occupation	Percent Self-Employed
Biological and life scientists	2.68
Metallurgical and materials engineers	2.68
Religious workers, n.e.c.	2.62
Fire inspection and fire prevention occupations	2.51
Crane and tower operators	2.48
Laborers, except construction	2.45
Separating, filtering, and clarifying machine operators	2.37
Aircraft engine mechanics	2.34
Nursing aides, orderlies, and attendants	2.33
Payroll and timekeeping clerks	2.30
Billing clerks	2.29
Supervisors, food preparation and service occupations	2.26
Billing, posting, and calculating machine operators	2.25
Biological technicians	2.23
Dispatchers	2.23
Boilermakers	2.20
Supervisors, mechanics and repairers	2.19
Managers; marketing, advertising, and public relations	2.17
Financial managers	2.15
Physical scientists, n.e.c.[a]	2.12
Production helpers	2.10
Inspectors, testers, and graders	2.03
Sawing machine operators	2.03
Machinists	2.02
Graders and sorters, agricultural products	2.01
Personnel and labor relations managers	2.00
Compressing and compacting machine operators	1.98
Assemblers	1.94
Social workers	1.86
Correspondence clerks	1.77
Structural metal workers	1.75
Inspectors and compliance officers, except construction	1.73
Public transportation attendants	1.70
Statistical clerks	1.66
Attendants, amusement and recreation facilities	1.66
Guards and police, except public service	1.66
Motor transportation occupations, n.e.c.[a]	1.64
Electrical and electronic technicians	1.57
Freight, stocks, and material handlers, n.e.c.[a]	1.55
Machinery maintenance occupations	1.53
Engineering technicians, n.e.c.[a]	1.52
Hand packers and packagers	1.52
Telephone installers and repairers	1.52
Millwrights	1.49
Purchasing managers	1.48
Office machine operators, n.e.c.[a]	1.44
Cashiers	1.43
Computer operators	1.42

Table 3.2 Percent of Self-Employed Workers, by Occupation, 1983–2002
(continued)

Occupation	Percent Self-Employed
Bus drivers	1.41
Slicing and cutting machine operators	1.39
Supervisors, motor vehicle operators	1.37
Registered nurses	1.36
Receptionists	1.35
Administrative support occupations, n.e.c.[a]	1.33
Mathematical science teachers	1.32
Records clerks	1.26
Electrician apprentices	1.23
Dental hygienists	1.23
Teachers, prekindergarten and kindergarten	1.19
Electrical power installers and repairers	1.15
Supervisors; distribution, scheduling, and adjusting clerks	1.12
Purchasing agents and buyers, n.e.c.[a]	1.07
Dental assistants	1.06
Mail clerks, except postal service	1.02
Kitchen workers, food preparation	1.02
Cost and rate clerks	1.00
Counselors, educational and vocational	0.98
Industrial engineers	0.98
Health technologists and technicians, n.e.c.[a]	0.96
Licensed practical nurses	0.94
Expediters	0.93
Elevator installers and repairers	0.92
Underwriters	0.89
Short-order cooks	0.89
Supervisors, computer equipment operators	0.89
Respiratory therapists	0.87
Photoengravers and lithographers	0.86
File clerks	0.84
Clinical laboratory technologists and technician	0.83
Supervisors, extractive occupations	0.83
Supervisors, production occupations	0.82
Machine operators, not specified	0.82
Miscellaneous machine operators, n.e.c.[a]	0.81
Industrial truck and tractor equipment operators	0.80
Lathe and turning machine operators	0.78
Investigators and adjusters, except insurance	0.78
Mining occupations, n.e.c.[a]	0.74
Meter readers	0.74
Interviewers	0.73
Supervisors, general office	0.72
Weighers, measurers, checkers, and samplers	0.71
Waiters and waitresses	0.70
Hotel clerks	0.67
Graders, and sorters, except agricultural	0.66
Librarians	0.65
Archivists and curators	0.65

Table 3.2 Percent of Self-Employed Workers, by Occupation, 1983–2002 (continued)

Occupation	Percent Self-Employed
Library clerks	0.64
Order clerks	0.61
Health aides, except nursing	0.61
Data-entry keyers	0.61
Electrical and electronic equipment assemblers	0.58
Marine and naval architects	0.51
Chemical technicians	0.51
Traffic, shipping, and receiving clerks	0.50
Furnace, kiln, and oven operators, except food	0.49
Operations and systems researchers and analysts	0.49
Helpers, construction trades	0.46
Stock and inventory clerks	0.44
Packaging and filling operators	0.44
Food counter, fountain, and related occupations	0.43
Garbage collectors	0.39
Stock handlers and baggers	0.38
Production coordinators	0.36
Telephone operators	0.34
Miscellaneous food preparation occupations	0.30
Production inspectors, checkers, and examiners	0.27
Mixing and blending machine operators	0.24
Personnel clerks, except payroll and timekeeping	0.23
Supervisors, guards	0.23
Teachers, special education	0.23
Telephone line installers and repairers	0.23
Waiters/waitresses' assistants	0.23
Art, drama, and music teachers	0.22
Radiology technicians	0.21
Duplicating machine operators	0.19
Firefighting occupations	0.19
Molding and casting machine operators	0.18
Teachers, secondary school	0.16
Bank tellers	0.15
Administrators and officials, public administration	0.13
Teachers' aides	0.11
English teachers	0.11
Postsecondary teachers, subject not specified	0.06
Police and detectives, public service	0.05
Teachers, elementary school	0.03
Mail carriers, postal service	0.02

Source: Adapted from data in the Bureau of Labor Statistics, Current Population Survey.

[a]n.e.c. = not elsewhere classified.

Table 3.3 Occupations for Which No One Reported Being Self-Employed between 1983 and 2002

Administrators in protective services
Agriculture and forestry teachers
Air traffic controllers
Apparel and fabric patternmakers
Atmospheric and space scientists
Automobile mechanic apprentices
Biological science teachers
Bookbinders
Brickmason and stonemason apprentices
Bridge, lock, and lighthouse tenders
Carpenter apprentices
Cementing and gluing machine operators
Chemistry teachers
Chief communications operators
Chief executives and general administrators, public administration
Classified ad clerks
Communications equipment operators
Computer science teachers
Cooks, private household
Correctional institution officers
Crossing guards
Crushing and grinding machine operators
Drilling and boring machine operators
Earth, environmental, and marine science teachers
Economics teachers
Education teachers
Elevator operators
Eligibility clerks, social welfare
Engineering teachers
Explosives workers
Extruding and forming machine operators
Fabricating machine operators
Folding machine operators
Foreign language teachers
Forging machine operators
Hand engraving and polishing occupations
Health record technologists and technicians
Health specialties teachers
Heat-treating equipment operators
Helpers, extractive occupations
Helpers, surveyor
History teachers
Hoist and winch operators
Home economics teachers
Industrial engineering technicians

Table 3.3 Occupations for Which No One Reported Being Self-Employed between 1983 and 2002 (continued)

Judges
Lathe and turning machine set up operators
Law teachers
Lay out workers
Legislators
Locomotive operating occupations
Longshore equipment operators
Machine feeders and offbearers
Machinist apprentices
Mail preparing and paper handling machine operators
Marine life cultivation workers
Material recording, scheduling, and distributing clerks
Mathematical scientists
Mechanical controls and valve repairers
Mechanical engineering technicians
Medical science teachers
Milling and planing machine operators
Miscellaneous metal and plastic processing machine operators
Miscellaneous metal, plastic, stone, and glass working machine operators
Miscellaneous precision metal workers
Miscellaneous printing machine operators
Motion picture projectionists
Nail and tacking machine operators
Natural science teachers
Numerical control machine operators
Patternmakers and model makers, metal
Patternmakers and model makers, wood
Peripheral equipment operators
Physical education teachers
Physics teachers
Plumber, pipefitter, and steamfitter apprentices
Political science teachers
Postal clerks, excluding mail carriers
Power plant operators
Precision assemblers, metal
Production samplers and weighers
Production testers
Protective service occupations
Psychology teachers
Punching and stamping press machine operators
Rail vehicle operators
Railroad brake, signal, and switch operators
Railroad conductors and yardmasters
Recreation workers
Rolling machine operators

Table 3.3 Occupations for Which No One Reported Being Self-Employed between 1983 and 2002 (continued)

Sailors and deckhands
Samplers
Science technicians
Sheet metal worker apprentices
Sheriffs, bailiffs, and other law enforcement officers
Shoe machine operators
Social science teachers
Social work teachers
Solderers and brazers
Stationary engineers
Statisticians
Stevedores
Supervisors, financial records processing
Supervisors, firefighting and fire prevention occupations
Supervisors, handlers, equipment cleaners, and laborers
Supervisors, police and detectives
Telegraphers
Theology teachers
Tool and die maker apprentices
Tool programmers, numerical control
Trade and industrial teachers
Urban planners
Ushers
Water and sewage treatment plant operators
Welfare service aides
Winding and twisting machine operators

Source: Adapted from data in the Bureau of Labor Statistics, Current Population Survey

anyone goes to work for him or herself. But as we can see from the data in table 3.3, there are a large number of occupations in which the odds of starting your own business are actually zero! For these occupations, the Bureau of Labor Statistics reports that *no one* went to work for themselves in any of the twenty years between 1983 through 2002.

Are Immigrants More Likely Than the Native Born To Be Entrepreneurs?

Are immigrants carriers of an entrepreneurial spirit that leads them to start new businesses, spurring our country's economic growth? If you read newspapers or magazines regularly, you probably think the answer to this question is "yes." The popular wisdom is that immigrants have the work ethic, gumption, willingness to take risks, and a host of other things that enable them to start businesses at a rate higher than the native-born population. As a result—the story goes—we can boost start-up activity in this country by bringing in more immigrants.

Once again, the popular wisdom turns out to be an urban legend. A variety of data sources indicate that, since 1980, immigrants have been no more likely than people born in this country to start businesses.[28] Moreover, immigrants are not a monolithic group, and there is substantial variation among the different immigrant groups in the likelihood of starting a business. For instance, one study showed that 29 percent of male immigrants from Israel and 28 percent of male immigrants from Korea were self-employed, while only 3.2 of male immigrants from Laos and 3.6 percent of male immigrants from Puerto Rico worked in their own businesses.[29] The greater variation between immigrant groups suggests that immigrant status per se doesn't explain who goes into business for themselves.

Although we do not know why immigrants from some countries are so much more likely than immigrants from other countries to go to work for themselves once they get to America, we do know that one explanation often bandied about in the press—that the rate of firm formation in the immigrants' country of origin explains their odds of starting a business in the United States—isn't the explanation. The data show that there is no relation between the rate of business formation in an immigrant group's country of origin and their rate of firm formation in the United States.[30] Instead, researchers think that the differences in rate of entrepreneurial activity among immigrant groups might have to do with their access to capital or their tendency to work in certain professions.

It's What You Know, Not Who You Know

One of the myths about entrepreneurship is that what you know is less important than who you know. Many people talk about how important social networks are to starting a business. If you have a better social network, you will be more likely to raise money, hire people, and do all of the other things that you need to do to get a business started. The belief in this conventional wisdom is so strong that one state government provides a guide for its residents, which identifies social networking as one of its five tips for starting a business![31]

While the idea that being a good networker will increase your odds of starting a new business is appealing to many people, the data don't support it. The Panel Study of Entrepreneurial Dynamics, which examined a representative sample of the working-age population in the United States, found that people starting new businesses are no different from the rest of the population on most measures of social networking. Moreover, on the few dimensions on which they are different, the study found that the entrepreneurs actually use their social networks for assistance *less* than the rest of the population. For instance:

- Only 63 percent of the entrepreneurs, but 74 percent of the rest of the population, indicate that other people were helpful to them in their work.
- The entrepreneurs indicated that they had only one or two career helpers, while the control group indicated that they had significantly more, with more than a third of the control group having more than five helpers.
- The entrepreneurs talked to their helpers about business matters at half the rate of people who were not in the process of starting a business.[32]

In short, it doesn't appear that being good at networking does much to increase your odds of starting a business when compared to the networking that generally takes place for others. If anything, being a lone wolf is more common. If we combine this evidence with the evidence that industry and management experience affect the odds of starting a business, then it appears that starting a business depends more on what you know than on whom you know.

Busted Myths and Key Realities

10. The typical entrepreneur isn't a Silicon Valley tycoon, but rather a white man, married and in his forties, who started his business because he didn't want to work for someone else and who is just trying to make a living.

11. Psychological factors account for very little of the difference between entrepreneurs and other people, much less than demographic factors like age, race, and gender.

12. The typical entrepreneur doesn't start a business because of a desire to make money, for the thrill of starting businesses, to support their families, or to become well known; the typical entrepreneur starts a business because he doesn't like working for someone else.

13. The characteristics that make people more likely to start businesses aren't all desirable; people are more likely to go into business for themselves if they are unemployed, work part-time, have changed jobs often, and make less money.

14. Entrepreneurship is not a young person's game; middle-aged people are more likely than anyone else to be entrepreneurs.

15. Education doesn't hinder entrepreneurship; getting an education makes people more likely to start businesses.

16. Studying business isn't that important to becoming an entrepreneur; studying things that correspond to occupations in which a lot of people run their own businesses is just as likely to increase your chances of starting a business.

17. Working for someone else increases the chances that a person will start his own business.

18. Immigrants are not more likely than the native born to start their own businesses.

19. Being a good networker doesn't increase a person's odds of starting a new business.

In Conclusion

So who starts new businesses? The typical entrepreneur looks a lot like your next door neighbor: a married white man in his forties, who started his business because he didn't want to work for someone else and who is just trying to make a living, not build a high-growth company.

The characteristics that make people more likely to start businesses aren't all the desirable ones that our myths associate with entrepreneurship. The data show that the likelihood that a person starts a business increase if he:

- is unemployed
- works part-time
- has changed jobs often
- makes less money

Finally, the kinds of experiences that make people more likely to start businesses aren't the ones you usually read about. The experiences often associated with being an entrepreneur—immigrating, dropping out of school, and networking—don't actually increase the odds that people will start businesses. Instead, going to college, getting a professional degree, and having some experience managing others in a business setting are the experiences that actually increase a person's odds of starting a company.

4

What Does the Typical Start-Up Look Like?

If you were to ask a random person on the street to describe what she thought of as a typical start-up company, what would she say? Many would likely describe a small, growing business, one that was generating a couple million dollars in sales and employing 10 or so people, and that was organized as a corporation by a team of entrepreneurs who were developing an innovative new product or service with the intent of challenging existing businesses through the deft exploitation of a competitive advantage. After all, that's the description put forth in most newspaper and magazine articles about start-ups. It's also the kind of description you would see in the how-to books and textbooks. But is it accurate?

If you believe that this is an apt description, then the information in this chapter will probably defy your expectations. The data paint a very different picture of the typical new business than do most of the media.

Most New Businesses Are Very Ordinary

The typical new business is extremely ordinary. So ordinary, in fact, that you would probably never read about it in a popular newspaper, book, or magazine as it's not exciting enough to hold most readers' interest. The typical start-up isn't innovative, doesn't intend to challenge existing companies, lacks a single competitive advantage, and is not intended to grow. It's just plain boring in comparison to the mythic start-ups that people want to hear about.

Most Start-Ups Aren't Innovative

The typical entrepreneur is often described as an innovator. Take, for example, the following passage from one commentator: "Entrepreneurs . . . see *new* opportunities and risk exploring them—[they are] the people who find *new* markets, create *new* products, think out *new* ways to handle commodities commercially, organize work in *new* ways, design *new* technology or transfer capital to more productive uses. The entrepreneur is an explorer, who ventures into uncharted territory and opens up the *new* routes along which we will all be traveling soon enough" (emphasis added).[1]

Although many people associate entrepreneurs with innovation, most new businesses aren't doing anything innovative at all. The data show that almost all new businesses produce the *same* products and services as existing businesses, and almost none of them provide a product or service that their founder views as unique.[2] Even among some of the best start-ups—the Inc. 500 firms, which are the fastest growing private companies in the United States—only 10 percent offer a product or service that other companies do not offer.[3]

Most new businesses don't *intend* to do something innovative enough to alter the market they are in. Data from the Entrepreneurship in the United States Assessment indicates that only 2 percent of new business founders *expect* their new companies to have a substantive effect on the markets in which they operate, and 91 percent expect to have little or no impact on those markets.[4]

Most Start-Ups Are Tiny

Most new businesses are really tiny. Only 24 percent of the new businesses founded each year employ anyone (and only 16.9 percent of the self-employed hire any employees).[5] Moreover, the firms that do have employees have very few.[6] Of the 578,543 new businesses with employees that were started in the average year between 1989 and 2003, only 10 percent had 5 or more employees, and only 4.5 percent were started with more than 20 employees.

The average new firm that has any employees has 3.8 of them. But because approximately 76 percent of new businesses have no employees,[7] the average start-up in the United States begins with 1 employee, including the founder.

New businesses are also small when measured by revenues. The Federal Reserve's Survey of Consumer Finances indicates that the median (typical) revenue of an owner-managed firm is $90,000;[8] while the Census Bureau's Characteristics of Business Owner Study, a survey of 125,000 self-employed owners of sole proprietorships, partnerships, or subchapter S corporations, found that the average revenues per business was $183,973.[9]

Few New Businesses Intend to Grow

Our myth of the growth aspirations of new businesses resembles those of venture capital-backed companies like Apple Computer. Although these businesses may begin in a garage, their founders aspire to create giant corporations.

While the stories of these companies are no doubt true, so are stories of people who get struck by lightning in their back yards. The problem with them, like the stories of people hit by lightning, is that they are told and retold with such frequency that people forget how rare they are. People start to believe the myths about the growth aspirations of entrepreneurs and don't pay any attention to the reality.

The reality of entrepreneurship is that the founders of very few new businesses have any intention of expanding. One study of a representative sample of the founders of new businesses started in 1998 showed that 81 percent of them had no desire to grow their new businesses.[10] Given the size of the typical start-up when it is founded, this means that fewer than *one in five* new business founders has any aspiration of building a business that is larger than one employee and about $174,000 in annual sales.

Another study showed that half of the founders of a representative sample of start-ups in the United States in 1993 expected to have only one employee in their business's first year of operation and only three employees in their third year of operation.[11] Other data, collected from a representative sample of new business founders in a variety of countries, indicate that almost two-thirds of firm founders do not expect their new companies to generate more than two jobs within five years.[12]

Even among the small number of entrepreneurs who do intend to expand their businesses, the size aspirations of the typical entrepreneur are very small. For instance, one study found that half of a representative sample of new business founders in the United States expect their firms to have sales of *less than $100,000* in their fifth year of operation.[13]

Many entrepreneurs do not think that their new businesses will become substantial enough to supplant their jobs. The data show that one-third of entrepreneurs don't expect their new businesses to replace their jobs, seeing them instead as a way to provide additional household income, much like a part-time job.[14]

Many New Businesses Lack a Competitive Advantage

As you no doubt know, the standard explanation for why some firms perform better than others is that they have a competitive advantage. Successful firms have some sort of unfair advantage—a patented technology, a superior production process, better economies of scale, a more talented workforce, and so on—that other firms can't match.

Because you know about the value of a competitive advantage to firm performance, you might expect that all start-ups would all have some sort of competitive advantage to use in their battles against other companies, or at least that the founders of those companies *believe* they have a competitive advantage. You wouldn't expect founders of new companies to report that their new businesses have no competitive advantages over other companies.

As it turns out, the founders of more than one-third of all new firms report that they do not have any kind of competitive advantage. This may be an understatement. Because most founders tend to believe in their new businesses, their self-reports about their companies may be inflated. Still, in the preliminary data from the Kauffman Firm Survey—a national probability sample of new businesses founded in the United States in 2004—only 63 percent of the founders of new businesses reported that their new business had a competitive advantage. That is, more than one-third of the founders of new businesses believe that their new companies have nothing that allows them to out-compete other firms—not a patented technology, better customer service, superior financing terms, or even better entrepreneurial hustle.

Every Other New Business Is Home-Based

Existing myths about entrepreneurship don't mention that every other new business in America is operating out of a spare bedroom or the

Table 4.1 Location of New Businesses

Space Used	Percent of Sample
Residence, such as a home or garage	48.40
Rented or leased space	40.64
Purchased space	5.20
Customers' premises	4.78
Other location	0.98

Source: Preliminary data from the Kauffman Firm Survey.

kitchen of someone's home. Some of our myths tell about start-ups that are founded in a garage and then transformed into great businesses, but they don't describe businesses that are started in a basement and stay there.

The reality is that almost half (46 percent) of new businesses that are founded in this country and manage to stay alive for five years are started as and remain home-based businesses.[15] The distribution of locations for businesses, based on the preliminary data from the Kauffman Firm Survey, can be seen in table 4.1. Almost half of all new businesses are home-based businesses. Moreover, other sources show that, when measured over a five-year period, less than 5 percent of home-based businesses move out of the home of their founders.[16]

How Do Entrepreneurs Come Up with Their Business Ideas?

How does the typical entrepreneur come up with the idea for his new business? The popular perception is that most entrepreneurs search for new business ideas. For instance, our image of the typical entrepreneur has him surveying people about their satisfaction with existing products, asking himself what products are missing in the marketplace, reading magazines and newspapers in search of new product ideas, or looking at regulatory or demographic changes to spot new business opportunities—all in the hope of finding an idea for a new business.

If you go to your local library and browse the shelves, you will likely find a large number of books that give advice on how to search for new business ideas. And if you do an Internet search, you will quickly come across Web pages that explain "how to come up with 30 business ideas in 30 days," as well as myriad offers to enroll in seminars on how to identify new business ideas, all of which provide techniques for searching new business ideas. Many Web sites offer worksheets you can use to come up with business ideas.[17] The proliferation of these Web pages, books, and seminars give the impression that most entrepreneurs use some sort of search technique to find ideas for new businesses.

The reality is different. Most entrepreneurs don't search for new business ideas. In fact, only one-third (33.2 percent) of new business founders surveyed in the Panel Study of Entrepreneurial Dynamics responded that they engaged in a deliberate or systematic search for their new business ideas.[18] This isn't because most entrepreneurs aren't experienced enough to figure out how to identify business ideas. A survey of business founders who were members of the National Federation of Independent Businesses showed that more experienced entrepreneurs, who presumably had a better idea of how to start a new business, *conducted less research* and *collected less information* about new business ideas than entrepreneurs with less start-up experience.[19]

Entrepreneurs may not search for new business ideas because they don't believe that people "discover" new business ideas in a single aha! moment, the way our myths would suggest. Rather, 70.9 percent of the founders of new businesses surveyed in the Panel Study of Entrepreneurial Dynamics indicated that the identification of their business opportunities wasn't a "one-time thing" but instead unfolded over time. Moreover, almost half (49.6 percent) of new firm founders indicated that their business ideas changed between the time they first identified them and the time when they were surveyed about them.[20]

Also, entrepreneurs may not search for new business ideas because they don't believe that systematically searching for ideas yields very good ones. Almost the same percentage (30.4) of business founders who search for new business ideas believe that the *best* business ideas come *without searching* for them.[21]

If entrepreneurs don't search for business ideas, how do they tend to find them? The data from a variety of sources suggest that most entrepreneurs get their ideas from their experience working in an industry. Most businesses are started by people who have a significant amount of experience working in the industry in which they are launching their new companies. According to preliminary data from the Kauffman Firm Survey, an overwhelming majority—92 percent—of new businesses founded in the United States in 2004 had at least one owner who had experience in the same industry as the new business. And they had a significant amount of experience. The preliminary data from the Kauffman Firm Survey showed that the typical (median) lead owner of a new business started in the United States in 2004 had ten years of prior experience in the industry in which the new business was started. Moreover, studies show that many entrepreneurs attribute their ability to identify their new business ideas to their industry experience.[22] For instance, the Panel Study of Entrepreneurial Dynamics found that 55.9 percent of new firm founders in the United States attribute the identification of their new business idea to their experience in a particular industry or market.[23]

The interactions that entrepreneurs had with customers in their prior jobs are a common source of new business ideas. Almost a third (30.9 percent) of entrepreneurs in the Panel Study of Entrepreneurial Dynamics indicated that discussions with potential or existing customers led to their business idea.[24] Similarly, a study of business founders who were members of the National Federation of Independent Businesses found that the founder's prior job was the source of the idea for a new business 43 percent of the time.[25]

The evidence that interactions with customers at their prior jobs is a major source of new business ideas for many entrepreneurs doesn't mean that most entrepreneurs spend a lot of time working with those customers to come up with novel business ideas that dramatically depart from how customers' needs historically have been met. Rather, the data show that many new business founders simply offer the same or similar products, to the same or similar customers, as their previous employers. For instance, a study of the business founders who were members of the National Federation of Independent Businesses showed that 61 percent of new businesses serve the same or similar customers as their founder's previous employer, and 66 percent of the new businesses were in the same or similar product line.[26]

How Do Entrepreneurs Evaluate Business Ideas?

Once entrepreneurs come up with their ideas for a new business, how do they evaluate them? Our myth is that entrepreneurs carefully consider a variety of business ideas, choosing the one that appears most promising. We have an image of an entrepreneur who spends some time conducting research or talking to people about the viability of his idea before deciding whether to invest further time or money.[27]

In truth, many entrepreneurs don't conduct feasibility studies or engage in any systematic evaluation, and many of them do not compare multiple ideas in the hope of finding the best one. Data from the Panel Study of Entrepreneurial Dynamics indicate that 27.8 percent of business founders never consider any opportunities other than the one they eventually pursue.[28]

Perhaps more surprising is the small number of entrepreneurs who even have an idea of what they will do at the time that they start their new businesses. Data from the Panel Study of Entrepreneurial Dynamics indicate that 42 percent of new business founders decide to start a company before they have identified a business idea; while 37 percent first identify the business idea before starting a company (21 percent reported doing the two things at the same time).[29] In other words, 4 in 10 entrepreneurs start a company before they have a business idea. That is, they invest some of their money, set up a new legal entity, scope out a location, and so on before they know what opportunity the business will pursue.

Moreover, it isn't clear that most entrepreneurs *think* about starting their new businesses before initiating action. Data from the Panel Study of Entrepreneurial Dynamics Survey indicate that only about half (52 percent) of new business founders "spent a lot of time thinking about the business" before they took an action to start it, for example, investing money, defining market opportunities, or purchasing equipment.[30] That is, every other entrepreneur acts to start a business without thinking about it first. That doesn't suggest that the typical entrepreneur spends much time evaluating his business idea.

Getting a New Business Started

Having an idea for a new business is one thing, starting a new company is another one entirely. How does the typical start-up get off the ground? What things does the founder do and when does he do them? Does he do them alone or with other people? How long does the start-up process take? These are important questions to answer if you want to understand entrepreneurship.

There is no shortage of answers. There is a lot of material available on the topic, but most sources provide an inaccurate description of the start-up process, one that is based on our common myth of how the process works. The myth holds that entrepreneurs start their new businesses in a linear fashion, quickly and painlessly responding to economic

Table 4.2 Percent of Start-ups Undertaking Different Business Activities

Activity	At Initiation	At End of First Year
Invest money	23.8	67.1
Define opportunities	20.2	61.7
Develop product/service	22.3	59.9
Purchase inputs	13.5	52.1
Promote product/service	5.0	37.8
Purchase/lease plant and equipment	8.3	36.7
Prepare financial projections	6.1	31.6
Establish supplier credit	2.9	23.7
Seek external financing	3.8	21.4
Pay social security tax	2.0	11.5
Seek IP protection	1.4	10.1
Hire employees	1.3	8.1
Pay unemployment tax	1.3	6.7

Source: Adapted from P. Reynolds, *New Firm Creation in the U.S.: A PSED I Overview,* (Berlin: Springer-Verlag, forthcoming).

opportunities. As the story goes, the typical entrepreneur searches for a business idea, finds one, evaluates it positively, and then systematically starts to create a legal entity, followed by assembling resources, developing a product or service, and marketing it to customers, all within a few months time. While this is a nice story—and logical—it doesn't describe the way things really work.

A Process, Not an Event

Starting a new business is a process, not an event. There is no single step that you can take to start a business. When you begin the process of starting a typical new business, you are starting with a blank slate. Your business probably won't have the capital, employees, products, sales, or a host of other things that it will need to survive. For instance, one study showed that only about 11 percent of new ventures managed to make their first sale at the end of their first month.[31] Steps that we might think necessary for starting up a new business in many cases aren't undertaken for months or years (see table 4.2). For example, less than 7 percent of new businesses have paid unemployment taxes by the end of their first year of life, indicating that they had no paid employees, including the founders, at that point in time.

Organizing a business takes a lot of time. Estimates show that the typical entrepreneur needs to spend one person-year of full-time effort to get his new business started—and that's if he starts a business that doesn't require a lot of capital, and he does it alone.[32] New businesses started by teams and businesses that require more capital take longer to organize.[33] Moreover, most entrepreneurs don't work full time on their start-ups, so it often takes them more than a year to turn their new businesses into going concerns. In fact, one study looked at the efforts of firm founders who got their new businesses up and running within seven years and found that the typical entrepreneur had undertaken only 8 out of 27 possible organizing activities by the end of the venture's first year; only 10 at the end of its second year; 12 at the end of its third year; 13 at the end of its fourth year; and 14 at the end of its fifth year.[34] One observer has argued that it may take six to seven years for a start-up effort to become an established firm.[35]

If we look at specific activities that entrepreneurs undertake to create their businesses, we can see how slowly the typical start-up is created. One study of a representative sample of start-ups founded in Sweden in 1998 showed that only 6 percent of the firms' founders had written a business plan within six months of starting their new ventures, and only 25 percent had written one by the end of the venture's first year. After eighteen months, 59 percent had written one, by twenty-four months 64 percent had done one; and two-and-a-half years after the start-up process had begun, 66 percent had completed a business plan.[36] On the basis of this information, it appears that for the majority of start-ups with business plans, the founders need at least a year-and-a-half just to get their plans written.

Not a Linear Process

Our myth holds that the start-up process is linear, beginning with an idea and progressing in an orderly fashion through a series of steps to become a company selling products in the market. The reality is much messier.

As noted above, many businesses are started before a business idea is identified. Just as starting a company doesn't necessarily begin with identifying a business idea, the actions that entrepreneurs take to build their companies don't occur in a set order. Studies have shown that people initiate new businesses by undertaking any of a wide variety of different activities, with almost every organizing activity that researchers measure—investing money, initiating marketing, filing tax forms, incorporating, selling products, buying raw materials and so on—being undertaken first by some start-ups.[37] (The only activity that no entrepreneurs start with is hiring employees.)

Despite the somewhat chaotic beginnings of many new businesses, some approaches are more advisable. The data show that writing business plans increases the odds that ventures will undertake other organizing activities and product development, as well as continue in business.[38] Completing a business plan also increases the pace of initiating product development, obtaining inputs, starting marketing, talking to customers, and asking for external funds. Similarly, establishing a legal entity increases the pace of initiating product development, obtaining inputs, initiating marketing, talking to customers, and asking for external funds.[39] In short, there are a couple of facilitative, helpful actions entrepreneurs can take, but the order and nature of ensuing events do not then emerge in a predictable, invariant way.

The Firm Formation Process Fails More Than It Succeeds

Our image of a quick, methodical, and painless start-up process gives us the sense that everyone who begins the process creates a new business. This image is so ingrained in our start-up mythology that we don't even talk about the people who fail to get their new companies off the ground. We just assume that everyone who tries to start a new company succeeds and move on from there.

As it turns out, most people who start companies don't get their new ventures up and running.[40] In fact, a remarkably large percentage of people who begin the start-up process terminate it less than one year later. One study that looked at representative samples of entrepreneurs who began the start-up process in the United States, Canada, and the Netherlands found that 20 percent of entrepreneurs in the United States, 27 percent in Canada, and 26 percent in the Netherlands had abandoned their start-up efforts one year later.[41]

The outcome is no better when we look at those entrepreneurs who manage to get a new business up and running. The data show that, after seven years, only one-third of people who initiate the start-up process had a new business with positive cash flow greater than the salary and expenses of the owner for more than three consecutive months.[42]

In fact, a large number of people appear to be stuck in the process of starting a business for years on end. One study showed that more than one-third (38 percent) of the people who were in the process of starting a business in 1998 had initiated the process five years before and yet their new businesses were still not "up and running."[43] In fact, one researcher estimates that one out of every five entrepreneurs is involved in the start-up process forever, never abandoning the effort but never completing it![44] We don't know for sure why so many start-ups remain in the nether region between idea and actual business. It's probably the result of a combination of factors: some entrepreneurs want to work for themselves but have no viable business concepts, so their businesses don't progress; other entrepreneurs don't devote enough time or effort to the firm creation process, so their businesses advance at glacial speed; and still others are enamored with the idea of starting a business and so treat the business creation process as a hobby that is pursued indefinitely.

Venture Teams?

One of the more popularly held beliefs about entrepreneurship is that new businesses tend to be started by teams. You see this belief in the academic research on new businesses,[45] in business plan competitions and networking sites for entrepreneurs, and in the media profiles of new businesses. So pervasive is our belief in the idea that new businesses are created by teams of people that the term *venture team* is now part of our entrepreneurship lexicon, leading many people to talk about "venture teams" rather than about "entrepreneurs." Yet a minority of new businesses are actually started by teams.[46] The data show that between 50 and 60 percent of all new businesses are founded by a single individual.[47]

Even fewer businesses are started by teams in the sense that most people use the term, which is to mean a group of coworkers, friends, neighbors, or strangers. When businesses are started by more than one person, they are rarely started by unrelated people. In fact, the term *mom and pop business* is a more accurate description of new businesses founded by more than one person than the term *venture team;* more than half of all businesses with more than one founder (53 percent) are started by spouses.[48] Because half of ventures are founded by people alone, this means that more than three-quarters of all new ventures (76 percent) are founded by people on their own or with their spouse.

Some businesses started by more than one person are started by relatives other than husbands and wives. In fact, the data from the Panel Study of Entrepreneurial Dynamics indicate that only 18 percent of team start-ups are with non spouse family members. This means that less than 10 percent of all new businesses are founded by teams of nonrelatives.[49]

Moreover, even when new businesses have a founding team, they tend to be started initially by one person. Different representative samples of entrepreneurs indicate that between 13 and 17 percent of them organize their venture teams during the first month of the venture's life. Obviously, businesses whose founders work on creating a venture team during the first month of the venture's life could not have been formed by a team. Because half of all new businesses are founded by individuals, this number means that between one-quarter and one-third of all ventures with a founding team involve the organization of the team by the lead entrepreneur after the start-up process began.

These numbers are more extreme if you assume that the ventures run by spouses don't set up their venture teams after the start-up process has begun. Factoring out spousal teams, we find that between one-half and two-thirds of all venture teams are organized after the lead entrepreneur has initiated the start-up process.[50] Thus we probably shouldn't think in terms of venture teams when we think about who is starting companies in this country. It appears that new businesses are rarely started by teams of unrelated individuals, despite fanciful images of college roommates or childhood friends building business empires together.

Busted Myths and Key Realities

20. Contrary to most people's mental image, the typical start-up is a very ordinary, not-very-innovative, home-based business that starts and stays tiny.

21. Most entrepreneurs don't systematically search for, or evaluate, their new business ideas, offering instead the same or

similar products, to the same or similar customers, as their previous employers.

22. Thinking about business opportunities isn't something that many entrepreneurs do; more people start companies before they have identified a business idea than the other way around.

23. Starting a new business isn't a quick, painless, linear, collective, or all-encompassing process.

24. There is no one way to start a business; entrepreneurs get started by first doing a variety of different things.

25. Venture teams are very rare; the typical business is started by a single person alone; and when more than one person is involved in starting a business, it is usually two spouses working together.

In Conclusion

We have a lot of inaccurate perceptions about what the typical start-up looks like and how it gets started. Contrary to most people's mental image, the typical start-up is a small, home-based business that provides a well known product or service.

Moreover, the typical founder of a new business doesn't come up with the idea for his new business in a way that resembles our popular conception of the process. Most entrepreneurs don't systematically search for, or evaluate, their new business ideas, instead offering the same or similar products, to the same or similar customers, as their previous employers.

In fact, thinking about business opportunities isn't something that many entrepreneurs do. More people start companies before they have identified a business idea than the other way around, and only about half of all entrepreneurs spend much time thinking about their new business ideas before they take an action to start their businesses.

Starting a new business isn't as quick, painless, linear, collective, or all-encompassing a process as our popular conception suggests. A remarkably small percentage of entrepreneurs—one-third—manage to get a business established within seven years of starting the process, and even then it often takes several years to do so.

In addition, there is no one way to start a business. Entrepreneurs get started by first doing a variety of different things—investing money, initiating marketing, filing tax forms, selling products, buying raw materials, and so on. What they do next over the first couple of years of their new businesses' lives varies a great deal across ventures.

Venture teams are very rare. The typical business is started by a single person. And when more than one person starts a business, it is usually two spouses or family members working together. In short, many of our beliefs about what the typical start-up looks like and how it gets started aren't very accurate.

5

How Are New Businesses Financed?

Think about the typical start-up for a minute. How do you think it is financed? How much capital does it require? Where does that money come from? Does it come in the form of debt or equity?

Many people think that the typical new business requires hundreds of thousands of dollars to start. Much of this money, they believe, comes from an outside investor—a venture capitalist, a business angel, a friend, or a family member—who gives the founder money in return for an equity stake in the business. This view is shared by a wide range of people: entrepreneurs who think about starting new businesses; investors who provide money to young companies; and government officials who develop policies toward entrepreneurship. It shapes how we approach entrepreneurship in America.

The only problem with this view is that it's wrong. Our collective perception how the typical start-up is financed is, once again, a myth.

How Much Money Do Entrepreneurs Need to Start Their Businesses?

Studies show that the typical new business is actually started with very little capital. For instance, the Panel Study of Entrepreneurial Dynamics found that the typical (median) start-up in the United States requires $20,000 in start-up capital (measured in 1998 dollars), while the Entrepreneurship in the United States Assessment found that the typical start-up needs $15,000 in initial capital.[1]

The cost to entrepreneurs who purchase a business are not very high either. The Federal Reserve's Survey of Small Business Finances asked respondents how much money they needed to start their businesses. It found that the typical new business initiated through a purchase of a company required $34,600 (in 1996 dollars), and the typical new business started from scratch needed $22,700 (in 1996 dollars) in initial capital.[2] Although the amount of initial capital for the typical start-up through a business purchase is about 73 percent higher than for the typical start-up from scratch, the actual numbers aren't that high: neither require very much money.

The Main Source of Financing Is the Founder's Savings

Entrepreneurs, experts tell us, look everywhere for start-up capital. They go to banks, government agencies, venture capitalists, business angels, friends, family members, and anyone else that they can think of. Although these sources provide some money to entrepreneurs, the most common source of start-up capital for a new business is actually the founder's savings. In fact, the majority of entrepreneurs get their businesses started without obtaining money from anyone, and more people finance their new businesses with their own savings than obtain money from banks and friends and family members combined.[3] Even in studies of firms as much as eight years old, researchers have found that one-half received no external financing; all of the money came from the founders.[4]

Many entrepreneurs don't look for start-up capital from other sources. One study of a representative sample of business founders in the United States showed that 61 percent of them did not intend to get external financing to start their businesses.[5] Another study showed that only 56 percent of the founders of new businesses ever sought money from an external source.[6]

But businesses that receive financing from an external source are capitalized at a much higher level than those that receive only founder financing. As a result, the amount of capital provided by founders is a lower percentage of the total capital received by new firms than is the percentage of new firms that receive founder funding. Nevertheless, the amounts are still substantial. Studies show that between 20 and 30 percent of the start-up capital of new businesses comes from their founders.[7]

Does Being Wealthier Make You More Likely to Start a Business?

If the main source of financing for a new business is the founder's savings, does this mean that people are kept from starting businesses because they lack adequate capital? It is tempting to think so. Although the typical start-up doesn't require very much money, many people believe that a lot of would-be entrepreneurs are stymied by their lack of capital. Because of this belief, government policies have been put in place in the United States and elsewhere to help would-be entrepreneurs get access to capital.

But is this belief accurate? The answer is both "yes" and "no." Research shows that when a person receives money that he didn't expect, such as occurs when someone wins the lottery, his odds of starting a business increase. But having more money appears to affect the odds that a person will start a business only among the wealthiest 10 percent of Americans, and even then, only among those people considering the creation of professional service firms, like law firms and accounting firms. For other kinds of start-ups and for the other 90 percent of Americans, how much money they have doesn't appear to effect whether or not they start new businesses.[8]

How can this be true? Studies (as well as general observation) show that people with a greater net worth, higher assets, and more income are more likely than other people to start their own businesses.[9] It would seem that rich people are more likely to become entrepreneurs than poor people, but the correlation between wealth and the odds of starting a business doesn't necessarily mean that people with low income, assets, or net worth are held back from starting businesses by their lack of money.

It's entirely possible that the correlation between the tendency to start a business and wealth exists because people with more money have more business smarts than other people, and these business smarts make them think that they would be good at running their own businesses. As a result, people with more money are more likely to start new businesses than other people. This explanation makes sense because people who work in business tend to make more money than those who work in education, health care, public service, or other nonbusiness jobs. And people who work in business probably do have better business smarts than people who do not work in business, at least on average.

To see if people don't start businesses because they lack sufficient capital, several researchers have looked at whether receiving an inheritance increases the odds that a person will start a business. If it does, it would suggest that receiving money overcomes the obstacle that prevents people who lack capital from starting businesses.[10] These studies show that receiving an inheritance has the same effect on the odds of whether someone will start a business whether it is received before or after a person starts a business. This pattern indicates that receiving an inheritance doesn't increase the odds that a person will start a business by overcoming the obstacle of a lack of start-up capital.[11]

To know for sure whether a lack of money holds people back from starting businesses, we would need to randomly give money to some people while withholding it from others and then observe the behavior of each group. If those who received money were more likely to start businesses, then money would be the determining factor given that everything else between the two groups is randomly determined.

Some researchers in Sweden conducted just this experiment. They examined whether winning the lottery made people more likely to become self-employed. Because people don't know in advance whether they will win the lottery, if lottery winners are more likely than other people to go into business for themselves, then winning the lottery must be overcoming the obstacle to starting a business created by a lack of start-ups funds. The results of the study showed that winning the lottery increased the odds that people will become self-employed, thus supporting the idea that some people are kept from starting businesses by a lack of start-up capital.[13]

Thus it would seem that having more money makes people more likely to start businesses because it overcomes the constraint of a lack of money that holds people back from starting businesses that they otherwise would start. But this constraint may be more perceived than real because it doesn't take much money to get a new business going. "Not having money" might be a self-limiting belief. Moreover, a lack of money doesn't hold back all would-be entrepreneurs. Careful examination of the data indicates that the effect of having more money on the probability that a person will start a business is concentrated among the wealthiest 10 percent of Americans (those with a net worth of more than $200,000), and it appears to affect only those households that are starting professional service businesses, like law firms and accounting firms. Moreover, the size of the wealth effect is very small. Increasing wealth by $100,000 (that is, almost tripling the median net worth of $55,000) increases the odds that a person will start a business by only 10 percent.[14]

So where does this leave us? A financial windfall, like winning the lottery, does make people more likely to start businesses. But the effect of having money on the odds of starting a business is pretty small. And the effect is concentrated among people who are already pretty rich and who are also starting professional service firms.

External Personal Debt Financing

Everyone has heard the stories of entrepreneurs who have taken out a second mortgage on their homes to finance their new businesses. These stories illustrate an important point about financing new businesses in America: entrepreneurs don't just use their savings to start companies; they also use their personal credit. In fact, studies show that 65 percent of the founders of new businesses in the United States use some kind of personal debt to finance their businesses.[15]

Where do entrepreneurs turn to for the personal credit that they need to finance their new businesses? You might think that they turn principally to their credit cards, and if you do, you'd be half right. Credit cards are the most common source of personal debt used to finance new businesses. Approximately 28.3 percent of the founders of new businesses surveyed in the Panel Study of Entrepreneurial Dynamics report that they used their credit cards to help finance their new businesses. Bank loans were the second most common source of personal debt financing, having been obtained by 23 percent of the founders.[16] But credit cards are a much less important source of financing than bank loans when measured by the amount of money that they provide to new businesses. Personal loans from banks provide the founders of new businesses more than seven times as much as personal credit cards, according to preliminary data from the Kauffman Firm Survey.

Personal debt also plays a large role in new business financing because entrepreneurs often need to provide personal collateral and personal guarantees to obtain business credit cards, bank loans, and lines of credit for their businesses. In addition, they can usually obtain more external capital for their businesses if they provide these guarantees.[17] A large portion of new firm founders guarantee the debts of their businesses. The Federal Reserve's Survey of Small Business Finances indicates that the owners of between 25.1 and 48.1 percent of small businesses less than five years of age personally guarantee their businesses' loans, with the exact percentage depending on whether the businesses are sole proprietorships, partnerships, S corporations, or C Corporations.[18]

Moreover, the simple fact that most American entrepreneurs start their new businesses as sole proprietorships—not as corporations—indicates that they are on the hook for their businesses' debts. A corporation protects a founder personally against liability for the obligations of the business, but a sole proprietorship does not. Thus by setting up a sole proprietorship, the typical American entrepreneur indicates that he is willing to personally guarantee the debt of his new business.

Which Firms Get External Financing?

Although most people use their savings supplemented by personal credit to finance their new businesses, some new businesses do raise money from external sources. Why are some new start-ups able to raise external capital when others cannot? If you read about entrepreneurship in the popular press or look at entrepreneurship Web sites, you probably think that the answer has to do only with the quality of the entrepreneurs and their business ideas. The popular notion of why some entrepreneurs raise external capital for their businesses while others do not is that the former are better entrepreneurs, smoother salespeople, or have bigger, higher-quality ideas. In reality, something else also matters: the willingness to ask for money.

Entrepreneurs who ask for money from such external sources as banks, finance companies, venture capitalists, and business angels are much more likely than the others to get it. But, surprisingly, only about one-third of entrepreneurs ask others for money when they start their businesses. In fact, one study found that only 37 percent of new business founders asked external sources for money during the first two-and-a-half years of their new ventures' lives.[19]

Why do so few entrepreneurs ask others for capital? Most entrepreneurs don't look for money when their businesses are very young but seek external capital only as their ventures age. Because most new businesses fail, and fail fairly quickly, a lot of start-ups go out of business before they reach the age when most founders seek external capital.

In addition, many entrepreneurs start businesses that don't require external capital. Except for businesses—like manufacturing—that require considerable initial capital, the financing requirements for a new business are small.[20] Most businesses these days are service businesses, which demand little capital, and the most capital-intensive start-ups—those in manufacturing—are rare. As a result, searching for external capital is not something that is a priority for most entrepreneurs.

Finally, many entrepreneurs get external capital only when they decide to grow their businesses.[21] The growth process is what makes many new businesses go cash flow negative and makes external financing important. But because very few founders manage to grow their businesses, most entrepreneurs never need to raise capital from an external source. They can capitalize their businesses just fine from their savings, their personal borrowing, and their businesses' retained earnings. In short, most entrepreneurs don't get external capital because they don't ask for it, and they don't ask for it because they don't need it.

But some entrepreneurs do seek external financing, and not all of them get it. Why are some new companies more likely than others to obtain external financing? Our popular perception focuses on the entrepreneurs and their business ideas. Talented entrepreneurs who network well with investors and who are pursuing business ideas that are in vogue, the story goes, are the ones who get external financing. The others do not.

Although entrepreneurial talent and valuable business ideas undoubtedly affect whether or not founders get external financing, some more basic things also have a big effect on which new businesses get financing and which do not. One is the age of the business. The odds that a new business will get either external debt or equity financing increases as the business gets older.[22] Simply surviving for a few years improves the odds that a new business will get money from external sources.

Another often-forgotten factor is the business's level of development. Informal investors, and banks and other debt providers, tend to put their money into new businesses that have sales, positive cash flow, and employees. As a result, new businesses that have made sales or achieved positive cash flow are more likely to get capital from outside sources.

Sadly, making sales or generating positive cash flow is no mean feat; only a third of start-ups manage to do this. The rarity of these outcomes, however, is what makes them a good signal to debt and equity providers that the business is worth considering. Thus, just by selling products and generating cash, you can greatly improve the odds that your new business will raise outside capital. But even smaller steps help your chances. Studies have shown that obtaining assets, engaging in business organizing activities, initiating marketing, and completing a business plan—that is, by showing that the start-up is developing—increase the odds that a new venture will get external financing.[23]

These patterns shouldn't be surprising. Because many new ventures never get up and running and many others fail in their early years, just picking the start-up efforts that have been organized into new businesses and have survived a few years is a good way for investors to separate the wheat from the chaff in deciding what to fund.

Debt or Equity?

When most people think about how new firms are financed, they think about sources of equity capital, like venture capitalists or business angels. This focus results from the common perception that new firms are financed primarily with equity. For instance, the National Federation of Independent Businesses Small Business Policy Guide (the guide to small business put out by the largest small business trade association in the United States) notes that "very young firms are often ineligible for business loans."[24] But why do most people believe that new firms are financed largely with equity? Because they think that new firms lack the track record to pay back loans on a fixed schedule. And because they believe that investing in start-ups is very risky, which means that investors expect higher rates of return than are possible with debt financing, given the usury laws that exist in this country.

As it turns out, the received wisdom—that investors provide mostly equity financing to new businesses—is inconsistent with the data. New businesses receive a surprisingly large amount of debt financing. In fact, several studies of young firms have found that new firms are financed by debt and equity in roughly equal proportions.[25] For instance, the Federal Reserve's Survey of Small Business Finances shows that approximately half the funding for businesses less than two years old takes the form of equity (47.9 percent), while the rest (52.1 percent) takes the form of debt.[26] Information provided by investors reveals similar patterns. A survey of a representative sample of informal investors who had made at least one investment in the previous three years in a young private company owned by another person showed that 45 percent of their investments took the form of equity and 55 percent took the form of debt.[27]

Moreover, start-ups are even more likely to be financed by debt than we commonly believe if we consider only external financing. The proportion of start-ups that receive *external debt* is much higher than the proportion of start-ups that receive *external equity* because most of the equity in new businesses is provided by the founders of the company. As a result, the funding that comes from outside sources is more likely to take the form of debt, thus producing the 50-50 balance between debt and equity that we see across the population of new businesses.

The number of firms that get external debt greatly exceeds the number of firms that get external equity. Because equity investments from outside sources tend to be much larger than loans from those sources, the proportion of new businesses that borrow money from external sources is much larger than the proportion of external financing that takes the form of debt. For instance, a study of young firms in Minnesota, Pennsylvania, and Wisconsin found that less than 10 percent of the firms had received an external equity investment, but half had borrowed money from an external source.[28]

Can Start-Ups Borrow from Banks?

Although new businesses may obtain debt financing, most people believe that start-ups are not able to get loans from banks because they lack tangible assets, like accounts receivable or equipment, that can be used as collateral.[29] As one entrepreneurship textbook explains, "Banks and other lending institutions are conservators of their depositors' money and their shareholders' investments. . . . In almost no circumstances are they in a position to lend money to start-ups."[30]

Once again, it turns out that "what everyone knows" is wrong. Banks frequently lend money to start-ups. Studies that gather data from many different sources show that banks are actually the *leading source* of external debt financing for new businesses.[31] In fact, the Federal Reserve's Survey of Small Business Finances shows that loans from commercial banks account for 16 percent of the total financing of businesses that are less than two years old, 3 percent more than the next highest source, trade credit.[32]

Moreover, commercial banks provide much more financing than do commonly thought of sources of loans—friends and family, government agencies, and strategic investors. The Federal Reserve's Survey of

Small Business Finances shows that strategic investors account for only 1.5 percent of the total financing of businesses that are less than two years old, and government agencies provide a paltry 0.3 percent of the total financing of new businesses. Both of these sources provide far less money than the third most important source of financing for new businesses, nonbank financial institutions, which account for 12 percent of the total financing of businesses less than two years old.[33] Similarly, the Panel Study of Entrepreneurial Dynamics indicates that banks, trade creditors, and nonbank financial institutions all provide much more capital than strategic investors, government agencies, or friends and family.[34]

Where do these studies put business credit cards? After all, credit card financing gets perhaps the most attention of all sources of external debt financing for new businesses, at least in the popular press. Interestingly, preliminary data from the Kauffman Firm Survey show that business credit cards are by far the most common source of external debt financing. More than 27 percent of all start-up founders borrow money on their business credit cards. But like many other studies, including the Federal Reserve's Survey of Consumer Finances,[35] the preliminary data from the Kauffman Firm Survey indicate that business credit cards do not account for very many dollars of new business loans, providing less than 2 percent of all business borrowing by new companies in their first year of operation.

External Equity Finance

Most books, magazine articles, and Web sites that discuss obtaining external equity capital for new businesses contain the same message: go to friends and family, business angels, venture capitalists, other businesses, and government agencies. Although correct in noting that there aren't many options in terms of equity financing, the information provided by the media is a bit deceptive. The sources usually don't mention how few start-ups receive any external equity investment. The numbers are well down in the single digits.

These patterns are nowhere more evident than in the books, articles, Web sites, and blogs that recommend going to friends and family for financing. The most common recommendation made in the media to entrepreneurs seeking external equity is to go to the three Fs—friends, family, and fools. Take, for example, the following comments:

- "Family and friends can be a great source for bootstrap financing. They've got a vested interest in your personal success, and they may be willing to take a chance on you that no bank would."[36]
- "The irony is that in this boom time for small business, there are many sources of loans or equity financing for startups. 'Money's not that hard to get from friends and family if you've got a really good idea.'"[37]
- "Asking people you know to pitch in on financing a new or growing business is anything but a radical idea. Before anyone ever heard of banks, informal, person-to-person loans were the way many businesses got started—and the way many investors made money."[38]

These comments give the impression that getting an equity investment from friends and family is pretty common. The reality is different; getting an investment from one of these groups is pretty rare. For instance, the Panel Study of Entrepreneurial Dynamics indicates that fewer than 1 in every 12 start-ups (7.8 percent) obtained an equity investment from family or friends.[39]

Another misconception is that government agencies are an important source of external investment for start-ups. Take the television infomercials, which urge you to "come to our seminar and find out how you can get your government grant to start a small business!" A breathless announcer intones, "Just $300." A smiling entrepreneur assures in a taped testimonial, "I got $40,000 for my small business!"[40]

Some people do obtain equity investments for their start-ups from some sort of government entity, but not very many do. In fact, the odds that some city, state, federal, or other government entity will make an equity investment in your business are roughly the same as the odds that you will be audited by the Internal Revenue Service (164 to 1 for the equity investment versus 175 to 1 for the audit).[41] Preliminary data from the Kauffman Firm Survey show that, in 2004, fewer than 1 percent of start-ups in the United States received an equity investment from a government agency.

Perhaps more important, in those rare instances when a start-up gets an external equity investment from a government agency, the magnitude of that investment is small—averaging a little over one-tenth the size of the average venture capital investment. Whether measured by the frequency of investment or by the amount of money provided, the government isn't a significant source of equity investment in new companies.

This brings us to another important point. How much money will you get from different equity investors if you are lucky enough to get it? There are huge differences in the average amount of money provided by sources of equity investment that have the same odds of giving money. For instance, although other businesses are roughly as common a source of external equity as spouses, preliminary data from the Kauffman Firm Study show that the typical (median) equity investment in a start-up from another company is more than 24 times as large as the typical (median) equity investment from a spouse. So it might be a better use of your time to look for an equity investment from a potential customer or supplier of your business than to go to your spouse unless, of course, you're married to someone like Donald Trump.

Venture Capitalists Matter Less Than You Think

Virtually every guide to financing a new business discusses venture capital (VC). That's understandable. Venture capital is a very exciting business, and venture capitalists have funded the start of some very important companies—Genentech, Microsoft, Federal Express, and Google to name a few. But the focus on venture capital in the news media creates the misconception that venture capital is an important source of financing to consider if you start a new businesses. The reality is different.

Unless you have an extraordinarily high-growth biomedical or information technology start-up, with a proprietary competitive advantage and a team that has taken a company public in the past, you might as well forget about venture capital as a financing source. Venture capitalists are very picky investors who put their money in a tiny percentage of the companies founded every year. In the United States, for instance, venture capitalists make investments in about 3,000 companies each year, of which only about 500 are start-ups.[42] In other words, venture capitalists finance less than 0.03 percent of all new businesses founded in this country every year.

Think about what this means for the odds of your getting venture capital for your start-up. The managing director of Garage.com, a venture capital firm in Silicon Valley, tells people that the odds of getting VC financing are the same as the odds of being hit by lightning if you are standing in a swimming pool while the sun is shining.[43]

It isn't that bad. The odds of getting venture capital for a seed stage start-up is about 1 in 4,000, while the odds of getting hit by lightning are actually 576,000 to 1. But the odds of getting venture capital are lower than the odds that you will get hurt mowing your lawn (3,623 to 1) or fatally slip in the bath or shower (2,232 to 1).[44] When you are thinking about your new business in the shower tomorrow, don't ponder getting venture capital, think about making sure you don't fall. The chances are that it will be a better use of your time.

If you have started a typical new business, don't think that venture capital is worth considering because the amount of money provided by venture capitalists makes up for the small portion of start-ups they fund. It turns out that venture capitalists don't provide that large a share of new firm capital. The Federal Reserve's Survey of Small Business Finance shows that venture capitalists account for only 1.9 percent of total small business financing.[45] While this is a large multiple on the number of businesses they finance, the very large size of their investments does not make up for the small numbers financed in a way that makes venture capital a major source of money for new businesses in this, or any other, country.

Moreover, the industries in which the typical start-up is created receive almost no venture capital because venture capital funds concentrate their investments in a very small number of industries. Estimates are that as much as 92 percent of all venture capital goes into the information technology and health care sectors.[46] So if you haven't started a company in one of those two sectors, your odds of getting venture capital may actually be the same as the odds of getting hit by lightning, at least on a rainy day.

The Real Informal Investors

The informal investors who put their money into start-up companies are a much more important source of external equity investment than venture capitalists. Several studies show this. For instance, the Entrepreneurship in the United States Assessment estimated that informal investors provide more than eight times the amount of money to start-ups as venture capitalists.[47] In fact, the accredited angel investor portion of informal investors—people whose net worth alone or with their spouse exceeds $1 million, or who had an individual income in excess of $200,000 in each of the two most recent years, or joint income with their spouses in excess of $300,000 in each of those years—provides almost twice the amount of small business financing as venture capitalists (3.6 percent versus 1.9 percent), according to the Federal Reserve Survey of Small Business Finances.[48]

Clearly informal investors in start-ups are an important source of capital for new companies. But who are these people? One informal funding source is an accredited investor, someone who is experienced as an entrepreneur and who is concerned about both return on investment and mentoring would-be entrepreneurs. This type of informal investor is often written about, but many other people make informal investments in start-ups. In fact, accredited investors account for only 13.4 percent of informal investments made in new businesses in the United States.[49]

Studies show that between 1 and 2 percent of the population of the United States between the ages of 18 and 70 made an investment to finance a new business founded by a nonrelative in the past three years.[50] And at any given point in time, approximately 1 percent of American households have an ownership stake in a private business that they do not manage.[51]

Why is there a misperception about what informal investors look like? Probably because the typical informal investor, and his investments, are not interesting enough to write about. The typical investor looks too much like you and me, and his investments are mundane at best. The typical informal investment is much smaller than the whopping $518,367 that the Center for Venture Research at the University of New Hampshire reports as the average investment made by an accredited angel investor.[52] The Entrepreneurship in the United States Assessment found that only 23 percent of the informal investments in the United States were more than $20,000, and 53 percent of the informal investments were less than $15,000.[53] In fact, for the period from 1997 to 2001, the average investment made by an informal investor in the United States was only $10,628, with an investment of $200,000 or more falling in the top 1 percent of all informal investments.[54]

Most informal investors in start-ups are ordinary people, not the wealthy former entrepreneurs of Silicon Valley described in most newspaper and magazine articles on angel investing. The typical unaccredited investor is a person like Ian McGlinn, a regular guy who owned a garage in Sussex, England, when he made an equity investment of £10,000 (about $17,000) in return for 50 percent ownership of a start-up business. That business? The Body Shop.[55]

The data show that the household income of 41.1 percent of the informal investors in start-ups in the United States is less than $50,000 per year. Moreover, these investors have little experience at investing in start-ups: 39 percent have made only one investment in a new venture, and only 33 percent have made more than three such investments in their lifetimes. Their experience starting businesses or working in the industries in which their investee companies operate is no better: 26 percent of the informal investors have no experience in the business sector in which the target firm is operating, and only 27 percent have experience starting or running their own business.[56]

In contrast to the popular image of groups of angel investors pooling their money and investing together, like the Band of Angels in Silicon Valley or Common Angels in Boston, most informal investors make their investments alone. According to the Entrepreneurship in the United States Assessment, only 15 percent of informal investors invest as part of a group. In fact, 30 percent of the time that he makes an investment, the typical informal investor is the sole person providing external capital to a start-up.[57]

Perhaps the most surprising information about informal investors is their motivation for making their investments. Our myth of informal investors is one of sophisticated individuals who are seeking to make money from their investments in start-ups. While perhaps not as sophisticated as venture capitalists, angel investors are seen as trying to make a buck. They are certainly not engaged in making charitable contributions when they invest their money.

But the reality is that, unlike venture capitalists and accredited business angels, most informal, nonaccredited investors in start-ups aren't very interested in achieving high financial returns. In fact, one study found that more than one-third (35 percent) of informal investors expected *no* return (that's zero, nada, zilch) on their investments in start-ups.[58] Clearly, the typical informal investor is investing in start-ups for nonfinancial reasons, such as to help out a friend.

Busted Myths and Key Realities

26. It doesn't take a lot of money to start a business; the typical new business established in the United States takes less than $25,000 in initial capital.

27. Most founders don't get money from others; the most common source of capital for a new business is the founder's savings.

28. New businesses don't borrow, their founders do; many entrepreneurs borrow personally to finance their new businesses, with personal bank loans being the most important source of personal debt for new businesses.

29. Receiving a financial windfall increases the odds that a person will start a new business, but wealthier people aren't more likely than other people to start businesses unless they are in the wealthiest 10 percent of people and are starting professional service firms.

30. One of the most overlooked reasons why some entrepreneurs get external financing is simply that they ask for it.

31. One reason some entrepreneurs who seek money get it when others don't is that their ventures are older and have undergone more development.

32. New businesses can obtain debt financing and, on average, are financed about half with debt and half with equity.

33. Banks do lend money to new businesses; the most common source of debt for new businesses is commercial banks.

34. The oft-cited friends and family aren't a very good source of external funds.

35. Venture capitalists provide money to less than one-tenth of 1 percent of all start-ups and account for less than 2 percent of all small business financing.

36. Informal investors are a more important source of capital for start-ups than venture capitalists.

37. Only 13.4 percent of informal investors are accredited

investors, and the typical informal investor is much less
wealthy, has much less experience, makes much smaller investments, and expects much lower returns than the accredited angels that we tend to hear about.

In Conclusion

It doesn't take very much money to start a business in the United States.
The typical start-up requires $24,920 in today's dollars; the typical new
business begun by acquisition takes $44,461.

Although new businesses are financed from a variety of sources,
the most common source of capital is the founder's savings. The amount
of money that founders contribute to their start-ups from their own savings underestimates how much money most entrepreneurs put into their
businesses. Many entrepreneurs borrow personally to finance their new
businesses, with personal bank loans being the most important source of
personal debt for new businesses.

Because entrepreneurs typically use their savings to capitalize their
new businesses, you might think that some people are prevented from
starting businesses because they lack the money to finance them. If you
did, you'd be partially right. Receiving a financial windfall increases the
odds that a person will start a new business, but wealthier people are no
more likely than other people to start businesses, except for the part of
the richest 10 percent that is starting accounting firms, law firms, and
medical practices.

There are a lot of reasons why some entrepreneurs get financing
from external sources and others don't. Things like the quality of their
business ideas or their talent as entrepreneurs make a difference. But
one reason some entrepreneurs get money from others is because they
seek it.

Of course, not all entrepreneurs who seek external financing get it.
There are many reasons why some entrepreneurs get money, while others don't, but one of the most basic is that their ventures are older and
have undergone more development. Investors use these factors—age

and level of development—to screen out ventures that are not worth funding.

In contrast to the common view that new firms can't get business loans, new businesses are financed about half with debt and half with equity. In fact, the most common source of debt for new businesses is commercial banks.

What most new firms are unable to obtain is equity investment from someone other than a founder of the firm. No external source provides external equity to more than a very small percentage of new firms. In fact, the oft-cited friends and family aren't a very good source of external funds, providing it to less than 6 percent of new firms. Venture capitalists matter much less than most people think, providing money to less than one-tenth of 1 percent of all start-ups and accounting for less than 2 percent of all small business financing.

Informal investors are more important than venture capitalists, providing between many times as much capital. Real informal investors don't look much like the business angels we see described in magazines and newspapers. Only 13.4 percent of informal investors are accredited investors, and the typical informal investor is much less wealthy, has much less experience, makes much smaller investments, and expects much lower returns than the accredited angels that we tend to hear about. In short, the financing of start-ups doesn't fit the pattern that most of us think it does.

6

How Well Does the Typical Entrepreneur Do?

How successful is the typical entrepreneur? If you read the popular press, you might get the impression that most entrepreneurs make a lot of money. Statements like this—"Self-employed people are four times more likely to be millionaires than those who work for others"[1]—give the impression that people who start businesses tend to be very successful and make good money. But this perception is inaccurate. In reality, the typical entrepreneur starts a company that goes under. Even the atypical entrepreneur, one whose business manages to survive over time, makes less money than he would have made if he had worked for others.

The data clearly support this position. In fact, if you think about it for a minute, the average entrepreneur almost *has to fail*. If the average new business were to survive over time, then the average existing businesses would have to fail, or the number of entrepreneurs in the United States would rise. Because we know that the number of entrepreneurs has been pretty much constant over the past few decades, and established businesses are not very likely to fail, then it must be the case that most newly started businesses fail.

But don't interpret the fact that the business started by the typical entrepreneur fails to mean that you shouldn't become an entrepreneur. The data also show that a few people become very wealthy. In fact, there are few ways for you to become very wealthy other than starting a company. If you aren't a good actor or singer, and if you have a poor fastball or jump shot, starting a business is probably the only avenue available to you.

There is another reason to become an entrepreneur: personal happiness. The data from a wide variety of studies show that people are much happier working for themselves than for others. Contrary to the common perception, the reason for starting your own business is not because doing so is likely to make you well off financially. Rather, the reason to do it is to get more psychic rewards from your work.

The Typical New Business Fails

Most new businesses fail. Pretty much all studies agree on that. The only question is how long it takes for a majority of them to go out of business (and why). Data on self-employment from several sources indicate that half of all people who become self-employed go back to work for someone else within seven years (see figure 6.1).[2] A minority of people who become self-employed remain self-employed. The numbers are pretty much the same for other measures of new businesses. Only 45 percent of new firms last five years, and only 30 percent last ten years (see figure 6.2).

These patterns are amazingly consistent across cohorts of new firms. The one-, two-, three-, and four-year failure rates of new single establishment firms founded in 1997 are identical to the one-, two-, three-, and four-year failure rates of new single establishment firms founded in 1992, and the five-year failure rate is only 1 percent higher. Moreover, the failure rates of the 1989 to 1992 cohorts of new employer firms over their first six years differ from each other by only 1 or 2 percent, and are almost identical to the failure rates for the 1992 and 1997 cohorts of new single establishment firms. And studies using data drawn from Dun and Bradstreet files for new firms founded between 1977 and 1978, different years of the Census of Business Owners, other census data on new businesses founded in 1982, and new employer firms founded in Michigan all show very similar survival patterns.[3]

Furthermore, this survival pattern is not unique to the United States. Studies have shown that it is the same in most developed economies. In short, no matter how you measure new firms, and no matter which developed country you look at, it appears that only half of new firms started remain in business for five years, and less than one-third last ten years.

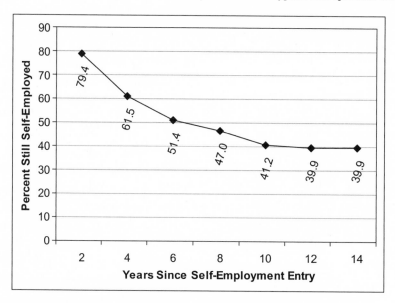

Figure 6.1. Percentage of Self-Employed People Remaining Self-Employed
Source: Adapted from data in D. Evans and L. Leighton, "Some Empirical Aspects of Entrepreneurship," *American Economic Review* 79, no. 3 (1989): 519–35.

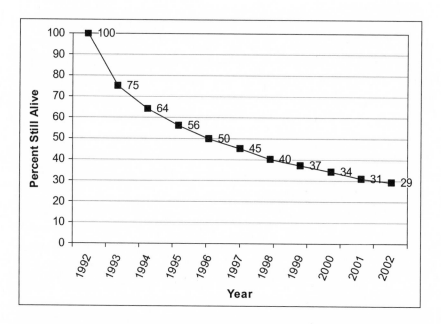

Figure 6.2. Proportion of New Businesses Founded in 1992 Still Alive, by Year
Source: Adapted from a special tabulation by the Bureau of the Census produced for the Office of Advocacy of the U.S. Small Business Administration.

Shutting Down a Business Matters

Some people argue that new business survival rates don't matter very much because there are a lot of reasons why companies cease operations. Because few of these firms go bankrupt, they say, we shouldn't interpret the fact that they go out of business as a negative. Their founders might not be unhappy with the outcome. As *Inc.* magazine commentator John Case explains, "Companies are terminated for all kinds of reasons. The owner sells out or decides to get a regular job. He or she closes one company to start another, maybe in a different industry or location. Those discontinuances are different from what we usually think of as business failures, meaning a closing in which creditors lose their money. . . . Discontinuances where creditors don't lose money account for the vast majority of all terminations. *Only about 18% of all new businesses . . . end in real failure.* The rest survive or are closed voluntarily."[4]

Should we think of closed businesses as successes as Mr. Case and others have implied, or should we think of them as failures as I have suggested? There's one way to figure that out: ask the founders of terminated businesses how they view the outcome of their entrepreneurial endeavors.

One study did just that, and the result is instructive. In contrast to Mr. Case's view that the termination of a new business isn't a negative, a survey of new employer and nonemployer firms founded between 1989 and 1992 that went under within four years showed that 70.1 percent of the founders felt that their start-up effort *was unsuccessful.*[5] If the founders think of their start-ups as unsuccessful because they ceased operations, it would seem a clear indication, then, that those businesses were unsuccessful, despite whether they ended in bankruptcy or not.

Moreover, the termination of a new business adversely affects its founder financially. Although many people believe that entrepreneurs are not personally liable for the debts of their businesses should they fail, this perception turns out to be inaccurate. Most entrepreneurs personally bear the financial obligations of their failed businesses because most new businesses are organized as sole proprietorships, an organizational form that does not provide limited liability (see table 6.1).[6] In short, most entrepreneurs are unhappy about the termination of their start-ups even if the businesses don't go bankrupt, perhaps because they are on the hook for the debt of the failed businesses.

Table 6.1 Legal Form of New Ventures, By Percent

Legal Form	Percent of New Firms
Sole proprietorship	59.8
General partnership	14.9
Limited partnership	6.4
Limited liability company	10.2
Subchapter S corporation	3.8
General corporation	3.8

Source: Adapted from P. Reynolds, "Nature of Business Start-Ups," in *Handbook of Entrepreneurial Dynamics,* ed. W. Gartner, K. Shaver, N. Carter, and P. Reynolds (Thousand Oaks, Calif.: Sage, 2004), and P. Reynolds *Entrepreneurship in the U.S.* (Miami, Florida International University, 2004).

Entrepreneurs Don't Earn Very Much

Not only do most new businesses fail, but the typical start-up that manages to survive over time isn't very profitable. Only one-third of all owner-operated businesses generate more than $10,000 in profits annually.[7] The typical level of profits isn't much higher. The Federal Reserve's Survey of Consumer Finances shows that the median (typical) profit of owner-managed firms is $39,000.[8] This number probably overstates how much money the typical new firm makes because the data include only those start-ups that survive until the time that the survey was conducted, and businesses are more likely to survive if they are making money.

And this lack of profits isn't because the owner-operator is pulling everything out of the business as compensation. Several studies have compared the total compensation of people running their own businesses with what they would earn working for others. The studies show that the average self-employed person *earns significantly less* than the average person who works for someone else.[9] In fact, the median (typical) earnings of people who have run their own businesses for ten years is 35 percent lower than what they would have earned working for someone else. Going out twenty-five years, this gap shrinks, but only to 25 percent. Moreover, no matter how long he works for himself, the typical entrepreneur always earns less than the entry-level salary for someone doing the same thing but employed by someone else![10]

It's possible that people who work for themselves are not as talented as people who work for others, and that their lesser talent is what explains their lower compensation. Researchers, however, have used a statistical technique that compares the earnings of *the same people* when they work for themselves and when they work for others to determine if this is the case. Using this technique, researchers have found that people with ten years of work experience and job tenure earn 18 percent less when they are entrepreneurs than when they work for someone else.[11] Add to this the fact that the average person who works for himself has fewer benefits, such as health insurance, than the average person who work for someone else,[12] and it becomes clear that compensation of the typical entrepreneur is significantly less than the compensation of the typical employee.

Returns from Entrepreneurship Are Uncertain

As if earning less money than the average employee were not bad enough, the range in incomes among entrepreneurs is much greater than the range in incomes among people who are employed by others to do the same job, in the same industry, serving the same customers. Moreover, entrepreneurs have much more variation in their incomes from month-to-month and from year-to-year than people who work for others.[13]

This income variability is problematic for entrepreneurs in two ways. First, it means that becoming an entrepreneur involves risking downward income mobility. Said another way, if you start a business, your chances are much higher that you will slip to a lower socioeconomic level than if you go to work for someone else. This risk is particularly great if your income is already high.[14] Starting a business means taking a chance that your family will become significantly worse off financially.

Second, the variability of self-employment income means that entrepreneurs pay higher average income taxes than people who work for others. Because their income fluctuates significantly from year to year, entrepreneurs often end up in high marginal tax brackets for the years in which they make a lot of money, but because of how the tax code is structured, they don't get corresponding tax reductions in the years when they make less money. As a result, if you average entrepreneurs' incomes over time, you will find that they pay more in taxes on the same amount of earnings than people who work for others because the latter tend to earn that money more evenly over time.

Entrepreneurs Earn No Extra Return on Their Invested Capital

You might think that the financial returns that entrepreneurs reap on the capital they invest in their businesses might make up for their lower and more variable incomes. After all, the popular conception is that entrepreneurs don't get as much in salary as they would have gotten working for someone else, but they cash in later when they sell their businesses. It's a nice story, but it doesn't jibe with the data. Researchers have looked at the financial returns that entrepreneurs earn on the capital they invest in their companies and have found that, on average, it is the same as they would have gotten had they invested their capital in publicly traded stocks.[15]

Actually, the typical entrepreneur is worse off than the typical employee even though they earn the same return on invested capital. Because the entrepreneur's investment is illiquid, he can't sell it quickly or easily if he needs to. If he needs cash, he has to get the money elsewhere, probably at a higher cost than he would have incurred if he sold the investment. In contrast, if the employee needs some cash, he can go to a discount broker and sell some of his stock, probably at a pretty low cost.

Moreover, the entrepreneur's investment is undiversified. He has all of his eggs in one basket—his business—while the employee, if he puts his money into a mutual fund, is able to invest in a variety of companies. Being diversified minimizes the amount of risk a person has to bear to get a given financial return. And since none of us like risk, the entrepreneur, who has to bear more risk, is worse off.[16]

Entrepreneurs Work More Than Others

In addition to earning less money, facing more variable compensation than the typical employee, and achieving no extra financial gain from investing his money in his own business, the typical entrepreneur also works more hours. Studies show that both the median (typical) and mean (average) number of hours worked by people who run their own businesses are higher than those of people who work for others.[17]

In fact, entrepreneurs are found to have a greater work load in all of the countries where it has been examined, except for Chile and Russia (see table 6.2). Moreover, entrepreneurs don't work just a little bit

Table 6.2 Average Number of Hours Worked Per Week for Self- and Wage-Employed by Country in 1999

Country	Self-Employed	Wage-Employed	Difference
East Germany	56.7	41.3	15.4
West Germany	54.2	39.7	14.5
Poland	56.5	42.9	13.6
France	49.9	37.1	12.8
Slovakia	56.3	43.5	12.8
Bulgaria	54.6	42.1	12.5
Northern Ireland	43.7	34.4	9.3
Slovenia	52.0	43.0	9.0
Sweden	47.2	38.5	8.7
Czech Republic	52.0	43.7	8.3
Norway	45.7	39.0	6.7
New Zealand	46.3	40.0	6.3
Hungary	51.8	46.1	5.7
Portugal	47.0	41.5	5.5
Spain	49.9	45.2	4.7
United States	44.7	40.3	4.4
Japan	51.6	47.3	4.3
Israel	42.8	38.5	4.3
Cyprus	42.6	38.4	4.2
Great Britain	42.6	38.6	4.0
Australia	39.4	36.4	3.0
Canada	41.4	39.1	2.3
Latvia	44.2	42.0	2.2
Chile	46.5	48.2	−1.7
Russia	36.5	39.0	−2.5

Source: Adapted from D. Blanchflower, "Self-employment: More May Not Be Better," *Swedish Economic Policy Review* 11, no. 2 15–74.

harder than other people. In some countries, for example, in Germany and Poland, the average self-employed person works an additional 13 or more hours per week.

Some people think that entrepreneurs work more hours because they love what they are doing. As the story goes, they spend more time at work because being at work makes them happy. This idea is one of our myths about entrepreneurship. Although the typical entrepreneur is more satisfied with his job than the typical employee, it isn't the long hours that make him more satisfied. Surveys have shown that self-employed people are more dissatisfied with their work hours than people who work for others.

Moreover, self-employed people report that this higher workload exacts a physical and psychological toll. People who have their own businesses are more likely than people who work for others to report that their work:

- is stressful and exhausting
- creates a strain and pressure in their lives
- causes them to lose sleep
- makes it difficult for them to enjoy their leisure activities
- causes conflict with their spouses
- makes them unhappy or depressed[18]

Entrepreneurs don't work more hours than other people because doing so makes them happy; they work more hours than other people, even though they don't like it.

Are Entrepreneurs Overoptimistic about the Prospects of Their Ventures?

The average entrepreneur works harder but earns less money than the guy who works for someone else. He receives no extra financial gain from investing his money in his own business, and he faces much more uncertain compensation. Given this dismal picture, why does anyone start a business? Is there something that makes up for the greater hours worked and the lesser earnings?

One answer is that the typical entrepreneur is just an overoptimistic fool. He systematically overestimates his chances of success, which motivates him to start businesses even though his prospects are, on average, pretty poor. Because the average entrepreneur doesn't live in Garrison Keeler's Lake Wobegon (where "all the children are above average"), he ends up worse off financially than he would have been had he not started a business.

There is some evidence that this is the case. Studies show that people who work for themselves tend to expect better financial outcomes over the coming year than those who work for other people, even though they tend to experience worse actual results.[19] Moreover, other studies show that the average entrepreneur assesses the probability that he "will succeed" with his new business at 81 percent, even though this probability is higher than the one-year *survival* rate of new businesses. The typical entrepreneur also assesses the probability of success of his businesses as higher than those of businesses "like his."[20]

A Few Entrepreneurs Are Very Successful

Despite the poor performance of the average start-up, people who start businesses aren't necessarily overoptimistic fools. Entrepreneurship is a lot like gambling. The average outcome is negative, just as it is in Las Vegas where, on average, the money goes to the house. But some people win, and they win big. That's why some people buy Powerball tickets, put coins into the slots, play blackjack, and start businesses. Although the average outcome is negative, the winners do really well.

How do we know? Take a look at the data. As you no doubt remember from the beginning of the chapter, most new firms simply fail, with 70 percent of start-ups gone ten years after starting. Those that survive show little growth. In fact, from year-to-year, between 65 and 75 percent of new businesses have the same employment that they had the previous year.[21]

Over longer periods, the record is little better, with studies showing that as many as two-thirds of surviving firms experience no employment growth at all over their first nine years of life.[22] If you combine the low survival rate of new businesses with the low percentage of new businesses that grow, you find that only about 10 percent of new firms are still around and have more than their initial number of employees ten years after their founding. That is, only 10 percent of new businesses ever grow.[23]

Even fewer firms grow a lot. One study showed that less than 3 percent of businesses add more than 100 employees.[24] And growing a lot consistently is rarer still. Studies show that the firms that show rapid growth in one year tend not to show that same level of growth the next year.[25] In short, the small number of new businesses that win account for almost all of the employment growth that we see. On employment, at least, the winners win big.

We can see similar patterns in entrepreneurs' incomes. Business-owning households make almost three times as much, on average, as non-business-owning households (one study showed $127,702 as compared to $45,177).[26] But almost all of the income difference between busi-

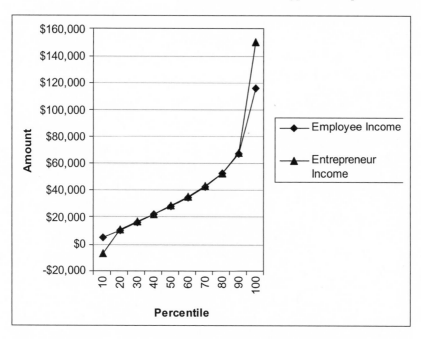

Figure 6.3. The Income Distribution of Entrepreneurs and Employees
   Source: Adapted from V. Quadrini, "The Importance of Entrepreneurship for Wealth Concentration and Mobility," *Review of Income and Wealth* 45, no. 1 (1999): 1–19.

ness-owning households and non-business-owning households comes from the most successful entrepreneurial households (see figure 6.3).

The same is true for entrepreneurs' wealth. One study showed that the wealthiest 10 percent of business owners have almost three-quarters (73 percent) of all business wealth, 38 percent of all personal assets, and 39 percent of all personal net worth.[27] Another study found that the average net worth of a business-owning household was $984,307, as compared to $190,023 for the average non-business-owning household.[28] Most of this difference, however, comes from the difference between the net worth of the most successful entrepreneurs and that of the most successful employees (see figure 6.4).

Lest you think that the greater wealth of business owners represents old money from businesses that are handed down from generation to generation, consider this additional fact: business-owning households are *more likely* than households where people do not own businesses to move up to a higher wealth category.[29] That is, having a business is a

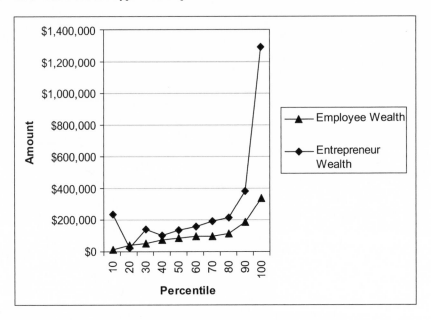

Figure 6.4. The Wealth Distribution of Entrepreneurs and Employees
   Source: Adaped from V. Quadrini, "The Importance of Entrepreneurship for Wealth Concentration and Mobility," *Review of Income and Wealth* 45, no. 1 (1999): 1–19.

path to upward mobility. Thus, entrepreneurship offers people the opportunity to generate a very high income, a very high net worth, and to move up in economic status, but only if they succeed.

Founder Satisfaction

There's another reason why people aren't necessarily foolish when they start businesses, despite the poor financial performance of the average start-up. Entrepreneurship provides a very important nonfinancial benefit: it makes people happier. In a wide variety of countries, studies show that people who work for themselves have higher job satisfaction than people who work for others.[30] This is true not just for one cohort of people; the studies show consistent results for young and old alike.

Moreover, the size of the difference in levels of satisfaction is substantial. In the United States, 62.5 percent of people who work for themselves are satisfied or very satisfied with their jobs, compared with only 45.9 percent of people who work for others.[31]

You might say that these patterns just reflect the fact that people who tend to be happier also tend to go into business for themselves. But we know this isn't the case because some studies have looked at the same people when they are working for themselves *and* when they are working for others. These studies have found that people are more satisfied with their jobs when they are working for themselves than when they are working for others. In fact, the studies show that to be as satisfied when he is working for others as he is when he is working for himself, the average person needs to earn two-and-a-half times as much money![32]

What makes entrepreneurs more satisfied with their jobs than people who work for others? For many women, it's the flexibility it allows to work and care for small children at the same time.[33] For both men and women, it's the ability to work in a small organization. The data show that as companies get bigger, the job satisfaction of people who work in them declines. Human beings, it seems, prefer to work in settings where they can interact directly with everyone else who is part of the company. Finally, entrepreneurs are more satisfied with their jobs because of the autonomy, flexibility, and greater control over their lives that being their own boss provides.[34] That is a big part of why people go into business for themselves and a big part of what they get out of it as well.

Busted Myths and Key Realities

38. Most start-ups do not succeed; the typical entrepreneur forms a business that is gone within five years and views his effort to start that company as unsuccessful.

39. The typical entrepreneur earns less money than he would have earned had he worked for someone else and has worse job benefits.

40. Making money as an entrepreneur is very uncertain; the typical entrepreneur has a more variable income than he would have had as an employee, which leads him to risk downward mobility.

41. The typical entrepreneur works more hours than people who work for others, and he isn't happy about it.

42. Many entrepreneurs start businesses despite the poor performance of the typical entrepreneur because they are overoptimistic about their chances of success.

43. The typical entrepreneur tolerates the lower earnings he receives from starting a business, compared to what he would have earned working for someone else, because he is happier working for himself.

44. Even though the typical entrepreneur experiences poor financial performance, a small number of entrepreneurs are very successful, earn a lot of money, increase their net worth substantially, and move up the economic ladder.

In Conclusion

The typical entrepreneur's financial performance isn't good.

- He forms a business that is gone within five years, and he views his effort to start that company as unsuccessful.
- He earns less money than he would have earned had he worked for someone else, and he has worse job benefits.
- He has a more variable income than he would have had as an employee, which leads him to risk downward mobility.
- He works more hours than people who work for others, and he isn't happy about it.

So why does he do it? In addition to the fact that the typical entrepreneur is overoptimistic about his chances, which leads him to start a businesses without realizing how poor his chances of success really are, he starts his business for two reasons. First, it makes him happy. People are happier working for themselves than for other people because they like the flexibility, autonomy, and control over their lives that being an entrepreneur provides. In fact, people are so much more satisfied when working for themselves that they need to be paid two-and-a-half times as much to be just as happy doing the same job for someone else. Second, a small number of entrepreneurs are very successful. If their new businesses survive and grow, entrepreneurs have a chance to earn a lot of money, increase their net worth substantially, and move up the economic ladder.

7

What Makes Some Entrepreneurs More Successful Than Others?

There is no shortage of answers to the question "What makes an entrepreneur successful?" In fact, there may be more answers to this question than there are entrepreneurs to look at them. According to the large number of experts who have offered their expertise in books or articles, or who have posted their insights on the Internet, the key to success as an entrepreneur is to:

- never start a business alone
- never start a business with anyone else
- keep things simple
- come up with a complex idea that no one can copy
- start with good people; they'll know what to do
- watch your people like a hawk
- make something customers want
- come up with something that customers don't know that they need
- spend as little money as possible
- remember that you get what you pay for
- have persistence
- don't throw good money after bad
- be self-confident
- be humble
- work hard
- work smart
- be a leader

- follow the lead of others
- spot a trend
- follow the beat of a different drummer

I could go on, but you are probably getting tired of my repeating the contradictions offered by the multitude of experts on what it takes to be a successful entrepreneur. Instead of offering another opinion, my own, I am going to do something simpler. I'm going to show you the data.

It Gets Easier Over Time

The most basic observation that researchers have found about the performance of start-ups can be summarized by the phrase "it gets easier over time." A host of studies have shown that the longer a business has been operating, the greater the likelihood that it will continue to operate in the future.[1] Looked at another way, the odds of your new business failing are highest when you first start and decline in relation to the length of time you have been in business.

And it isn't just the chance of staying alive that increases over time. The data also show that the average start-up also becomes more profitable as it gets older.[2] The first thing we know about being a successful as an entrepreneur is: if you can make it through the early years, your odds of success will go way up.

Industry Matters—A Lot

One of the strange things about much of the advice about how to be a successful entrepreneur that you find on the Web or in newspapers, magazines, and books is that it doesn't point out one of the most important things you can do to improve your odds of success: pick a favorable industry. This advice may not be given very often because, as we saw in chapter 2, most entrepreneurs don't compare industries when starting a business. They tend to stay in the industry where they are currently working or pick another industry that matches their business skills. I suspect many experts don't want to deflate the hopes of their readers by pointing out that they have already made a big mistake: they've started a business in an unfavorable industry.

Discouraging or not, you need to know that picking the right industry in which to start a company is going to dramatically increase your odds of success. Your start-up will be more likely to survive, will grow

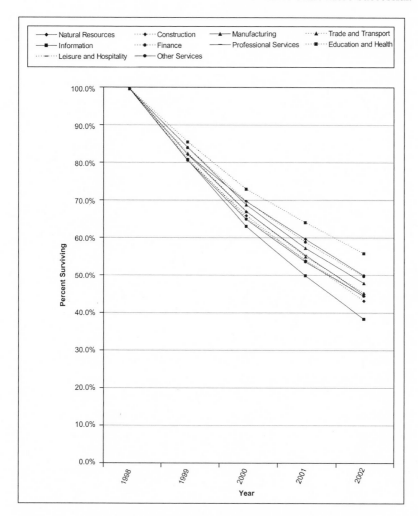

Figure 7.1. New Employer Firm Survival by Industry Sector, 1998–2002
   Source: Adapted from A. Knaup, "Survival and Longevity in Business Employment Dynamics Data," *Monthly Labor Review,* May 2005, 50–56.

more, and will be more profitable if you choose some industries over others.[3] The difference in your odds is not trivial. There is a 17-percentage-point difference in the four-year survival rates of firms across industry sectors, ranging from a low of 38 percent for start-ups in the information sector to a high of 55 percent in the education and health services sector (see figure 7.1).

Within these broad sectors, the performance of the average start-up

Table 7.1 Business Outcomes for Owner-Operated Businesses, by Industry

Industry	Average Sales	Average Number of Employees	Percent with More than $10,000 Profit
Agriculture, forestry, fishing	$106,859	0.9	31.0
Construction	$167,862	1.2	38.5
Manufacturing	$872,526	7.1	41.2
Transportation, communication	$186,053	1.7	44.8
Wholesale trade	$1,190,794	3.2	54.0
Retail trade	$291,646	2.8	33.6
Finance, insurance, and real estate	$166,021	0.9	42.1
Services	$84,954	1.2	27.1
Professional	$103,455	1.2	
Personal	$71,344	1.2	

Source: Adapted from R. Fairlie, and A. Robb. *Race, Families, and Business Success: A Comparison of African-American-, Asian- and White-Owned Businesses* (New York: Russell Sage Foundation, forthcoming).

also differs.[4] For example, in the manufacturing sector, the two-, four-, six-, eight-, and ten-year survival rates of businesses vary across industries, with one study showing a 17-percentage-point gap in the ten-year survival rate between the lowest (textiles and apparel with a survival rate of 27.3 percent) and the highest (paper and printing with 45.2 percent survival rate).[5]

The choice of industry affects more than just survival. The sales, employment growth, and profitability of start-ups also depend a lot on the industry that they are in (see table 7.1).

Perhaps the most shocking information about the effect the choice of industry has on your chances of entrepreneurial success is how it improves or worsens the odds that your business will be *very successful.* The Inc. 500 is a list of the 500 fastest growing private companies in America. The percentage of companies started in different industries that made it to the Inc. 500 between 1982 and 2002 are listed in table 7.2. As we can see from the table, the odds that your new company will become one of these super successful start-ups depends a great deal on which industry it is in. For instance, between 1982 and 2002, start-ups in the software industry were 608 times more likely than start-ups in the restaurant industry to become one of the 500 fastest growing private

Table 7.2 The Proportion of New Firms That Become Inc. 500 Firms, by Industry, 1982–2000

SIC[a]	Industry	Number of *Inc.* 500 Firms	Firm Starts	Percent of Starts
261	Pulp mills	6	33	18.182
357	Computer and office equipment	99	2,359	4.197
376	Guided missiles, space vehicles, parts	2	60	3.333
335	Nonferrous rolling and drawing	14	581	2.410
474	Railroad car rental	3	136	2.206
382	Measuring and controlling devices	49	2,482	1.974
262	Paper mills	3	152	1.974
381	Search and navigation equipment	6	310	1.936
366	Communications equipment	29	1,543	1.880
283	Drugs	20	1,092	1.832
384	Medical instruments and supplies	55	3,025	1.818
316	Luggage	3	172	1.744
314	Footwear, except rubber	4	271	1.476
623	Security and commodity exchanges	2	141	1.418
496	Steam and air-conditioning supply	1	83	1.205
356	General industrial machinery	26	2,173	1.197
386	Photographic equipment and supplies	7	646	1.084
276	Manifold business forms	3	281	1.068
363	Household appliances	4	390	1.026
362	Electrical industrial apparatus	11	1,080	1.019
811	Legal services	10	129,207	0.008
581	Eating and drinking places	34	494,731	0.007
175	Carpentry and floor work contractors	4	66,383	0.006
651	Real estate operators	5	90,042	0.006
701	Hotels and motels	2	39,177	0.005
172	Painting and paper contractors	2	43,987	0.005
546	Retail bakeries	1	22,165	0.005
541	Grocery stores	5	112,473	0.005
593	Used merchandise stores	1	24,442	0.004
753	Automotive repair shops	5	124,725	0.004
723	Beauty shops	3	79,081	0.004
836	Residential care	1	27,710	0.004
784	Videotape rental	1	27,793	0.004

Source: Adapted from data contained in J. Eckhardt, "When the Weak Acquire Wealth: An Examination of the Distribution of High Growth Start-Ups in the U.S. Economy," (Ph.D.Diss., University of Maryland, 2003).

[a]SIC = Standard Industrial Code.

companies in the United States—608 times more likely! What else could increase the odds of your business's success 608 times?

Now, of course, you probably want to know why some industries are better for start-ups than others. Unfortunately, I can't provide you with a definitive explanation, but let me at least lay out for you the few patterns that we do know from the data. We know that the technology intensity of an industry is one factor that increases the odds of a start-up reaching the Inc. 500. The more people in an industry that are employed in occupations that make use of technology, the better the odds for the start-ups being among the 500 fastest growing companies.[6] In particular, industries in which you can get a barrier to imitation, for example, a patent or a trade secret to keep others from duplicating your new technology, are the ones with the highest proportion of Inc. 500 companies. Of course, the smart money already knows this. Just look at where venture capitalists put their money. The industry distribution of their investments is tech focused like the industry distribution of Inc. 500 companies.

There are a couple of other factors that make some industries better for start-ups than others. New firms do better in industries that have large, more rapidly growing markets.[7] They do worse in capital-intensive industries, such as steel and autos that require a lot of expensive equipment, and in industries, like mining, where the average size of firms is large.[8]

What's the message here? It's simple. You can improve your chances of success as an entrepreneur by starting a company in an industry that is better for start-ups.[9] Don't delude yourself into thinking you'll be fine if you are considering starting a new business in an industry that's lousy for start-ups. Think about doing something else instead. Just as you shouldn't play the games with the worst odds when you gamble in Las Vegas, you shouldn't start a company in an industry where the chances are you will almost certainly lose.

Are Most Entrepreneurs Stupid?

Most of our myths about entrepreneurs glorify them. They portray entrepreneurs as brilliant business people who make such shrewd decisions that they can do the business equivalent of turning lead into gold. If these myths are right, we should expect the average entrepreneur to make shrewd business decisions.

But he doesn't. The data show that the typical entrepreneur makes many decisions that actually *reduce* the chances that his business will be successful. For example, most entrepreneurs start businesses in industries that are unfavorable to start-ups. As a result, his odds of success are lower than if he started his business in a better industry.

This is not the only unwise choice made by the typical entrepreneur. Take a look at some other examples:

- Most entrepreneurs start their businesses at a really small size, with few assets or employees, even though many studies, conducted in many countries and in many industries, show that larger start-ups have greater access to capital, are more profitable, have higher sales and employment growth, and are less likely to fail.[10]
- Many entrepreneurs capitalize their new businesses with very little money, even though studies show that the size of a business's start-up capital enhances new business survival; in fact, firms with more than $100,000 in start-up funds are 23 percent more likely to survive over time than firms capitalized with less than $5,000.[11]
- New businesses are much more likely to be set up as sole proprietorships than as corporations, even though new corporations outperform new sole proprietorships on almost every possible measure: speed of business development, access to external capital, survival, sales growth, employment growth, and profitability.[12] Moreover, setting up a corporation, which takes a couple hundred dollars and can be done in a few minutes on the Internet, shields an entrepreneur from personal liability from the debts of his business.
- Most entrepreneurs start businesses on a part-time basis, even though many studies show that the acquisition of external capital—and the business's survival, profitability, and growth—is higher if entrepreneurs work on developing the venture on a full-time basis.[13]
- More than 90 percent of entrepreneurs start their new businesses from scratch even though start-up efforts are much less likely to fail if an entrepreneur purchases a business from someone else.[14]
- Most entrepreneurs start their businesses on their own, even though the performance of new businesses founded by teams is better.[15]
- Many entrepreneurs never write business plans, yet writing a business plan enhances product development, improves the organization of new ventures, increases the likelihood that they will obtain

external capital, increases the level of venture sales, and reduces the likelihood that the venture will fail, particularly if the plan is developed before the entrepreneur begins marketing or talking to customers.[16]

• Most entrepreneurs start businesses to serve the same or similar customers as their previous employers, with the same or similar products, even though studies have shown that new firm performance is enhanced by seeking customers missed by others.[17]

• Most start-ups sell products or services to individual consumers, even though 90 percent of the fastest growing private companies in this country sell to businesses.[18]

I could go on, but I think you get the point. Many of the decisions made by the typical entrepreneur about a variety of things—from who their customers are, to the industry that they are in, to the strategy they follow, to the legal form that they adopt—are the very choices that research has shown are associated with *worse* outcomes for start-ups.

Of course, these patterns might reflect the limited choices most entrepreneurs have when it comes to setting up their businesses. For instance, many people want to be entrepreneurs, but because entrepreneurs tend to start businesses in the industries where they have experience, they tend to start their businesses in unfavorable industries. These patterns might also suggest that the typical entrepreneur isn't paying attention to what the data tell us about creating successful new businesses. Unfortunately, we can't know for sure which explanation accounts for the poor entrepreneurial decisions we observe.

If you are an entrepreneur starting a company or an investor backing one, you have two choices. You can say that you have no alternative and start or back a new company that makes a series of decisions that lower its odds of success, or you can say that you do have an alternative and pay attention to the data. There *are* many things that we know enhance the performance of start-ups that *most* entrepreneurs aren't doing. You can take the atypical (and better) approach. If you do, you won't guarantee your success, but you will increase your odds.

Is There Anything Else You Can Do?

Many real-life entrepreneurs differ from the mythic creatures described in most articles and books on the topic for their sins of omission as well

as their sins of commission. Not only do many entrepreneurs take actions that make their new businesses less successful, but they also don't
do many of the things that studies have shown make start-ups more successful. For instance:

- Many entrepreneurs don't emphasize marketing, even though new
companies that start marketing sooner, and that emphasize the im-
plementation of marketing plans, perform better than other start-
ups.[19]
- Many entrepreneurs don't stress the importance of financial controls and don't put careful financial controls in place in their new
businesses, even though this emphasis makes new businesses more
likely to survive and grow.[20]
- Many entrepreneurs compete on price, even though this strategy
hinders the performance of new ventures, which are better off competing on service, quality, or some other dimension.[21]
- Many entrepreneurs fail to focus their activities on a single product or market when they first start out, even though new businesses
that focus their activities perform better than those that do not.[22]
- Many entrepreneurs don't organize their new businesses in an orderly manner—starting with the identification of the idea; proceed-
ing to business planning, the evaluation of the idea, the acquisition of
resources, and the development of a product or service; and ending
with the marketing of the new product or service—even though the
order in which firm founders undertake start-up activities affects the
performance of new businesses.[23]

Overall, the message is pretty straightforward. The choices that you
don't make will have an effect on the performance of your new business
just like the decisions that you do make will. Because several careful
studies have identified a variety of things that you can do to enhance
your business's odds of success, you should learn what these things are
and be ready to implement them.

You Can Prepare Yourself To Be a Better Entrepreneur

Much of what we hear about entrepreneurship gives the impression that
there is little you can do to prepare yourself to become a better entrepreneur. A lot of the discussion in newspaper and magazine articles of what
makes a person a better entrepreneur focuses on a set of psychological

characteristics, which are either inborn or, if they are not, are pretty much determined by the time you are out of diapers. When the discussion turns to things you can do to make yourself a better entrepreneur, it tends to focus on very proximate factors, for example, how to network with investors or how to interview prospective employees. Almost never does it address the kinds of things that you can undertake over the course of your career. The reality is that you can manage your career to become a better entrepreneur.

Go to School

There are hundreds of stories about entrepreneurs like J. R. Simplot, the inventor of the frozen French fry, who quit school at age 14 to start a company, which grew into a $3-billion business. These stories have led to the myth that education doesn't help you become a successful entrepreneur and that it may even hinder your efforts.

Don't be deluded by this myth. People with little education who become successful entrepreneurs are few and far between. If you want to become a successful entrepreneur, your odds are much better if you graduate from high school and go on to college. Many studies show that better educated entrepreneurs have greater access to external capital, lower business failure rates, greater business sales and employment growth, and more profitable ventures.[24] In fact, the data show that the average start-up founded by a college graduate has 25 percent greater sales than the average start-up founded by a high school dropout, and the average start-up founded by a person with a graduate degree has 40 percent greater sales than the average start-up founded by a college graduate.[25]

Don't Rush Off to Start a Business

Stories, like the one of Michael Dell's creation of a multibillion-dollar company in a University of Texas dorm room, give many people the impression that young people are more successful as entrepreneurs than older people. In fact, much of the discussion on this topic gives you the impression that working for someone else before starting a company will actually make you a worse entrepreneur. Working as an employee, the story goes, will make you think like a corporate cog instead of like an entrepreneur, which will come back to haunt you later. But the data show that the stories of young people becoming successful entrepreneurs are extreme examples. On average, businesses founded by people between the ages of 45 and 54 tend to perform better than those founded by people less than 35 years old.[26]

Moreover, working for someone else will help, rather than hurt, your efforts to become a successful entrepreneur. The data show that the longer entrepreneurs work for someone else before starting their companies, the less likely their businesses are to fail, the more profitable they tend to be, and the more likely they are to grow.[27] In particular, the performance of a new venture is particularly enhanced if the founder had professional, management, or supervisory experience in his prior jobs.[28]

Not only does work experience help you to develop a more successful start-up, but experience in the industry in which your new company is operating also seems to help. Start-ups have faster product development, greater access to capital, higher likelihood of survival, higher profitability, greater sales, and more employment if their founders have prior experience in the industry in which they are starting their companies.[29]

Of course, nothing helps the performance of a start-up as much as the founder's prior experience as an entrepreneur. Businesses founded by experienced entrepreneurs develop faster, have higher incomes, grow faster, and are less likely to fail than businesses founded by inexperienced entrepreneurs.[30] But you don't need a lot of prior experience to realize the benefits. Research shows that what matters is the difference between having no experience and having some experience. Having started more than one company gives you no added benefit over that which comes from having started only one business previously.[31]

Have the Right Motivations for Starting

People start new businesses for a variety of reasons. Some people can't find a job and have nothing better to do. Others don't like working for a boss and are attracted by the freedom and autonomy that entrepreneurship offers. Some people just want to earn money. Do these different motivations make any difference to the performance of start-ups? It turns out that they do.

As you may remember from chapter 3, most people start businesses to avoid working for other people. Unfortunately, people who start businesses for this reason don't do very well as entrepreneurs. Their businesses tend to make less money, grow more slowly, and are more likely to fail than those of people who start with the goal of making high profits.[32]

This shouldn't be surprising. New businesses often reflect what their founders want. People who start businesses to avoid working for others tend to want autonomy, not money, and as a result, they tend to accept lower financial performance in their businesses. In contrast, founders who want their businesses to make money are more likely to have businesses that perform well financially because they strive to meet this goal, which leads others—investors, employees, and customers—to respond positively.[33]

What about people who start businesses because they have no better alternative, like the unemployed? How do their businesses tend to perform? The answer to this question is important because of the number of programs in different cities, states, and countries that are designed to help unemployed people become entrepreneurs. Companies started by the unemployed—pay attention policy makers—perform *worse* than companies founded by the employed. In fact, the longer a person is unemployed before he starts his new business, the worse his earnings from his new business tend to be.[34] The unemployed who become entrepreneurs might be better off as entrepreneurs than they were as unemployed people, but they aren't likely to be high-performing entrepreneurs. Policy makers should take this information into consideration when considering the value of programs to turn the unemployed into entrepreneurs.

Busted Myths and Key Realities

45. All industries are not equal; the industry in which a start-up operates has a large effect on its performance.

46. Success as an entrepreneur is not all about your personality; there are many decisions that you can take that affect the performance of your start-up, from what strategy you adopt, to the market you target, to the internal controls in your business.

47. Doing what most entrepreneurs do is a mistake; the majority of entrepreneurs are wrong about how to run a new company.

48. New businesses are not better than established busi-

nesses; as your business gets older, its performance is likely to improve.

49. Why you start your business matters; if you want your business to survive, grow, and generate a good income, start your business to achieve those goals and not because you are unemployed or want to escape a bad boss.

50. Getting an education will help, not hinder, your performance as an entrepreneur.

51. Knowing your industry matters; working in an industry before starting a business in it will improve your odds of success.

In Conclusion

There are a lot of opinions floating around about why some entrepreneurs are more successful than others. All this clutter makes it difficult to find information that comes from careful, scientifically designed studies. But these studies are out there, and they identify several things that make start-ups more successful. First, they show that industry matters a lot. The difference in performance between the average start-up in different industries is pretty large. Picking an industry that is favorable to start-ups is an important first step in having a successful new company.

Second, there are many decisions that you can take that affect the performance of your start-up, from what strategy you adopt, to the market you target, to the internal controls in your business. Although it might sound trite, knowing what works and what doesn't will help you to do what it takes to have a more successful start-up. In particular, you need to remember that the majority of entrepreneurs are wrong about how to run a new company. The majority of entrepreneurs fail. Don't follow the choices of the majority—from the capitalization of a business to its legal form—as it may actually hinder performance.

Third, it gets easier over time. As your business gets older, its performance is likely to improve. Don't be discouraged if at first the going is very tough.

Fourth, start your business for the right reasons. Although you might be tempted to start a business because you are unemployed or to escape your tyrannical boss, those aren't good reasons. If you want your business to survive, grow, and generate a good income, start your business to achieve those goals.

Finally, don't forget that you can make yourself a better entrepreneur by taking a couple of simple steps. Go to school. And work for a while before starting your company, preferably in the industry in which you are thinking of entering. If you do, the data show that you will greatly improve your odds of success.

8

Why Don't Women Start More Companies?

Forget about all of the psychological tests that predict who is an entrepreneur and who is not. None of them are as accurate as this simple test. Go to your nearest mall and stand outside of the restrooms for an hour. If you don't get arrested first, keep a tally of the number of people who go into the men's room and the ladies' room. Using only the criterion of which bathroom people enter, you will be more likely to accurately identify which people are entrepreneurs and which ones are not than if you administer all of the available psychological tests currently used to identify entrepreneurs.

Because this statement can easily be misinterpreted, at the risk of being redundant, I am going to restate it. I am definitely, unequivocally, and absolutely *not* saying that women can't or shouldn't be entrepreneurs. And I am definitely, unequivocally, and absolutely *not* saying that they can't or shouldn't be just as good at entrepreneurship as men. All I am saying is that the reality in the United States today is that women are so much less likely than men to start their own businesses that if the only thing you know about a person is his or her gender, you can predict whether or not he or she is an entrepreneur with greater accuracy than if you use all of the psychological tests that are believed to identify entrepreneurs.

This fact shows that it is very important to understand why women are less likely than men to become entrepreneurs and how well the typical female entrepreneur does at running her own business.

Women Are Not Very Likely to Become Entrepreneurs

This chapter opened with a very strong statement: that gender is a powerful predictor of whether or not a person becomes an entrepreneur. Such a strong statement has to be backed up with some facts. Regardless of what source you look at, the data show that women are much less likely than men to become entrepreneurs. For instance:

- In 2004, women made up 51 percent of the U.S. population and almost half (47 percent) of the nonmilitary workforce, yet they composed only 27 percent of business owners.[1]
- Women-owned businesses make up 25 percent of nonfarm businesses in the United States.[2]
- Men are twice as likely as women to be involved in starting a new business at any point in time.[3]
- In 2003, only 34.2 percent of self-employed people in the United States were female.[4]
- In 2004, 7.1 percent of women in the U.S. labor force were self-employed, as compared to 12.4 percent of men in the labor force.[5]

The data are consistent. Women are much less likely than men to be entrepreneurs in the United States today.

Why Is the Rate of Female Entrepreneurship So Low?

The fact that women start businesses at roughly half the rate of men begs the question: why? Like many puzzling and potentially uncomfortable phenomena about entrepreneurship, this one has no shortage of answers—some credible and some implausible. People are certainly entitled to their beliefs, but to tease apart fact from fiction, let's take a look at some of the most common explanations offered and see how consistent they are with the data.

One explanation that is commonly offered for why women are less likely than men to start new businesses is that women have more difficulty obtaining financing for new companies, and this greater difficulty keeps them from pursuing entrepreneurial endeavors.[6] The available data really don't support this explanation. As you no doubt remember from chapter 5, most entrepreneurs self-finance the start-up of their businesses, seeking external capital only later. Thus the ease of obtaining external capital can't be used to explain the decision by most entrepreneurs to *start* a business.

In addition, unlike the case for some minority groups, the household wealth of men and women is the same, on average.[7] The typical woman doesn't lack adequate personal capital to finance the start-up of a new business. In fact, the initial capitalization of start-ups led by women is actually much lower than that of start-ups led by men. Therefore, if anything, women should be *more* likely than men to start their own businesses if access to sufficient capital to get started is an issue. Having the same amount of household wealth as the average man but needing less money to start her business,[8] the average woman should have an easier time financing her start-up than the average man.

A second explanation that is frequently offered for why women are so much less likely to start businesses than men is that they lack access to business opportunities.[9] Lacking the right social networks or business experiences, the story goes, they are less likely than men to come up with new business ideas and so are less likely than men to start companies. But the data don't support this explanation either. No serious, careful studies have shown that women have less access to information about new business ideas or opportunities than men. Moreover, many entrepreneurs don't have a business idea in mind when they start their businesses (see chapter 4). For the 42 percent or so of entrepreneurs who start businesses without a business idea, it is hard to see how lack of access to information about business ideas could keep them from starting businesses, regardless of their gender.

Furthermore, the evidence in chapter 4 about the kinds of businesses that the typical entrepreneur starts, and the sources of the ideas for those businesses, indicates that it isn't very hard for anyone, male or female, to come up with them. The typical idea is to start a company in the same industry as the entrepreneur's prior employer to serve the same or similar customers, with the same or similar products. There's no reason to believe that gender would affect a person's knowledge that it is possible to sell the same products to the same customers as their current employer. In short, it appears unlikely that a lack of access to business ideas or opportunities explains the lower rate of business formation among women.

A third explanation offered for why women are less likely than men to start businesses is that women have lesser human capital (e.g., management experience and education) than men. This lesser human capital makes a smaller percentage of women *capable* of starting new businesses than men, resulting in the lower rate of business creation among women.[10]

The data do not support this explanation either. As you no doubt remember from chapter 3, one aspect of human capital that increases the odds that a person will start a business is his or her level of education. But lesser education cannot account for the lower rate of business formation by women because, on average, women have *more* education than men. In the United States at least, women are more likely than men to graduate from both high school and college.[11]

Another aspect of human capital that increases the odds that a person will start a business is management experience. But again, lesser management experience cannot account for the lower rate of new business creation by women because, on average, women are *more* likely to be found in managerial and professional occupations than men.[12] Specifically, they are more likely to have professional specialty, sales, and technical and support occupations. (For those of you, who are puzzled by these facts, remember how our myths about business play tricks on us. The typical person with management experience is not the CEO or CFO of a Fortune 500 company. Rather, that person is a low level manager. So it shouldn't be surprising that women are more likely than men to have managerial and professional occupations.)

A fourth explanation for why women are less likely to start businesses is that women are less likely than men to have the prime motivation that leads most people to start businesses: a desire for autonomy. The idea that men care more about autonomy than women is not borne out by the data. For instance, if you look at the responses to survey questions that measure desire for autonomy in a representative sample of the working-age population in the United States, you will see that men are actually *less* likely than women to have a desire for autonomy.[13] If anything, the fact that a desire for autonomy motivates people to start businesses should make women *more* likely than men to start businesses.

If these four factors don't explain why women are less likely to start businesses than men, then what does? The data indicate that women are less interested in being entrepreneurs. Part of this is a result of the greater tendency of men to be in the labor force. Across almost all countries for which data are collected, women are significantly less likely than men to enter the labor force, perhaps because they have more household and child care responsibilities. Because people who are not in the workforce (stay-at-home moms, students, and retirees) are much less likely to start companies than people in the workforce, the higher labor force participation rate of men accounts for some of the difference between men and women in the tendency to start businesses.[14] But even among women who are in the labor force, women are *half as likely* as men to start businesses, suggesting that labor force participation is only part of the story. Although the data show that women are half as likely as men to initiate the business start-up process, they are just as likely to get a business up and running once they begin.[15]

The data show that women are less likely than men to initiate the process of starting a new business because, on average, women are less interested than their male counterparts in working for themselves. In fact, surveys that have asked people in 23 different countries in the Organization for Economic Cooperation and Development (OECD) if they would prefer to work in their own businesses or work for someone else have shown that women are less likely than men to want to work in their own businesses.[16] Even among high school students, women are less likely than men to want to own their own businesses, and are less likely to say that they will pursue the creation of a business.[17] Therefore, it's the lower tendency of women to want to begin the start-up process that accounts for their lower rate of business creation.

Given their tendency to prefer working for others, many women start businesses only when they have to work but cannot find jobs. As a result, in countries where it is easier for women to get jobs working for other people, women are less likely to start businesses than in places where it is more difficult for women to get paid work.[18] Moreover, in countries where many women can afford not to work, the rate at which they start businesses is much lower than in countries where few women can afford not to work. Specifically, the data show that women in richer countries are half as likely as women in poorer countries to start businesses because the former can afford to choose not to work whereas the latter have to work to support their families.[19]

How Do Women-Owned Start-Ups Perform?

It may be that fewer women start businesses than men, perhaps because they are less interested in having their own businesses. But what about the performance of new businesses led by women? How well do they do?

Many people believe that the average start-up run by a woman is doing just fine. In fact, many books and articles that discuss entrepreneurship by women give the impression that the typical new business run by a woman is doing just as well as the typical new business run by a man. But unfortunately, equality between the sexes in the performance of new businesses is a wish, not a reality. Across all economic sectors, new businesses led by women perform worse on almost every performance measure—survival, sales, growth, employment, and income—than new businesses led by men.[20] For instance:

- Women-owned firms that have at least one employee generated an average of $87,585 in sales in 2002, as compared to $1,862,159 for similar businesses owned by men.[21]
- Women-owned businesses with at least 1 employee had an average of 7.79 employees in 2002, as compared to 12.04 for comparable businesses owned by men.[22]
- For women who were self-employed in 1998, 46 percent had an income of less than $15,000, while only 21 percent of self-employed men had this low a level of income; in contrast, 16 percent of men had self-employment income of more than $95,000, as compared to 4 percent of women.[23]
- The average business owned by a woman generates only 78 percent of the profit of the average business owned by a man.[24]
- Start-ups led by women are less likely to grow over time than start-ups led by men.[25]
- The four-year survival rate of new businesses with at least 1 employee that are founded by women is 8.6 percent lower than that of comparable new businesses founded by men.[26]

Why Is the Performance of Businesses Created by Women So Poor?

There are a host of explanations for why businesses founded by women do not perform as well as those started by men. Rather than summarize all of the explanations that are proffered by others, I'm going to take two of the most common and compare them to the data. Then I'm going to offer a less common explanation and see how it fares.

One common reason for the lesser performance of start-ups led by women is that they lack access to the capital that their businesses need because the capital markets discriminate against women. As a result, their businesses can't perform as well as new businesses led by men, who have easier access to capital.[27]

Although discrimination against female entrepreneurs by banks and investors is always possible, it's pretty unlikely to be a major explanation for the lesser performance of start-ups led by women for several reasons. First, careful studies that have tried to explain why start-ups led by women perform worse than those led by men show that the difference in financial capital doesn't account for the performance difference.[28] Second, careful studies that have examined whether lenders discriminate against businesses led by women don't show any evidence of discrimination. While businesses run by women have more difficulty borrowing from banks and other lenders than businesses run by men, they are also less likely to meet the lenders' standards for making loans:

- Businesses led by women are capitalized at lower levels.[29]
- They pursue opportunities that are less profitable and are more likely to be found in less attractive industries, such as retail trade and personal services, rather than more attractive industries, such as professional services, mining, wholesale trade, finance, insurance and real estate, and construction.[30]
- And they are more likely than businesses led by men to be home-based.[31]

When researchers account for the kinds of factors that lenders consider in making loan decisions, such as the age and size of the business, its industry, its legal form, its financial performance, the owner's credit rating and history, and the owner's financial assets and history, start-ups led by women are no less likely than start-ups led by men to apply for loans, get loans or trade credit, or have outstanding loans. In other words, the differences in the financing patterns of start-ups led by men and women is explained by things other than gender, such as the age of the business, its legal form, the industry that it is in, the financial history

of the business and the founder, and the work experience of the entrepreneur.[32]

Another common explanation for the lesser performance of businesses started by women is that women are, on average, less experienced entrepreneurs. Because they have less work and start-up experience than men, the story goes, female entrepreneurs are less adept at
managing their businesses. As a result, their businesses do not perform
as well as those founded by men.

The data do not bear out this explanation. My examination of the
data from the Panel Study of Entrepreneurial Dynamics reveals that
there are no statistical differences between male and female entrepreneurs in terms of the number of start-up companies founded; the number
of start-up classes or workshops taken; and the tendency to be self-
employed, manager of a business owned by others, or a business owner,
controlling for a variety of demographic factors, such as age, race, education, income, and geographic location. Moreover, male entrepreneurs
are *more likely* than female entrepreneurs to indicate that a lack of mentors was a problem when they started their companies. If female entrepreneurs have the same amount of entrepreneurial experience as male
entrepreneurs, then differences in the performance of start-ups founded
by people of the two genders cannot be the result of differences in entrepreneurial experience.

The data from the Panel Study of Entrepreneurial Dynamics also
show that, controlling for demographic factors, male and female entrepreneurs have the same amount of experience in the industries in which
they start their businesses. As a result, it is not surprising that careful
studies that compare male- and female-led new businesses show that differences in the experience of male and female entrepreneurs don't account for the differences in the performance of start-ups led by men and
women.[33]

So what's a better explanation for the lesser performance of start-ups
led by women than the ones that people commonly offer? Their goals
and aspirations. Female entrepreneurs have lesser financial goals for
their businesses than male entrepreneurs.[34] For instance, the data from
the Panel Study of Entrepreneurial Dynamics show that female entrepreneurs are less likely than male entrepreneurs to start their businesses to
make money, and they have lesser financial aspirations for those busi-

nesses, even after controlling for a variety of other explanatory factors. These data also show that female entrepreneurs work fewer hours per day on their new businesses than male entrepreneurs, which is what we would expect if they are less motivated to create high performing businesses.

Not only do female entrepreneurs have lower profit and sales targets for their businesses, but research by Dr. Brian Headd of the Office of Advocacy at the U.S. Small Business Administration shows that they also are more likely to view a failed new start-up as "successful."[35] Because the average female entrepreneur has lower sales, profit, and employment goals than the average male entrepreneur, it should not be surprising that her business has lower sales, lesser employment, and lower profits. If she doesn't want to make as much money or hire as many people as her male counterpart, she probably won't.[36]

Rather than starting businesses to make a lot of money, many women become entrepreneurs to create flexible work schedules that will allow them to care for their families, particularly their children.[37] A variety of types of data support this observation. American women are more likely to become entrepreneurs when they are of childbearing age, and women in countries with higher birth rates and less governmental support for maternity leave and child care are more likely than women in other countries to become entrepreneurs.[38]

Studies show that becoming a mother increases the likelihood that a woman will start her own business because home-based work allows a woman to work and care for her children simultaneously, something that is not possible when she works outside the home.[39] It is difficult to find a job working for someone else out of your home, so the vast majority of women who work at home run their own businesses (62.9 percent of women between the ages of 25 and 55 who are home-based workers work for themselves).[40] Thus, it appears that many women become entrepreneurs when they have children because entrepreneurship provides the opportunity to work while simultaneously caring for children. That is a laudable goal and for many women it's the right one. Nevertheless, because work flexibility is the aim for many female entrepreneurs, the average performance of start-ups led by women is lower in financial terms than the average start-up led by men.

Busted Myths and Key Realities

52. Women are so much less likely than men to start businesses that gender is one of the best predictors we have of who is an entrepreneur and who is not.

53. Lack of access to money and business opportunities, lesser human capital, and a lack of desire for autonomy don't explain why women are less likely than men to start business; however, a lesser interest in running their own businesses does.

54. Compared to start-ups led by men, new businesses led by women have lower sales, fewer employees, less productivity, lower profits, and worse survival rates.

55. The lesser performance of female-led new ventures depends a lot on the lesser financial goals that female entrepreneurs have.

In Conclusion

Women are much less likely than men to start businesses. In fact, they are so much less likely that gender is one of the best predictors we have of who will become an entrepreneur.

Although there are many explanations for the low rate at which women start businesses—from lack of access to money and business opportunities to lesser human capital and a lack of desire for autonomy—the data don't support these explanations. Instead they show that women are less likely than men to start businesses because, on average, they are less interested in running their own businesses.

Compared to start-ups led by men, new businesses led by women have lower sales, fewer employees, lesser productivity, lower profits, and worse survival rates. Many observers attribute the lesser performance of female-led new ventures to external forces, particularly the lack of access to capital. The data, however, support another, less insidious, explanation. On average, female entrepreneurs have lesser financial goals than male entrepreneurs because many women start businesses so that they can have flexible work schedules that will allow them to care for their children. And because fewer women start businesses to achieve financial goals than men, female entrepreneurs tend to run new businesses with lower financial performance.

9

Why Is Black Entrepreneurship So Rare?

No myths about entrepreneurship are more pervasive than those about black entrepreneurs. One stubborn tall tale maintains that because blacks face a glass ceiling in corporate America, entrepreneurship among them is very common.[1] The ostensive high rate of start-ups in the black community is evidenced by such statements as:

- "We are now in an era when the educated members of the African American community are going into the business world."[2]
- "A wave of black entrepreneurs is forming businesses at a record clip."[3]
- "The most active group of entrepreneurs in American [*sic*] is black men and women."[4]

Although many of us wish these assertions were true, unfortunately they are not. Entrepreneurship is quite rare in the black community. Consider, for instance, the following statistics:

- Only 5.1 percent of business-owning households have a black head as compared to 12.7 percent of non-business-owning households.[5]
- More than twice the proportion of whites are self-employed than the proportion of blacks; 13.1 percent of white men and 7.4 percent of white women are self-employed, as compared to 5.1 percent of black men and 2.7 percent of black women.[6]

Clearly, the myth of black entrepreneurship is just that: a myth. Blacks are much less likely than whites to become entrepreneurs. Once again, the real question is "why?"

Why Is the Rate of Black Entrepreneurship So Low?

Why are whites so much more likely than blacks to become entrepreneurs? Let's start by considering what the data say *isn't* the reason why blacks are less likely to start businesses than whites. It isn't a lesser interest in entrepreneurship. If anything, the data show that the opposite is true. For instance, a survey of a random sample of high school students conducted by Gallup showed that significantly more black students are interested in starting their own businesses than white students.[7]

This isn't just an issue of what children want to do when they grow up. A survey of a representative sample of the U.S. working-age population revealed that blacks are 78 percent *more likely* to be in the process of starting a business than whites, and these higher rates are present after taking into account a variety of demographic factors.[8]

If blacks are more interested than whites in starting businesses, why then are they so much less likely to have their own businesses? One explanation frequently offered is the lack of parental role models for the next generation of black entrepreneurs. As one black entrepreneur commented, "Many black business owners are first-generation entrepreneurs. . . . You don't grow up with an innate thought that 'It's possible for me to own a business.' There's not this underlying current throughout the family [of that] whole entrepreneurial sense."[9]

But the data don't support the argument that a lack of parental role models explains the low rate of black entrepreneurship. The best evidence on this question has been gathered by Professor Rob Fairlie of the University of California at Santa Cruz, who examined data from the Panel Study of Income Dynamics from 1968 to 1989. He looked at the effect that having a self-employed father has on the likelihood that someone would go into business for himself. He found that having a self-employed father accounts for only a small amount of the difference in the tendency of blacks and whites to start their own businesses.[10]

Another possible explanation offered by many people is that of human capital. Blacks, the story goes, don't have as much education as whites, and this handicaps their efforts to start new businesses. This view is expressed quite clearly by Emma Chappell, the founder of the United Bank of Philadelphia, in an interview that appeared on Businessweek.com. She said, "They may have a great business idea and make a lot of money—we have found that those people who come to our classes typically could run a fine business—but they do not have the management skills that are required today to run a business."[11]

Again, the careful research of Robert Fairlie provides two important pieces of information that suggest that a lack of education is not the primary explanation for the difference in the rates at which whites and blacks start businesses. The first piece of data comes from research he conducted on the ratio of black and white self-employment rates since the beginning of the twentieth century. Professor Fairlie finds—quite astonishingly actually—that the rate of self-employment of whites was consistently three times that of blacks from 1910 to 1990.[12]

If education accounts for the difference in rates of self-employment among whites and blacks, then clearly we should have seen some movement in the ratio of white-to-black self-employment since 1910. The level of education among blacks has changed dramatically since 1910, in no small part because of the civil rights movement of the 1960s. For example, in 1940, whites were more than three times as likely as blacks to graduate from high school (26.1 percent to 7.7 percent). In 2000, this ratio was much smaller, with 83.6 percent of whites and 72.3 percent of blacks making it through high school. Similarly, in 1940, 5.4 percent of white men completed college, as compared to 1.4 percent of black men. In 2000, 28.5 percent of white men, and 14.2 percent of black men, had competed college,[13] a change in the white-to-black ratio from 3.9 to 1 to 2 to 1. If lack of education were the culprit for low levels of black entrepreneurship, one would expect that narrowing of the gap between black and white education levels would have had an effect on the gap in black and white self-employment. But it didn't.

Professor Fairlie also looked at the effects of education on the tendency of black and white male heads of household to work for themselves from 1968 to 1989. He found that the differences in education between the two groups explained very little of the difference in the rates of self-employment between the two races.[14] Thus, it appears that differences in education do not account for differences in the tendency of whites and blacks to be entrepreneurs.

A third possible explanation offered by many people for the lesser tendency of blacks to start businesses is that blacks lack the social networks necessary to facilitate new business formation.[15] Because black people don't know the right people to talk to about starting a business, the argument goes, they are less likely than white people to get the information they need to start a new business.

But data from representative samples of Americans show that new business founders are no more likely to have or use social networks than people who don't start businesses, so it's not even clear that having a "better" social network influences a group's rate of firm formation. Moreover, it turns out there isn't any difference in the size or use of social networks by black and white Americans.[16] Even if social networks were to matter, they can't account for the difference between black and white rates of firm formation. In short, the data don't support the idea that a problem with the social networks of black Americans inhibits their ability to start businesses.

If the lower likelihood of blacks going into business for themselves cannot be explained by interest, education, social networks, or a lack of parental role models, what could be the reason? The answer appears to be money. The average black person simply doesn't have enough money to start his own business. Even though starting the typical business doesn't take much capital, that amount is quite large in comparison to the median family income of a black household. The amount of capital needed to start a typical business in this country is $20,852 (in 2000 dollars; see chapter 5).

This amount is a manageable sum for the typical white prospective entrepreneur, given that in 2000, the median (typical) net worth of a white household was $79,400. It is, however, a lot of money for the typical black household to scrape together; in 2000, the median (typical) net worth of a black household was only $7,500.[17] In other words, starting a business takes 2.8 times the net worth of the average black household as compared to 26 percent of the net worth of the average white one. As a result, many black would-be entrepreneurs simply can't afford to start businesses, depressing the black start-up rate.

Professor Fairlie once again provides the systematic analyses necessary to show that the limited net worth of black households keeps blacks from starting businesses at the same rate as whites. Looking at data from 1968 to 1989 on the tendency of male heads of household to go into business for themselves, Professor Fairlie found that differences in the households' level of assets accounted for between 14 and 15 percent of the difference in the rate at which blacks and whites go into business for themselves.[18]

How Do Black-Owned Start-Ups Perform?

Not only are blacks much less likely than whites to start businesses, but virtually all sources of data indicate that black-owned start-ups perform worse than white-owned new businesses. And the differences aren't trivial. On some measures, the performance of start-ups led by blacks is as low as one-quarter that of start-ups led by whites. For instance:

- Blacks are 50 percent less likely than whites to get a new business up and running within seven years of beginning the start-up process.[19]
- The four-year survival rate of black-owned start-ups is 34.8 percent as compared to 48.7 percent for white-owned start-ups.[20]
- Blacks exit from self-employment at twice the rate of whites.[21]
- The average sales of a black-owned business are $86,478 as compared to $448,294 for a white-owned business.[22]
- While 75.1 percent of white-owned businesses show a positive net profit, only 60.7 percent of black-owned businesses do.[23]
- White-owned firms have an average of 3.1 paid employees, while black-owned firms have an average of 0.9 paid employees.[24]

Moreover, black-owned businesses aren't "catching up" to white-owned businesses. The performance of black-owned businesses was closer to that of white-owned businesses in the 1980s than it is today. For instance, in 1982, the average black-owned firm had sales that were 38 percent of those of the average white-owned firm, but this ratio had dropped to 17.5 percent by 2002; and the average black-owned firm had 35 percent of the employment of the average white-owned firm in 1992, but that ratio had fallen to 21.4 percent by 2002.[25]

Why Is the Performance of Black-Owned Start-Ups So Poor?

Overwhelming evidence from a variety of sources shows the lesser performance of black-owned start-ups, raising an important question: why? Keep in mind that answering this question is not just an intellectual exercise. We need to come up with the right explanation for this gap if we are to get rid of it, which many policy makers, entrepreneurs, investors, and concerned citizens would like to do. If we are wrong about *why* black-owned start-ups perform poorly, then any solution we might propose won't do any good. In looking for reasons why the average black-owned start-up underperforms the average white-owned one let us start by ruling out some of the rationales provided.

One explanation that we can eliminate is that black entrepreneurs have less knowledge than white entrepreneurs about how to run new businesses because they don't have as many entrepreneurial role models. Once again we can turn to the work of Rob Fairlie, who with his colleague Alicia Robb, looked at data from the Census Bureau's Characteristics of Business Owners Survey. Their analysis shows that black entrepreneurs are, indeed, less likely than white ones to have family members who started their own businesses, and they are less likely to have worked previously in family businesses. But Fairlie's and Robb's analysis shows that these differences don't account for much of the difference in the performance of black- and white-owned businesses.[26]

Similarly, the researchers who conducted the Panel Study of Entrepreneurial Dynamics asked entrepreneurs whether the lack of mentors and others who could provide support were problematic for their start-up efforts. My analysis of the data from this survey, which controls for a variety of potentially confounding factors, indicates that black entrepreneurs are no more likely than entrepreneurs of other races to perceive that the lack of mentors was a problem. These data also show that black entrepreneurs are no less likely than entrepreneurs of other races to believe that they have the skills and abilities to develop their new ventures; are no less likely to have friends and relatives who started businesses; have taken no fewer number of courses on starting businesses; have no less education or work experience in sales and marketing, production and plant management, transportation and distribution, financial and capital management, or technology and innovation management; and actually have taken *more* courses in economics and accounting and control (and have no less work experience in these two areas). The lack of differences between black and white entrepreneurs on these dimensions suggests that a lack of knowledge is not a likely explanation of the lesser performance of black entrepreneurs.

Another possible explanation that we can reject is that black entrepreneurs start their businesses in less desirable locations than white entrepreneurs, such as in inner cities where customers have lower incomes and where the costs of doing business may be higher. Again, Fairlie's and Robb's analysis of the Characteristics of Business Owners Survey shows that the greater tendency of black entrepreneurs to own businesses in urban areas doesn't account for the difference in performance of black- and white-owned businesses.[27]

A third possible explanation is that the lesser human capital of black entrepreneurs—their lower education and lesser business experience—hinders the performance of their new businesses. Again, the analysis shows that black-white differences in human capital explains little of the difference in the performance of black- and white-owned start-ups. The lesser experience of black entrepreneurs in management positions and in jobs for companies selling similar products doesn't account for any difference in the performance of black- and white-owned start-ups. And the difference in the education levels of white and black entrepreneurs explains only between 2.4 and 6.5 percent of the variance in the performance of black- and white-owned new businesses.[28]

Moreover, my analysis of the data from the Panel Study of Entrepreneurial Dynamics reveals that, controlling for a variety of potentially confounding factors, black entrepreneurs have started the same number of companies as entrepreneurs of other races; have the same amount of experience in the industries in which their new companies would operate; have the same number of years of full-time work experience; have the same number of years of administrative and supervisory experience; and have supervised the same number of employees. If black entrepreneurs are not lower on any of these dimensions than entrepreneurs of other races, then lesser human capital is not a likely explanation for the poorer performance of black entrepreneurs.

A final possibility is that the lower performance of black entrepreneurs results from the greater proportion of women among black entrepreneurs, making the racial performance gap a function of the gender performance gap. (As we saw in chapter 8, female-led start-ups do not perform as well as male-led ones.) Again, the research by Fairlie and Robb shows that the differences between whites and blacks in the proportion of female-owned businesses accounts for only a little of the difference in the performance of white- and black-owned start-ups.[29]

If these four explanations don't account for much of the difference in the performance of new businesses founded by white and black entrepreneurs, then what does? Two things appear to matter a lot. First, the average black entrepreneur starts his business in a less desirable industry than the average white entrepreneur. As you no doubt remember, the industry in which you start a business has a large effect on the new company's performance. Blacks are more likely than whites to start businesses in the personal services sector, which isn't very favorable to start-ups, and are less likely to start them in the agriculture, mining, construction, manufacturing, wholesale and retail trade, and finance sectors, which are more favorable. According to the analysis conducted by Fairlie and Robb, the concentration of black-owned start-ups in the personal services sector accounts for as much as 20.5 percent of the difference in the performance of white- and black-owned start-ups.[30]

Second, black entrepreneurs capitalize their start-ups at much lower levels than do white entrepreneurs. In fact, data from the Characteristics of Business Owners Survey indicate that the average initial capitalization of black-led start-ups is only 57 percent of that of white-led new businesses. New businesses started with a higher level of initial capitalization are more likely to survive and grow and are more profitable (see chapter 7). Analysis by Fairlie and Robb shows that the difference in the start-up capitalization of new businesses led by black and white entrepreneurs has a huge effect on their performance, explaining as much as 43.2 percent of the difference in the performance between the two groups of firms.[31]

But why does the average black entrepreneur undercapitalize his business if doing so has such an adverse effect on its performance? The answer is that he has no choice. The average black-led start-up has much lower capitalization than the average white-led one because the average black household has a much lower net worth. Because entrepreneurs need to provide a lot of their initial capitalization out of their savings, black entrepreneurs simply don't have enough money to properly capitalize their businesses. In fact, black entrepreneurs often start businesses that demand less capital and deliberately create businesses of smaller financial scale because of their lack of money.[32]

As if the lack of founder savings were not enough of a problem, black-led start-ups are also undercapitalized because black entrepreneurs face more obstacles than white entrepreneurs to financing their businesses. In response to surveys by the Federal Reserve Bank and the Census Bureau, blacks report having more trouble raising money, being less likely to apply for loans because they believe that they would not get them, and having to close their businesses because they lack access to personal or business credit.[33]

Moreover, the amount of money that a new business can borrow is related to the size of the owner's investment in the business. As a result, black-led start-ups can't borrow as much money as white-led businesses (because their owners cannot capitalize them at the same level). This point is clearly shown by data from the U.S. Small Business Administration. Even though blacks own 4.24 percent of businesses in the United States and receive 4.15 percent of the 7(a) loans—the SBA's most common loan program, in which the loans entrepreneurs receive from banks are at least partially guaranteed against loss by the government—they obtain only 2.8 percent of the value of those loans.[34] In other words, black entrepreneurs receive SBA-guaranteed loans roughly in proportion to their share of start-ups but at just over half the value of the loans made to white entrepreneurs.

Finally, the data indicate that financial institutions discriminate against black entrepreneurs. Studies show that black entrepreneurs with the same level of wealth and credit histories as white entrepreneurs, who are starting the same-sized businesses in the same industries, are more likely to have their business loans denied by banks or to have to pay higher interest rates. White entrepreneurs can borrow approximately 15 percent more from financial institutions per dollar of equity capital in their businesses than can blacks.[35]

The undercapitalization of black-led start-ups hinders their performance in a fairly straightforward way. Because their businesses have less money, black entrepreneurs cannot ride out periods of low sales or high costs the way white entrepreneurs can, and they cannot invest as much in growing their businesses. Consequently, the survival, growth, and profitability of black-owned start-ups are hindered by lack of capital, leading to their lesser performance in comparison to white-owned ones.

Busted Myths and Key Realities

56. Blacks create new businesses at only one-third the rate of whites, and this pattern has persisted for decades.

57. The low rate of new business creation among blacks
is not a function of a lack of desire, inadequate role models,
insufficient social networks, or an absence of business experience or education, but rather is the result of a shortage of
capital.

58. The performance of black-led start-ups is much worse
than that of white-led ones on all dimensions.

59. The lower performance of black-led start-ups does not
result from a greater tendency to start businesses in center cities, lower human capital, or a lack of entrepreneurial role models in black families but occurs because black-led businesses
are undercapitalized and are founded in less favorable industries.

60. The capital problem that hinders the formation and
performance of black-led start-ups is not going to go away of its
own accord.

In Conclusion

Blacks are much less likely than whites to create new businesses. The
data on this are very clear. Moreover, the low rate of new business creation among blacks is not a function of a lack of desire, inadequate role
models, insufficient social networks, or an absence of business experience or education. Rather, it's the result of a shortage of capital. Black
households have less than one-tenth the net worth of white households,
which means that fewer would-be black entrepreneurs can come up with
the money to start a business.

The performance of black-led start-ups is much worse than that of
white-led ones on virtually every measurable dimension: survival, sales,
profits, employment, and so on. Although there are many explanations
floating around for why this is so—including the tendency of blacks to
start businesses in city centers, the lower human capital of black entrepreneurs, and the lack of entrepreneurial role models in black families—
the data show that the primary reason why black-led start-ups perform
worse than white-led start-ups is that they are undercapitalized. Black
businesses are undercapitalized because blacks have less money than

whites, and because black entrepreneurs have a harder time getting external financing than white entrepreneurs.

Moreover, this problem isn't going to go away on its own. The ratio of white net worth to black net worth has shrunk only from 11.5 to 1 to 9.5 to 1 since 1983.[36] Because blacks earn lower incomes than whites, have lower investment performance, and receive smaller inheritances, this wealth gap persists over time. As a result, blacks are no more likely to have the capital necessary to start new businesses or to have them perform effectively now than they did twenty years ago.

10

How Valuable Is the Average Start-Up?

Many people believe that entrepreneurs are an unbelievable resource. Entrepreneurs are thought to take people out of poverty, encourage innovations, create jobs, reduce unemployment, make markets more competitive, and enhance economic growth.[1] As Steve Case, a columnist for *Inc.* magazine, wrote, "Start-ups take the place of companies that shut down. They replenish the business population and sow the seeds of growth. They provide jobs, income, and hope for the future. Often, they create new markets, just by nosing their way into niches no one knew were there. . . . When a region booms, part of the reason is always the creation of new companies."[2]

Because entrepreneurship is seen as a panacea for many of society's ills, elected officials often view helping people to start businesses as a fundamental goal of public policy.[3] Take, for example, the perspective of Utah's Governor Michael Leavitt, the chairman of the National Governors Association, who said, "States must rethink the way they provide services in the twenty-first century. Developing policies that assist entrepreneurs are crucial to the success of state economies."[4] Or consider the following statement made by President George W. Bush: "Two out of every three new jobs are created by the entrepreneur. That's why it makes sense to have the small business at the cornerstone of a pro-growth economic policy.[5]

Given these views, local, state, and federal governments in the United States and elsewhere in the world have adopted a wide array of policies to increase the number of entrepreneurs. Among these are:

- giving transfer payments to people if they start businesses[6]
- providing loans and subsidies to new businesses[7]
- protecting entrepreneurs against the loss of wealth in the event of bankruptcy[8]
- reducing taxes on entrepreneurs[9]
- exempting new businesses from regulations[10]

The data show that these policies achieve their goals: more new businesses have been formed in places where and at times when these policies are adopted.[11] But are they good public policy?

Perhaps not. We have no evidence that in the absence of government intervention, people were creating too few businesses or that without government action the wrong firms would get started or financed. Moreover, we have no evidence that creating additional new companies is a good thing. The data do not show that creating more typical start-ups generates additional economic growth, spurs more innovation, or generates more good jobs.[12]

In contrast, there is ample evidence that when governments intervene to encourage the creation of new businesses, they stimulate people to start new companies disproportionately in competitive industries with lower barriers to entry and high rates of failure.[13] Nor do the businesses formed in response to government intervention generate much employment or substantially enhance productivity.[14]

You might be startled by this position, as it goes against the grain of most popular arguments. It might even seem illogical to you. After all, companies like Apple in computers, Microsoft in software, Google in Internet search, and Genentech in biotechnology are all examples of wildly successful start-ups. The list need not stop there. Federal Express and Wal-Mart were also start-up companies not too long ago. Surely these companies have contributed to economic growth and job creation.

Yes, of course they have. But, they are not the average start-up. Even when these companies were first founded, they weren't anything like the typical new business. A small number of start-up companies significantly enhance economic growth and job creation, but the typical start-up does not. As a result, encouraging the creation of *more* start-ups, in general, isn't very good public policy.[15] To show why, I'm going to focus on three things: the effect of new firm formation on economic growth; the effect of new business creation on job creation; and the quality of jobs created by start-ups.

Economic Growth

The common wisdom is that the number of new companies created in an economy is a prime driver of economic growth. Take, for example, the following statements expressed in the media, by public policy makers, and by the experts and pundits:

- "Entrepreneurship means growth."[16]
- "Nothing is as important to the state of small business—or to the health of the U.S. economy—as the rate at which entrepreneurs are creating new companies."[17]
- "Entrepreneurial companies are engines of economic growth and innovation to a greater extent than other types of firms and hold greater potential to enhance local and regional economies. . . . Some experts attribute nearly 70 percent of economic growth to entrepreneurial activity and suggest that 'one-third of the differential in national economic growth is due to the impact of entrepreneurial activity.'"[18]

Those are pretty strong statements. Basically, they suggest that economic growth is more dependent on new firm formation than on anything else.

This view isn't rare. Not only is it widely shared by the popular press and among policy makers, but many academics claim that it is backed up by a variety of studies.[19] If you look closely at the research supporting this view, however, you will see that the evidence is flimsy, at best. All the studies that support this position examine correlations between new firm formation and economic growth. (A correlation is the degree to which two things move in the same direction.) That is, new firm formation tends to be higher at times when, and in places where, growth in the gross domestic (or gross state) product is higher.[20]

For instance, the authors of the Global Entrepreneurship Monitor, a study that examines new firm formation in more than 40 countries, show a positive correlation between a measure of a country's rate of new firm formation and its real (after inflation) per capita GDP growth. From this correlation, they infer that having more start-up activity *makes* GDP grow faster in some countries than in others.[21] But does this evidence really mean that new firm formation *causes* economic growth?

The answer is "no." As people often say, "correlation doesn't imply causation." When two things are correlated, like start-up rates and economic growth, the first could cause the second, or the second could cause the first, or both could be caused by something else. Having more start-ups might not make an economy grow faster. Instead, having a faster growing economy could make more people start companies. If you don't believe me, think back to the roaring 1990s for a minute. Didn't everyone think that the new economy meant we were all going to get rich by starting Internet companies?

The evidence from carefully conducted studies shows that more people start companies in economic booms than in economic busts because good economic times give people the resources to start businesses and lead them to think that the benefits from entrepreneurship are high and the risks are low. For instance, a study by Professor Zoltan Acs of George Mason University and his colleague Catherine Armington that looked at the rate of firm formation between 1993 and 1998 in 394 metropolitan areas in the United States found that those metro areas that had higher per capita income growth *in the prior year* had a more firm formation in the next year.[22]

Moreover, even if the correlations in these studies did indicate that having more start-ups would cause economic growth to increase, it doesn't mean that the best way to encourage economic growth is to create more new companies. The reason why has to do with what these studies measure and don't measure. The studies *do* tell us that when there are more new businesses, economic growth is higher. But they *don't* tell us anything about the relation between the expansion of existing businesses and economic growth. It could very well be that the effect of new business formation on economic growth is *less* than the effect of the expansion of existing businesses. Because these correlations don't tell us whether we get more economic growth from each dollar or hour invested in the creation of a new business than we get for each dollar or hour invested in the expansion of an existing business, we don't know whether our economy would grow faster or slower if more people started businesses. In fact, if we were to get more economic growth for each dollar or hour invested in the expansion of existing businesses, then having more start-ups would actually be a drag on economic growth.

One way to know if we would get more economic growth by having more start-ups would be to look at the relative productivity of new and existing companies. *Productivity* is just a term for any measure of the benefit of putting one dollar or hour of resources into something. Simply put, one activity is more productive than another if we get more benefit from each dollar or hour invested in it.

Given the enormity of the effort to compile the data necessary to test this question, there aren't a lot of studies that look at it. One very careful study conducted by Professor John Haltiwanger of the University of Maryland and his colleagues combined data from the U.S. Census and other sources to look at the relation between firm productivity (in this case, sales divided by employment) and firm age. The results showed that firm productivity *increases* with firm age.[23] This means that the average new firm makes worse use of resources than the average existing firm, which is not what you would expect if economic growth benefits more from the creation of new firms than from the expansion of existing ones.

Another problem with inferring that new firm formation causes economic growth from correlations between the two is that countries with more new business creation could have higher GDP growth because something about those countries makes both new firm formation and GDP growth higher than in other countries. If that is the case, then higher firm formation is *not* evidence that new firm formation causes economic growth.

To make this point clearly, let me give you a humorous example. People in different countries approach meals differently. In some countries, like the United States, Australia, and Canada, people tend not to make a big deal about eating. They eat simple food, gobble it down quickly, often in their cars, and they buy a lot of fast, frozen, and prepared food. In other countries, like France, Spain, and Greece, people eat more complex food, savor it more slowly, sitting down at a table, and they buy much less fast, frozen, or prepared food. The rate of economic growth is higher in the first group of countries than in the second. But you probably don't think that how people eat *causes* economic growth.

Because a lot of things are different about different countries, and these differences are often correlated with each other, economists use a statistical technique called *fixed effects* regression to try to tease out whether the rate at which people start companies, or a number of other things that are correlated with firm formation, account for the differences in economic growth across countries. This statistical technique compares the changes in firm formation and economic growth to each country's average for those things over time. By comparing each country to itself at other points in time, this technique allows economists to look at the relation between firm formation and economic growth while holding constant all other factors that differ between nations—their distribution of industries, the structure of their capital markets, their regulatory environments, their legal systems, what their citizens eat and drink, the language that they speak, how often they argue about politics at the dinner table, and anything else that you might think of that differs between countries.

I conducted a fixed effects regression to predict the effect of total entrepreneurial activity, the measure of new firm formation in the Global Entrepreneurship Monitor data, on real per capita GDP, using the same data that other researchers had used to examine the correlation between firm formation and GDP growth. What I found was very different from the positive correlations between entrepreneurial activity and GDP growth reported in many studies. Removing the effect of *all* other factors that differ between countries, the rate of new firm formation in a particular year has a *negative* effect on a country's real per capita GDP in the following year.

This means that increasing the rate of at which typical start-ups are formed in our, or any other, country is unlikely to cause economic growth to increase. Rather, there is something about some countries that causes them to have both more new firm formation and more economic growth than other countries.

Unfortunately, we don't know what that something is. It could be their distribution of industries, the structure of their capital markets, their regulatory environments, their legal systems, what their residents eat and drink, the language they speak, how often they argue about politics at the dinner table, or something else. But we do know that when you hold that something—whatever it is—constant, increasing the rate of new firm formation is correlated with a *decline* in a country's economic growth.

This pattern makes sense because there shouldn't be positive correlation between economic growth and the rate at which typical start-ups are formed over the long term, given the evidence described in chapter

1. As you no doubt remember from that chapter, richer countries have less new firm formation than poorer ones because economic development leads real wages to rise and more capital to be used in production processes. This, in turn, increases the average size of firms and reduces the rate of new business creation.

Rich countries are richer than poor countries because they had more economic growth. If we measure new business creation and economic growth over a long enough horizon to see real differences in economic growth between countries, the countries that have had consistently faster economic growth (the rich ones) should display *declining* rates of new firm formation over time.

In fact, if we look at the correlations between rates of new firm formation and economic growth over the medium to long term, we see that firm formation declines as economic growth increases. For instance, the correlation between real GNP growth rates and the rate of self-employment in France, West Germany, and Italy between 1953 and 1987, and in Sweden between 1962 and 1987 is negative,[24] as is the correlation between self-employment and economic growth in the 19 OECD countries for which data are available from 1975 to 1996.[25]

What's the message here? Very simply, the popular belief that we can *cause* economic growth to increase by upping the rate at which new firms are formed is probably incorrect. Having more "average" start-ups isn't likely to be the answer to the problem of economic growth. If firm formation is implicated in growth, then its involvement is much more complex than many surmise.

Job Growth

New firm formation might not enhance economic growth, but as everyone knows, new firms create more jobs than existing firms.[26] As John Case, commentator for *Inc.* magazine explained, "Most of the 20 million new jobs created during the past 15 years came not from established giants, the companies that had led America's growth up till then. The jobs came from companies that were smaller, newer—or both. They came from that 'independent entrepreneurial sector.'"[27]

This view isn't unique to Mr. Case. It has been voiced by politicians on countless occasions, and newspapers and magazines include it in their reporting over and over again, leading us to believe that start-ups create most new jobs. Once again the data tell a different story.

New Firms Don't Account for Much Job Growth

Let's start with some basic facts. Very few people work in new firms. According to research by Professor Zoltan Acs and Dr. Catherine Armington, companies less than two years old and with at least one employee account for only 1 percent of all employment in the United States. By contrast, companies that are more than ten years old and have at least one employee account for 60 percent of all employment in this country.[28]

But companies add and shed jobs every year: companies that didn't exist last year can hire employees, while firms in existence last year can add or lose jobs. So how many of the new jobs do new businesses create? Gross job creation by new firms is very easy to calculate. Data from the Bureau of Labor Statistics show that 31,472,000 jobs were created in the United States in 2004.[29] That year, 580,900 new firms with at least 1 employee were started, each of which had an average of 3.8 employees. Thus, in 2004, new firms created 2,207,420 jobs, or 7 percent of the total number of jobs created in that year.

Measuring net job creation—new jobs created minus old jobs lost— is a lot harder than measuring gross job creation, and so we have fewer estimates of it. But estimates of net job creation by new firms are remarkably similar to the estimates of gross job creation. One study by Professors Steven Davis of the University of Chicago and John Haltiwanger of the University of Maryland shows that in manufacturing, one-year-old firms created 6.4 percent of the net new jobs, an estimate that is consistent across industries, regions, firm size, and type of firm ownership.[30] In short, few people work in start-ups, and start-ups create few of the gross or net new jobs in this country.

So what should you think about the often-made statement that entrepreneurs create half of all new jobs created in this country? Without getting too philosophical, the answer depends on what you think an entrepreneur is. Clearly, if an entrepreneur is someone who created a firm that is one year old, then this statement is just plain wrong. As we just saw, one-year-old firms create less than 7 percent of all new jobs. But what about people who create firms that are two years old? Three years old? Four years old? If we think of these people as entrepreneurs, how many jobs do entrepreneurs create?

There is not a lot of data available on this question, but we do have data on the six-year period from 1991 to 1996. Over that period, the total number of jobs created by the expansion of existing establishments exceeded the total number of jobs that came from the birth of new establishments. In fact, 42.6 percent of employment growth came from the formation of new single-establishment businesses, while 57.4 percent came from the expansion of single- or multiple-establishment businesses or from the formation of new establishments by multi-establishment businesses.[31] This means that if businesses that are six years old or less are considered new firms, then entrepreneurs create just shy of 43 percent of jobs. To reach the point where 50 percent of net new jobs were created by new firms, we would have to consider all firms that are nine years old or less to be "new."

Within manufacturing, however, firms that are ten years old and younger do not account for a majority of job creation. One study showed that manufacturing firms that are ten or more years old account for 59.6 percent of all new jobs created. In manufacturing, for a majority of jobs to be created by "new" firms, we would need to include all firms that are less than fifteen years old. If we redefine "new" to include these firms, we could attribute 52.3 percent of jobs created to "new" firms.[32] But as those of you who have kids or drive a car know, fifteen years old is hardly "new."

All the Job Growth Occurs in the First Year

Every year a cohort of new firms is founded, and this cohort generates about 7 percent of the new jobs created in that year. But how many jobs does that cohort of firms account for in its second year? In its third year? In years that follow? On average, the answer is none. Studies conducted in the United States, Sweden, and Germany show that each cohort of new firms employs more people in its first year than it employs in any year after that.[33] For instance, the cohort of new employer firms founded in the United States in 1998 employed 798,066 people in its first year but only 670,111 people in 2002 (see table 10.1).[34] In other words, the number of jobs lost by new firms that close down in their second year, third year, fourth year, and so on exceeds the number of jobs added by the expansion of the new firms that survive.[35]

How Many Start-Ups Equal One Employer Firm in Ten Years?

How many people have to try to start a business to have one company that employs anyone ten years later? The answer: 43. Estimates show

Table 10.1 Employment of the 1998 Cohort of New Employer Firms in the United States, 1998–2002

Sector	1998	1999	2000	2001	2002
Overall	798,066	792,131	781,506	721,103	670,111
Natural resources and mining	21,809	19,781	19,945	17,636	16,789
Construction	98,750	94,468	84,550	75,256	69,426
Manufacturing	45,670	51,271	52,055	50,073	45,732
Trade, transportation, and utilities	139,125	140,472	137,448	127,135	118,266
Information	17,794	22,064	25,085	22,131	18,241
Financial activities	46,098	47,745	46,314	43,855	41,665
Professional and business services	137,908	154,160	170,016	158,281	147.618
Education and health services	57,068	64,594	67,017	65,534	64,881
Leisure and hospitality	156,668	139,041	126,323	114,154	105,941
Other services	69,736	55,664	49,639	45,027	39,932

Source: Adapted from A. Knaup, "Survival and Longevity in the Business Employment Dynamics Data," *Monthly Labor Review,* May 2005, 50–56.

that only about one-third of all start-up efforts result in the creation of a new firm.[36] Thus if three people initiate the start-up process, one new firm will result. But because just under one-fourth of firms (24 percent) employ anyone, we will need 12.5 people to try to start a new firm to get one new firm that employs anyone. Carrying this further, only 29 percent of new employer firms live ten years, and so 43.1 start-up efforts are needed today to have one new firm that employs anyone ten years from now.

And how many jobs will that start-up have, on average, ten years after it was founded? The answer is 9. In short, 43 people have to try to start companies to create 9 jobs a decade from now. That's not the spectacular yield that you might be expecting if you've been reading press reports about the job creation potential of start-ups.

Quality of Jobs

We have been talking about the jobs created by start-ups as if they were equivalent to jobs in existing companies. But they're not. They're worse. The average new firm is smaller than the average existing firm, which is an issue because small firms pay less, offer fewer fringe benefits, provide less job security, and do not provide the same opportunities for training as large firms.[37]

The data show that jobs in new firms are more likely to be part-time than jobs in existing firms.[38] Moreover, jobs in the average new firm do not pay as well as jobs in the average existing business. One study by Professor Paul Reynolds and his colleague Dr. Samis White showed that the average new-firm job paid 72 percent of the state's average wage in the firm's first year, and that the wages in those firms were still below the state average four years later.[39]

Jobs in new firms offer fewer benefits than jobs in existing firms. Studies show that older businesses are more likely to offer a pension plan or health insurance coverage to their employees.[40]

The size of the difference in the tendency of new and existing firms to offer health insurance is substantial. One study showed that men who work for others are three times as likely, and women who work for others are five times as likely, to have health insurance as those who work for themselves.[41] Moreover, preliminary data from Kauffman Firm Survey show that, in 2004, only 23.2 percent of new firms offered health insurance to their full-time employees. In contrast, approximately 47 percent of all businesses in the United States, of the same size of the average start-up with employees—between 3 and 9 employees—offered health insurance to their employees in the same year.[42]

Jobs in new firms are less likely to be around in the future than jobs in existing businesses, largely because the survival rate of new firms is so low. One study showed that the probability that jobs created by new firms in the services sector would still be around four years later was 10 to 13 percent lower than the probability for all (new and established) businesses in that sector. In manufacturing, the numbers were worse. The probability that a job created in a new firm would still be around four years later was 20 percent below that of jobs created in all firms.[43]

Busted Myths and Key Realities

61. Our public policies toward entrepreneurship—the transfer payments, loans, subsidies, tax reductions, exemptions

from regulation, and bankruptcy laws—work; they increase the number of start-ups in the United States.

62. Encouraging start-ups is lousy public policy because we have no evidence that people create too few or the wrong businesses in the absence of government intervention, and a lot of evidence that these policies lead people to start marginal businesses that are likely to fail, have little economic impact, and generate little employment.

63. We have no evidence that new firm formation causes economic growth; rather, economic growth probably causes people to start businesses.

64. Investing a dollar or an hour of time in the creation of an average new business is a worse use of resources than investing the same resources in the expansion of an average existing business.

65. New firms don't create more jobs than existing firms; to reach the halfway point of 50 percent of net new jobs, we would have to consider as "new" all firms up to nine years old.

66. All the job growth created by a given cohort of new firms comes in its first year; in every subsequent year, the cohort loses more jobs through company failure than it adds through company expansion.

67. The jobs in start-ups pay less, offer fewer benefits, and are more likely to disappear over time than jobs in existing companies.

In Conclusion

Many people believe that entrepreneurs take people out of poverty, encourage innovation, create jobs, reduce unemployment, make markets more competitive, and enhance economic growth. As a result, public policy in many countries, states, and locales is designed to encourage the creation of new companies. Governments give transfer payments to entrepreneurs; provide loans and subsidies to new businesses; protect entrepreneurs against the loss of wealth in the event of bankruptcy; reduce taxes on entrepreneurs; and exempt new businesses from following regulations, all to increase the number of start-ups.

And it works. Where these policies are used, there are more new businesses.

But encouraging start-ups is lousy public policy. We have no evidence that in the absence of government intervention people make bad decisions and create too few or the wrong kinds of businesses. In contrast, there is a lot of evidence that these policies lead people to start marginal businesses that are likely to fail, have little economic impact, and generate little employment.

In fact, the data do not support the two most oft-made claims about the typical new business: that it enhances economic growth and that it creates good new jobs. Despite a wealth of data that shows a correlation between new firm formation and economic growth, we have no evidence that new firm formation causes economic growth. Rather, economic growth probably causes people to start businesses.

Moreover, because firms become more productive as they get older, investing resources in the creation of an average new business is a worse use of resources than investing in the expansion of an average existing business. Indeed, having more new firm formation might actually slow economic growth. If we control for other factors that account for differences between countries in their rate of firm formation and their economic growth, this is exactly what we see.

The idea that new firms create more jobs than existing firms is a misconception. New companies—those that are one or two years old—employ only 1 percent of people in this country, while those that are ten or more years old employ 60 percent of them. Newly formed firms account for only 6 to 7 percent of gross or net new jobs created every year. In fact, companies less than six years old account for less than 43 percent of all net new jobs created in the United States. For "new" firms to create 50 percent of net new jobs, we would have to expand the definition of "new" to include all firms that are nine years old and younger.

The job growth from new firms is concentrated in a few companies and occurs primarily when those companies are first founded. That is, all of the job growth created by a given cohort of new firms comes in its first year; in every subsequent year, the cohort loses more jobs through company failure than it adds through company expansion.

Finally, the jobs in start-ups aren't as good as the ones in existing firms. They pay less and offer fewer benefits. In particular, jobs in start-ups are less likely to provide pensions or health insurance, and they are more likely to disappear over time than jobs in existing companies.

In short, the typical start-up is a lot less valuable than most people—and most policy makers—think. Which makes you wonder: why do we have so many policies to encourage ever more new companies to be founded?

Conclusion

We need to change the way we think about entrepreneurship. Our collective belief that the typical entrepreneur is a hero with special powers that lead him to build a great company, which innovates, creates jobs, makes markets more competitive, and enhances economic growth, is a myth. And our sense that the typical new business provides a great deal of benefit for its founder, his employees and customers, and society at large is also wrong. Our myths about entrepreneurship, and the policies we have developed in response to them, are leading too many people to become entrepreneurs, causing financial hardship for many, and hindering our economic well-being.

The Reality of Entrepreneurship

The reality of entrepreneurship lies in stark contrast to our myths about it. Entrepreneurship is a very common activity, undertaken by many people at some time during their lives. The typical entrepreneur is not a special person with hidden psychological powers that allow him to build great companies or great wealth; he's a middle-aged white guy who just wants to earn a living and doesn't want to work for somebody else. The typical entrepreneur could be your next door neighbor—and he might not be your most successful neighbor. People are more likely to start businesses if they are unemployed, have changed jobs often, and have made less money in their previous employment.

The typical start-up is no more impressive than the typical entrepreneur. It is a home-based sole proprietorship that employs one person—the founder—and it isn't innovative and has no intention, or prospects, of growing. The typical new business requires only about $25,000 of start-up capital and is financed largely from the founder's savings, supplemented by bank loans guaranteed by the founder.

The average new business is started in a mundane, run-of-the-mill industry—one in which a lot of companies fail and where profit margins are slim. The founder of the typical start-up spends little time coming up with his new business idea, and the business is likely to offer the same product or service that his previous employer provided to his customers.

The performance of the typical new business isn't very good. Its life-span is less than five years. Even the atypical start-up that survives over time provides its founder with less money and fewer job benefits than he would have earned working for someone else, despite working more hours and having more variable compensation.

The outcomes are worse for businesses started by women and blacks. For many decades, women and blacks have been less likely than white men to start businesses. When they do start those businesses, they face higher failure rates, lower sales, and lesser profits than do white men.

At the aggregate level, the story of the typical entrepreneur is no better. Having more start-ups in a country or region doesn't cause more economic growth. Moreover, start-ups don't generate as many jobs as most people think, and the jobs that they create aren't as good as the jobs in existing companies.

The good news is that this isn't a particularly entrepreneurial era, and America isn't a particularly entrepreneurial place. That honor is reserved for developing countries like Peru and Uganda, which are poorer and more agricultural.

I realize that much of this is depressing. It is a story of poor outcomes for individuals, cities, states, and countries. People don't like depressing stories; perhaps that is the reason why so many people ignore the data and perpetuate the myths about entrepreneurship. But someone has to reveal what the data say.

What Should We Do?

Now that I have poured the cold water of reality on the myths that we tell ourselves about entrepreneurship, it is only fair that I offer some suggestions about what we should and should not do.

Let me start with what we shouldn't do. We shouldn't get rid of start-ups. Despite the dismal story about the typical start-up portrayed in this book, getting rid of start-ups isn't the answer. Entrepreneurship is central to the success of a capitalist economy. But the formation of the typical start-up is not. The fine print that many people seem to miss is that new company formation per se isn't what matters; rather it's the creation of a small number of super-high-potential new companies, which among them generate almost all the economic growth and job and wealth creation that comes from having an entrepreneurial economy.

Take, for example, the handful of venture capital-backed companies that are formed every year. Since 1970, venture capitalists have funded an average of 820 new companies per year. These 820 start-ups—out of the more than 2 million efforts to start businesses in this country every year—have enormous economic impact. In 2003, companies that were backed by venture capitalists employed 10 million people, or 9.4 percent of the private sector labor force in the United States, and generated $1.8 trillion in sales, or 9.6 percent of business sales in this country.[1] In 2000, the 2,180 publicly traded companies that received venture-capital backing between 1972 and 2000 comprised 20 percent of all public companies in the United States, 11 percent of their sales, 13 percent of their profits, 6 percent of their employees, and one-third of their market value, a figure in excess of $2.7 *trillion* dollars.[2] Between 2003 and 2005, venture capital-backed start-ups made up 23 percent of the companies that went public.[3] In short, almost all of the value generated by start-ups comes from this handful of firms.

Rather than believe that we will be better off, both as individuals and as a society, simply if more people become entrepreneurs, we need to change our basic assumptions. A strategy that revolves around increasing the number of new businesses created every year is flawed. Increasing the number of people founding construction firms and hair salons and taxi services that don't do anything innovative isn't going to do us much good. In fact, it might hinder our economic growth because new businesses are, on average, less productive than existing ones.

Instead of believing naively that all entrepreneurship is good, we need to recognize that only a select few entrepreneurs will create the businesses that will take people out of poverty, encourage innovation, create jobs, reduce unemployment, make markets more competitive, and enhance economic growth. Therefore, as unfair as it might sound, we need to "stop spreading the peanut butter so thin." We need to recognize that all entrepreneurs are not created equal. We need to think like venture capitalists and concentrate our time and money on extraordinary entrepreneurs and worry less about the typical ones. That means identifying the select few new businesses, out of the multitude of start-ups created each year, that are more productive than existing companies and investing in them—as entrepreneurs, as investors, and as a society.

When we put time and money into new companies, we need to have evidence that they are worth it. This means putting resources into entrepreneurs who have the education and work experience to allow them to be successful. It also means putting resources into companies with well-thought-out ideas; the ones that are exploiting innovations that have the potential to generate economic value, that seek to meet real needs of customers, and that are pursuing opportunities worth going after.

We also need to change our public policies toward entrepreneurship. We need to reduce the incentives for marginal entrepreneurs to start businesses by reducing the transfer payments, loans, subsidies, regulatory exemptions, and tax benefits that encourage more and more people to start businesses. Because the average existing new firm is more productive than the average new firm, we would be better off economically if we eliminated policies that encourage people to start businesses instead of taking jobs working for others.

Some commentators argue that we can't focus solely on the small number of highly successful start-ups because we don't know which start-ups will become high-growth businesses and which won't. These commentators believe that the answer is to throw mud against the wall and see what sticks. This view may be politically appealing, but it is naïve. It assumes that we can't identify the things that make new businesses more likely to survive, generate profits, increase sales, and hire people. Unless the beliefs of venture capitalists and sophisticated business angels are completely wrong, and the research discussed in this book is completely incorrect, we know what criteria to focus on. From the human capital of the founder and his motivations, the industries in which companies are founded, their business ideas and strategies of these companies, and their legal forms and capital structure, among other things, we have a lot of information to help us distinguish likely winners.

In fact, you already know how to select the companies to bet on. Take, for example, the following two businesses:

• A personal cleaning business started by an unemployed high school dropout that is pursuing the customers of another personal cleaning business, is capitalized with $10,000 of the founder's savings, and is set up as a sole proprietorship.

• An Internet company that is started by a former Microsoft employee with fifteen years of experience in the software industry, an MBA and a master's degree in computer science, that is pursuing the next generation of Internet search, is capitalized with $250,000 in money from the founder and the Band of Angels in San Francisco, and is set up as a corporation.

Which one would you put your resources behind? It's obvious that the second business has a far better chance of success than the first one and that, on average, we would be better off putting our resources into such businesses. Why, then, are we encouraging and subsidizing the creation of businesses like the first one?

We also need to educate would-be entrepreneurs about what makes start-ups successful. We need to make sure they are not making poor decisions out of ignorance. Anyone who is thinking of becoming an entrepreneur needs to know the factors that contribute to the success of new businesses. For instance, they need to be aware that larger businesses that are more heavily capitalized, organized as corporations, started on a full-time basis by a team of entrepreneurs who have a written business plan and are seeking to provide products to customers missed by others will, on average, be more successful than other new businesses. Moreover, entrepreneurs need to know that such things as emphasizing marketing and financial controls, focusing their activities on a single market, and not competing on price will enhance their performance. Furthermore, they need to be aware that start-ups founded by people who obtain an education and then get experience working in the industry in which they plan to start a business, and who are starting their businesses with the goal of making money, have better financial performance, on average, than other start-ups.

The first step to improving your performance in any activity is recognizing that you need to get better. We've now reached the end of the first step in creating better entrepreneurs. We've busted many of the myths that led to the misconceptions that kept us from realizing what we need to do to improve entrepreneurship in this country. Armed with a better understanding, we can now begin the process of starting better companies and improving public policy toward entrepreneurship in America.

Notes

Introduction

1. The major sources include: (1) government databases, such as Internal Revenue Service Statistics and the Longitudinal Establishment and Enterprise Microfile (a database containing annual information on all U.S. establishments from 1988 to 2001); (2) U.S. Census Bureau surveys, such as the Survey of Business Owners (a survey of all nonagricultural U.S. businesses with sales of $1,000 or more that filed tax forms); Characteristics of Business Owners Survey (a survey of all businesses with more than $500 in sales that filed taxes as a sole proprietorship, partnership, or subchapter S corporation); Decennial Census (the long form U.S. census questionnaire collected every ten years); Survey of Income and Program Participation (a series of national panel surveys conducted on between 14,000 and 36,700 households over a two-and-a-half-to-four-year period); (3) surveys by the U.S. Bureau of Labor Statistics, such as the Current Population Survey (a survey of a representative sample of the U.S. population to gather information on the labor force) and the National Longitudinal Survey of Youth (a nationally representative sample of 12,686 men and women between the ages of 14 to 22 in 1979 that were surveyed annually from 1979 to 1994 and every two years thereafter); (4) surveys by the Federal Reserve's Board of Governors, such as the Survey of Consumer Finances (a survey on household finances of a nationally representative sample of 4,500 households conducted every three years); and the Survey of Small Business Finances (a survey on the finances of a nationally representative sample of 3,500 for-profit nonagricultural businesses with fewer than 500 employees conducted every five years; (5) representative studies conducted by academic institutions, such as the Panel Study of Entrepreneurial Dynamics (an annual panel study conducted from 1998 to 2003 on a representative sample of 830 people who were in the process of starting a business when they were surveyed in 1998), the Entrepreneurship in the United States Assessment (a nationally representative survey of 34,181 working-age people in the United States conducted between 2000 and 2004); the Kauffman Firm Survey (a national probability survey of new firms

founded in the United States in 2004); the National Federation of Independent Business Survey (a survey of new members of the largest business trade association in the United States, conducted in 1985 with follow-ups in 1986 and 1987); and the Panel Study of Income Dynamics (a longitudinal study of a representative sample of 7,000 U.S. families conducted since 1968); (6) representative studies of entrepreneurship in other countries, such as the Global Entrepreneurship Monitor (an annual survey of the working-age population in 39 countries to identify people who have begun and have completed the business formation process); the British Household Panel Survey (a nationally representative survey of 5,500 British households conducted from 1991 to 1997); Swedish Entrepreneurship Research Consortium Survey (a representative sample of 405 people in the process of starting a new business in Sweden in 1998 and tracked over the next two-and-a-half years); Survey of the Dutch Chamber of Commerce (an annual survey of all newly registered firms in Holland in the first quarter of 1994 from 1995 to 1997); and the National Child Development Study (a longitudinal study of a cohort of residents of the United Kingdom that were born in the first week of March 1958 and who were surveyed at birth, and ages 7, 11, 16, 23, and 33).

2. http://www.m-w.com/dictionary/entrepreneur.

3. *Wikipedia,* http://en.wikipedia.org/wiki/Entrepreneurship.

4. http://www.bbc.co.uk/radio4/news/inbusiness/inbusiness_20020620.shtml (accessed October 2, 2006).

5. Ann Winblad at Hummer Winblad Venture Partners quoted in "Can Entrepreneurship Be Taught," http://money.cnn.com/magazines/fsb/fsb_archive/2006/03/01/8370301/index.htm.

6. P. Reynolds and S. White, *The Entrepreneurial Process: Economic Growth, Men, Women, and Minorities* (Westport, Conn.: Greenwood, 1997).

7. W. Gentry and R. Hubbard, "Entrepreneurship and Household Saving" (working paper, Columbia University, New York, 2005); G. Haynes and C. Ou, "A Profile of Owners and Investors of Privately Held Businesses in the United States, 1989–1998" (paper presented at the annual conference of Academy of Entrepreneurial and Financial Research, New York, April 25–26, 2002).

8. Gentry and Hubbard, "Entrepreneurship and Household Saving"; Haynes and Ou, "A profile of Owners and Investors."

9. P. Reynolds, *Entrepreneurship in the United States* (Miami: Florida International University, 2005).

10. P. Reynolds, *Entrepreneurship in the United States: The Future is Now* (New York: Springer, forthcoming).

11. Reynolds, *Entrepreneurship in the United States.*

12. Reynolds and White, *Entrepreneurial Process.*

Chapter 1. America: Land of Entrepreneurship in an Entrepreneurial Era?

1. http://forum.belmont.edu/cornwall/archives/003928.html (accessed October 2, 2006).

2. P. Hise, "Everyone Wants To Start a Business," http://money.cnn.com/2007/01/22/magazines/fsb/entrepreneurship.boom.fsb/ (accessed February 1, 2007).

3. W. Poole, "Staying Out of the Way of Entrepreneurs" (speech to the Conference on Striking the Right Notes on Entrepreneurship, Memphis, Tenn., April 19, 2005), www.stlouisfed.org/news/speeches/2005/4_19_05.html (accessed October 2, 2006).

4. B. Bucks, A. Kennickell, and K. Moore, "Recent Changes in U.S. Family Finances: Evidence from the 2001 and 2004 Survey of Consumer Finances," *Federal Reserve Bulletin,* 2006, A1–A35; A. Kennickell and J. Shack-Marquez, "Changes in U.S. Family Finances from 1983 to 1989: Evidence from the Survey of Consumer Finances," *Federal Reserve Bulletin,* 1992, 1–18.

5. P. Reynolds, *Entrepreneurship in the United States: The Future is Now* (New York: Springer, forthcoming).

6. M. Manser and G. Picot, "The Role of Self-Employment in U.S. and Canadian Job Growth," *Monthly Labor Review,* April 1999, 10–21.

7. J. Bregger, "Measuring Self-Employment in the United States," *Monthly Labor Review,* January–February 1996, 3–9.

8. www.bls.gov/opub/ted/2004/aug/wk4/art02.txt (accessed August 30, 2006).

9. R. Fairlie and B. Meyer, "Trends in Self-Employment among White and Black Men during the Twentieth Century," *Journal of Human Resources* 35, no. 4 (2000): 643–69.

10. D. Blanchflower, "Self-Employment in OECD Countries," *Labour Economics* 7 (2000): 471–505.

11. R. Finnie and C. Laporte, "Setting Up Shop: Self Employment among Canadian College and University Graduates," *Industrial Relations* 58, no. 1 (2003): 3–32.

12. Reynolds, *Entrepreneurship in the United States.*

13. P. Reynolds, "Understanding Business Creation: Serendipity and Scope in Two Decades of Business Creation Studies," *Small Business Economics* 24 (2005): 359–64.

14. Ibid.; H. Schuetze, "Taxes, Economic Conditions and Recent Trends in Male Self-Employment: A Canada–U.S. Comparison," *Labour Economics* 7 (2000): 507–44.

15. T. Garrett, "Entrepreneurs Thrive in America," *Bridges,* spring 2005, www.stlouisfed.org/publications/br/2005/a/pages/2-article.html (accessed October 2, 2006).

16. S. Folster, "Do Lower Taxes Stimulate Self Employment?" *Small Business Economics* 19 (2002): 135–45.

17. Reynolds, *Entrepreneurship in the United States: The Future is Now.*

18. N. Noorderhaven, R. Thurik, S. Wennekers, and A. Van Stel, "The Role of Dissatisfaction and Per Capita Income in Explaining Self-Employment across Fifteen European Countries," *Entrepreneurship Theory and Practice,* fall 2004, 447–66; Fairlie and Meyer, "Trends in Self-Employment."

19. M. Carree, A. Van Stel, R. Thurik, and S. Wennekers, "Economic Development and Business Ownership: An Analysis Using Data of Twenty-three OECD Countries in the Period 1976–1996," *Small Business Economics* 19 (2002): 271–90.

20. D. Blau, "A Time Series Analysis of Self-Employment in the United States," *Journal of Political Economy* 95, no. 3 (1987): 445–65.

21. D. Blanchflower, "Self-Employment: More May Not Be Better," *Swedish Economic Policy Review* 11, no. 2 (2004): 15–74; Y. Georgellis and H. Wall, "What Makes a Region Entrepreneurial? Evidence from Britain," *Annals of Regional Science* 34 (2000): 385–403.

22. S. Hippel, "Self-Employment in the United States: An Update," *Monthly Labor Review,* July 2004, 13–23.

23. This correlation is not being driven by the effect of Uganda, the country with more than 30 percent of its GDP from agriculture. When Uganda is removed from the analysis, the correlation is almost the same ($r = 0.60$).

24. Z. Acs and C. Armington, "Using Census BITS to Explore Entrepreneurship, Geography and Economic Growth" (report for the U.S. Small Business Administration, contract no. SBAHQ-03-M0534, 2005).

25. Georgellis and Wall, "What Makes a Region Entrepreneurial?"

26. Finnie and Laporte, "Setting Up Shop."

27. R. Fairlie, *Kauffman Index of Entrepreneurial Activity National Report, 1996–2005* (Kansas City, Mo.: Ewing Marion Kauffman Foundation, 2006).

28. Reynolds, *Entrepreneurship in the United States.*

29. Fairlie, *Kauffman Index.*

30. Z. Acs, and C. Armington, *Entrepreneurship, Geography, and American Economic Growth* (Cambridge: Cambridge University Press, 2006).

31. Ibid. Technically the authors measured labor market areas.

32. Ibid.

33. Ibid.

34. P. Reynolds, N. Carter, W. Gartner, and P. Greene, "The Prevalence of Nascent Entrepreneurs in the United States: Evidence from the Panel Study of Entrepreneurial Dynamics," *Small Business Economics* 23 (2004): 263–84; P.

Davidsson, L. Lindmark, and C. Olofsson, "New Firm Formation and Regional Development in Sweden," *Regional Studies* 28, no. 4 (1994): 395–410; B. Guensnier, "Regional Variations in New Firm Formation in France," *Regional Studies* 28, no. 4 (1994): 347–58; D. Audretsch and M. Fritsch, "The Industry Component of Regional New Firm Formation Processes," *Review of Industrial Organization* 15 (1999): 239–52; P. Reynolds, "Autonomous Firm Dynamics and Economic Growth in the United States, 1986–1990," *Regional Studies* 28, no. 4 (1994): 429–42; H. Pennings, "Organizational Birth Frequencies: An Empirical Investigation," *Administrative Science Quarterly* 27 (1982): 120–44; Pennings, "The Urban Quality of Life and Entrepreneurship," *Academy of Management Journal* 25, no. 1 (1992): 63–79; O. Sorenson and P. Audia, "The Social Structure of Entrepreneurial Activity: Geographic Concentration of Footwear Production in the United States, 1940–1989," *American Journal of Sociology* 106, no. 2 (2000): 424–62; D. Keeble and S. Walker, "New Firms, Small Firms, and Dead Firms: Spatial Patterns and Determinants in the United Kingdom," *Regional Studies* 28, no. 4 (1994): 411–27; D. Schell and W. David, "The Community Infrastructure of Entrepreneurship: A Sociopolitical Analysis," in *Frontiers of Entrepreneurship Research,* ed. K. Vesper (Babson Park, Mass.: Babson College, 1981), 563–90; W. Dennis, "Explained and Unexplained Differences in Comparative State Business Starts and Start Rates," in *Frontiers of Entrepreneurship Research,* ed. R. Rondstadt, J. Hornaday, R. Peterson, and K. Vesper (Babson Park, Mass.: Babson College, 1986), 313–27; B. Schiller and P. Crewson, "Entrepreneurial Origins: A Longitudinal Inquiry," *Economic Inquiry* 35 (1997): 523–31; P. Reynolds, D. Storey, and P. Westhead, "Cross National Variations in New Firm Formation Rates," *Regional Studies* 28 (1994): 443–56.

35. Acs and Armington, "Using Census BITS"; Schell and David, "Community Infrastructure"; Guensnier, "Regional Variations"; D. Grant, "The Political Economy of New Business Formation across the American States, 1970–1985," *Social Science Quarterly* 77, no. 1 (1996): 28–42; S. Black and P. Strahan, "Entrepreneurship and Bank Credit Availability," *Journal of Finance* 42, no. 6 (2002): 2807–33.

36. M. Taylor, "Self-Employment and Windfall Gains in Britain: Evidence from Panel Data," *Economica* 68 (2001): 539–65; J. Ritsila and H. Tervo, "Effects of Unemployment on New Firm Formation: Micro-Level Panel Data Evidence from Finland," *Small Business Economics* 10 (2002): 103–15; P. Johnson, *New Firms: An Economic Perspective* (London: Allen and Unwin, 1986); D. Storey, *Entrepreneurship and the New Firm* (London: Croom Helm, 1982); Guensnier, "Regional Variations"; Audretsch and Fritsch, "Industry Component"; A. Kangasharju, "Regional Variations in Firm Formation: Panel and Cross-Section Data Evidence from Finland," *Papers in Regional Science* 79 (2000): 355–73; Reynolds, "Autonomous Firm Dynamics"; D. Storey and A. Jones, "New Firm Formation—A Labour Market Approach to Industrial Entry," *Scottish Journal of Political Economy*

34, no. 1 (1987): 37–51; Davidsson, Lindmark, and Olofsson, "New Firm Formation"; D. Bogenhold and U. Staber, "The Decline and Rise of Self-Employment," *Work, Employment and Society* 5, no. 2 (1991): 223–39; Grant, "Political Economy"; D. Audretsch and Z. Acs, "New Firm Start-Ups, Technology, and Macroeconomic Fluctuations," *Small Business Economics* 6 (1994): 439–49.

There are some studies that have found a negative correlation between self-employment or new firm formation and unemployment rates. These studies, however, are suspect on methodological grounds because they also show a strong positive correlation between the rate of GDP growth and the rate of new firm formation. Because unemployment tends to rise when economic growth falls (your standard recession scenario), unemployment rates and economic growth rates are highly negatively correlated. (Since the beginning of the 1950s, there has been a negative correlation between unemployment and GDP growth rates of between 0.66 and 0.72.) This high correlation gives rise to a technical problem in measuring effects that econometricians call multi-collinearity.

If two things are correlated perfectly (say economic growth and unemployment), you can't use both of them to predict new firm formation because once the effect of unemployment is measured, there is no variance in entrepreneurship left that economic growth can use to predict new firm formation. When measures are highly but not perfectly correlated, like unemployment and economic growth, the second variable (unemployment) has very little variance to use to explain new firm formation once the first variable's effect (economic growth) is measured. As a result, what these studies are really showing is that economic growth is positively correlated with new firm formation only in those few places and points in time where unemployment is low *and* economic growth is low.

37. Georgellis and Wall, "What Makes a Region Entrepreneurial?"; Blau, "Time Series Analysis."

38. Pennings, "Organizational Birth Frequencies."

39. S. Kreft and R. Sobel, "Public Policy, Entrepreneurship, and Economic Freedom," *Cato Journal* 25, no. 3 (2005): 595–616.

Chapter 2. What Are Today's Entrepreneurial Industries?

1. B. Kirchhoff, *Entrepreneurship and Dynamic Capitalism* (Westport, Conn.: Praeger, 1994).

2. P. Reynolds, *Entrepreneurship in the United States* (Miami: Florida International University, 2005).

3. P. Kim, H. Aldrich, and L. Keister, "Access (Not) Denied: The Impact of Financial, Human, and Cultural Capital on Entrepreneurial Entry in the United States," *Small Business Economics* 27 (2006): 5–22; P. Reynolds, "Who Starts New Firms?—Preliminary Explorations of Firms-in-Gestation," *Small Business Economics* 9 (1997): 449–62.

4. W. Gentry and R. Hubbard, "Entrepreneurship and Household Saving" (working paper, Columbia University, New York, 2005); Reynolds, *Entrepreneurship in the United States;* P. Reynolds, "Nature of Business Start-Ups," in *Handbook of Entrepreneurial Dynamics,* ed. W. Gartner, K. Shaver, N. Carter, and P. Reynolds (Thousand Oaks, Calif.: Sage, 2004), 244–58.

5. S. Hipple, "Self-Employment in the United States: An Update," *Monthly Labor Review,* July 2004, 13–23.

6. D. Blanchflower, "Self-Employment: More May Not Be Better," *Swedish Economic Policy Review* 11, no. 2 (2004): 15–74; Z. Acs, P. Arenius, M. Hay, and M. Minniti, *Global Entrepreneurship Monitor 2004 Executive Report* (Babson Park, Mass.: Babson College, 2004).

7. P. Reynolds and S. White, *The Entrepreneurial Process: Economic Growth, Men, Women, and Minorities* (Westport, Conn.: Greenwood, 1997).

8. P. Johnson, "Differences in Regional Firm Formation Rates: A Decomposition Analysis," *Entrepreneurship Theory and Practice* (fall 2004): 431–45.

9. M. Van Praag and H. Van Ophem, "Determinants of Willingness and Opportunity to Start as an Entrepreneur," *Kyklos* 48, no. 4 (1995): 513–40.

10. M. Cincera and O. Galgau, "Impact of Market Entry and Exit on EU Productivity and Growth Performance" (European Economy Discussion Papers, no. 222, 2005); J. Mata, "Firm Growth during Infancy," *Small Business Economics* 6 (1994): 27–39; T. Dean and G. Meyer, "New Venture Formation in Manufacturing Industries: A Conceptual and Empirical Analysis," in *Frontiers of Entrepreneurship Research,* ed. N. Churchill, S. Birley, W. Bygrave, D. Muzyka, C. Wahlbin, and W. Wetzel (Babson Park, Mass.: Babson College, 1992), 173–87; Z. Acs and C. Armington, "Using Census BITS to Explore Entrepreneurship, Geography and Economic Growth" (report for the U.S. Small Business Administration, contract no. SBA-HQ-03-M0534, 2005).

11. P. Reynolds, *New Firm Creation in the U.S.: A PSED I Overview* (Hanover, Mass.: Now Publishers, 2007).

Chapter 3. Who Becomes an Entrepreneur?

1. "Everyday Economics," http://www.dallasfed.org/educate/everyday/ev3.html.

2. National Federation of Independent Businesses, *Small Business Policy Guide* (Washington, D.C.: National Federation of Independent Businesses, 2000); D. Blanchflower and A. Oswald, "What Makes an Entrepreneur?" *Journal of Labor Economics* 16, no. 1 (1998): 26–60; I. Bernhardt, "Comparative Advantage in Self-Employment and Paid Work," *Canadian Journal of Economics* 27 (1994): 273–89; P. Robinson and E. Sexton, "The Effect of Education and Experience on Self-Employment Success," *Journal of Business Venturing* 9, no. 2 (1994): 141–56; Z. Lin, G. Picot, and J. Compton, "The Entry and Exit Dynamics of Self-Employment in

Canada," *Small Business Economics* 15 (2000): 105–25; M. Taylor, "Earnings, Independence or Unemployment: Why Become Self-Employed?" *Oxford Bulletin of Economics and Statistics* 58, no. 2 (1996): 253–66; B. Schiller and P. Crewson, "Entrepreneurial Origins: A Longitudinal Study," *Economic Inquiry* 35, no. 3 (1997): 523–31; D. Evans and L. Leighton, "Some Empirical Aspects of Entrepreneurship," *American Economic Review* 79, no. 3 (1989): 519–35; G. Borjas, "The Self-Employment Experience of Immigrants," *Journal of Human Resources* 11 (1986): 485–506; E. Johansson, "Self-Employment and Liquidity Constraints: Evidence from Finland," *Scandinavian Journal of Economics* 102, no. 1 (2000): 123–34; T. Lindh and H. Ohlsson, "Self-Employment and Windfall Gains: Evidence from the Swedish Lottery," *Economic Journal* 106 (1996): 1515–26; D. MacPherson, "Self-Employment and Married Women," *Economic Letters* 28 (1988): 281–84; J. Butler and C. Herring, "Ethnicity and Entrepreneurship in America: Toward an Explanation of Racial and Ethnic Group Variations in Self-Employment," *Sociological Perspectives* 34, no. 1 (1991): 79–95.

3. See, for example, a speech by Nigel Griffiths, a minister of Parliament in the United Kingdom, which can be downloaded from www.dti.gov.uk/ministers/archived/griffiths150302.html, or an article by Jim Hopkins in the *USA Today,* which can be found at http://www.usatoday.com/money/smallbusiness/2006–07–30-starting-your-business_x.htm.

4. Take a look at http://www.sba.gov/young/columbiacollege/k_12.nsf/vwHTMLPages/worksht.html.

5. We do have some data from carefully conducted studies that indicate that psychological characteristics make people more likely than others to become self-employed. For instance, one study (C. Van Praag and J. Cramer, "The Roots of Entrepreneurship and Labour Demand: Individual Ability and Low Risk Aversion," *Economica* 68, no. 269 [2001]: 45–62) surveyed 1,763 Dutch elementary school children in 1952 and again in 1993 and found that risk tolerance at age 12 predicted whether the people ever became self-employed over the next forty-one years. Another study (A. Burke, F. Fitzroy, and M. Nolan, "When Less Is More: Distinguishing between Entrepreneurial Choice and Performance," *Oxford Bulletin of Economics and Statistics* 62, no. 5 [2000]: 565–86) showed that those who were more tolerant of anxiety-provoking situations as measured in childhood were more likely to become self-employed later in life. Similarly, a study of 37,000 recruits to the Finnish army in 1982 (R. Uusitalo, *"Homo entreprenaurus?"* *Applied Economics* 33 [2001]: 1631–38) showed that the psychological dimension of cautiousness reduced the likelihood that the recruits would be working for themselves twelve years later.

In addition, the Panel Study of Entrepreneurial Dynamics, which surveyed a representative sample of the working-age population in the United States in

1998, compared those people who were in the process of starting a business with a control group of people who were not. They found only a few differences between the two groups on psychological characteristics—for instance, people for whom achieving recognition or meeting role expectation and who have greater confidence in themselves in social settings, a cognitive style that is focused on better approaches rather than novelty, and a preference for individual work are more likely than the rest of the population to be in the process of starting a business. On most of the psychological dimensions measured, there was no difference between the entrepreneurs and the control group. (See P. Reynolds, *New Firm Creation in the U.S.: A PSED I Overview* (Hanover, MA: Now Publishers, 2007.)

6. P. Reynolds, *New Firm Creation in the U.S.: A PSED I Overview* (Hanover, Mass.: Now Publishers, 2007).

7. L. Ross, "The Intuitive Psychologist and His Shortcomings: Distortions in the Attribution Process," in *Advances in Social Psychology,* vol. 10, ed. L. Berkowitz (New York: Academic Press, 1977).

8. Downloaded from www.dallasfed.org/educate/everyday/ev3.html.

9. M. Van Gelderen, R. Thurik, and N. Bosma, "Success and Risk Factors in the Pre-Start-Up Phase," *Small Business Economics* 26 (2006): 319–35; P. Reynolds and S. White, *The Entrepreneurial Process: Economic Growth, Men, Women, and Minorities* (Westport, Conn.: Greenwood, 1997); A. Burke, F. Fitzroy, and M. Nolan, "Self-Employment Wealth and Job Creation: The Roles of Gender, Non-pecuniary Motivation and Entrepreneurial Ability," *Small Business Economics* 9 (2002): 255–70; R. Uusitalo, *"Homo entreprenaurus?"* People also start businesses because they want jobs that allow them to "take initiative" and "to do important work" and because they have a low desire for job security (see M. Cowling, M. Taylor, and P. Mitchell, "Job Creators," *Manchester School* 72, no. 5 (2004): 601–17; Burke, Fitzroy, and Nolan, "Self-Employment Wealth").

10. Evans and Leighton, "Empirical Aspects"; J. Ritsila and H. Tervo, "Effects of Unemployment on New Firm Formation: Micro-Level Panel Data Evidence from Finland," *Small Business Economics* 19 (2002): 31–40; P. Dolton and G. Makepeace, "Self-Employment Among Graduates," *Bulletin of Economic Research* 42, no. 1 (1990): 35–53; Blanchflower and Oswald, "What Makes an Entrepreneur?"

11. Cowling, Taylor, and Mitchell, "Job Creators"; P. Reynolds, "Labor Force Participation and Residential Tenure," in *Handbook of Entrepreneurial Dynamics,* ed. W. Gartner, K. Shaver, N. Carter, and P. Reynolds (Thousand Oaks, Calif.: Sage, 2004), 62–77 ; R. Fairlie, "Self-Employment, Entrepreneurship, and the NLSY79," *Monthly Labor Review,* February 2005, 40–47. Ritsila and Tervo, "Effects of Unemployment"; Reynolds and White, *Entrepreneurial Process;* M. Taylor, "Self-Em-

ployment and Windfall Gains in Britain: Evidence from Panel Data," *Economica* 68 (2001): 539–65.

12. Dolton and Makepeace, "Self-Employment among Graduates"; Evans and Leighton, "Empirical Aspects"; A. Alba-Ramirez, "Self-Employment in the Midst of Unemployment: The Case of Spain and the United States," *Applied Economics* 26 (1994): 189–204.

13. Evans and Leighton, "Empirical Aspects"; Johansson, "Self-Employment and Liquidity Constraints"; Dolton and Makepeace, "Self-Employment among Graduates"; R. Amit, E. Muller, and I. Cockburn, "Opportunity Costs and Entrepreneurial Activity," *Journal of Business Venturing* 10, no. 2 (1995): 95–106; Taylor, "Earnings, Independence or Unemployment"; Bernhardt, "Comparative Advantage."

14. Fairlie, "Self-Employment."

15. "College Offers Fertile Ground for Starting a Business," http://www.quintcareers.com/college_entrepreneurs.html.

16. M. Levesque and M. Minniti, "The Effect of Aging on Entrepreneurial Behavior," *Journal of Business Venturing* 21 (2006): 177–94.

17. The Kauffman Firm Survey is a "national probability" sample when data from it are weighted by the nonresponse-adjusted sampling weight. The sample is based on Dun and Bradstreet listings of firms with a start date of 2004 and which perform business-initiating activities (such as establishing a legal status or an employer identification number, or paying unemployment insurance or social security taxes) in 2004.

18. Reynolds, *New Firm Creation;* Alba-Ramirez, "Self-Employment"; Taylor, "Earnings, Independence or Unemployment"; T. Bates, "Self-Employment Entry across Industry Groups," *Journal of Business Venturing* 10, no. 2 (1995): 143–56.

19. Bates, "Self-Employment Entry."

20. A. Henley, "Job Creation by the Self-Employed: The Role of Entrepreneurial and Financial Capital," *Small Business Economics* 25 (2005): 175–96; Fairlie, "Self-Employment"; P. Davidsson and B. Honig, "The Role of Social and Human Capital among Nascent Entrepreneurs," *Journal of Business Venturing* 18 (2003): 301–31; F. Delmar and P. Davidsson, "Where Do They Come From? Prevalence and Characteristics of Nascent Entrepreneurs," *Entrepreneurship and Regional Development* 12 (2000): 1–23; P. Kim, H. Aldrich, and L. Keister, "Access (Not) Denied: The Impact of Financial, Human, and Cultural Capital on Entrepreneurial Entry in the United States," *Small Business Economics* 27 (2006): 5–22; Ritsila and Tervo, "Effects of Unemployment."

21. "Hitting the Books," http://www.businessweek.com/magazine/content/06_38/b4001848.htm?chan=smallbiz_smallbiz+index+page_today's+top+stories.

22. R. Finnie and C. Laporte, "Setting Up Shop: Self Employment among Cana-

dian College and University Graduates," *Industrial Relations* 58, no. 1 (2003): 3–32; Dolton and Makepeace, "Self-Employment among Graduates"; Reynolds, *New Firm Creation.*

23. Bates, "Self-Employment Entry"; Evans and Leighton, "Empirical Aspects"; Schiller and Crewson, "Entrepreneurial Origins"; Lin, Picot, and Compton, "Entry and Exit Dynamics."

24. Experience starting a business also increases the odds that a person will start a business again. (See Evans and Leighton, "Empirical Aspects"; G. Carroll and E. Mosakowski, "The Career Dynamics of Self-Employment," *Administrative Science Quarterly* 32 [1987]: 570–89; Lin, Picot, and Compton, "Entry and Exit Dynamics"; P. Reynolds, "Who Starts New Firms?—Preliminary Explorations of Firms-in-Gestation," *Small Business Economics* 9 [1997]: 449–62; C. Praag and H. Pohem, "Determinants of Willingness and Opportunity to Start as an Entrepreneur," *Kyklos* 48, no. 4 [1995]: 513–40.) One study indicated that having prior start-up experience more than doubles (increases by 217 percent) the likelihood that a randomly sampled person will be in the process of starting a business at a given point in time. (See Davidsson and Honig, "Social and Human Capital"; and Delmar and Davidsson, "Where Do They Come From?") Many start-up efforts are undertaken by people with previous start-up experience. (See G. Haynes and C. Ou, "A Profile of Owners and Investors of Privately Held Businesses in the United States, 1989–1998" [paper presented at the Annual Conference of Academy of Entrepreneurial and Financial Research, New York, April 25–26, 2002]; P. Reynolds, N. Carter, W. Gartner, and P. Greene, "The Prevalence of Nascent Entrepreneurs in the United States: Evidence from the Panel Study of Entrepreneurial Dynamics," *Small Business Economics* 23 [2004]: 263–84; Van Gelderen, Thurik, and Bosma, "Success and Risk Factors"; J. Pratt, "Homebased Business: The Hidden Economy" [paper prepared for the Office of Advocacy, U.S. Small Business Administration, contract no. SBAHQ-97-M-0862, 1999]; Van Gelderen, Thurik, and Bosma, "Success and Risk Factors.")

25. R. Boyd, "Black and Asian Self-Employment in Large Metropolitan Areas: A Comparative Analysis," *Social Problems* 37, no. 2 (1990): 258–74; Taylor, "Earnings, Independence or Unemployment"; Henley, "Job Creation"; Reynolds and White, *Entrepreneurial Process.*

26. Reynolds, *New Firm Creation.*

27. Delmar and Davidsson, "Where Do They Come From?"; Kim, Aldrich, and Keister, "Access (Not) Denied"; Honig and Davidsson, "Social and Human Capital."

28. P. Reynolds, "Labor Force Participation and Residential Tenure," in *Handbook of Entrepreneurial Dynamics,* ed. Gartner et al., 62–77; J. Sanders and V. Nee, "Immigrant Self Employment: The Family as Social Capital and the Value of

Human Capital," *American Sociological Review* 61 (1996): 231–49; S. Hipple, "Self-Employment in the United States: An Update," *Monthly Labor Review,* July 2004, 13–23.

29. R. Fairlie and B. Meyer, "Ethnic and Racial Self-Employment Differences and Possible Explanations," *Journal of Human Resources* 31, no. 4 (1996): 757–93.

30. Ibid.

31. http://www.michigan.gov/documents/
071604StartingaBusinessFactSheet_101302_7.pdf.

32. H. Aldrich and N. Carter, "Teams," in *Handbook of Entrepreneurial Dynamics,* ed. Gartner et al., 324–35.

Chapter 4. What Does the Typical Start-Up Look Like?

1. J. Norberg, "Humanity's Greatest Achievement," *Wall Street Journal,* October 2, 2006, A11.

2. P. Reynolds, "Understanding Business Creation: Serendipity and Scope in Two Decades of Business Creation Studies," *Small Business Economics* 24 (2005): 359–64.

3. A. Bhide, *The Origin and Evolution of New Businesses* (Oxford: Oxford University Press, 2000).

4. P. Reynolds *Entrepreneurship in the United States: The Future is Now* (New York, Springer, Forthcoming).

5. J. Bregger, "Measuring Self-Employment in the United States," *Monthly Labor Review,* January–February 1996, 3–9; S. Hipple, "Self-Employment in the United States: An Update," *Monthly Labor Review,* July 2004, 13–23; A. Henley, "Job Creation by the Self-Employed: The Role of Entrepreneurial and Financial Capital," *Small Business Economics* 25 (2005): 175–96.

6. B. Kirchhoff, *Entrepreneurship and Dynamic Capitalism* (Westport, Conn.: Praeger, 2004).

7. A. Knaup, "Survival and Longevity in the Business Employment Dynamics Data," *Monthly Labor Review,* May 2005, 50–56; B. Headd, *Business Estimates from the Office of Advocacy: A Discussion of Methodology* (working paper, Office of Advocacy, U.S. Small Business Administration, June 2005), table 1; P. Reynolds, *New Firm Creation in the U.S.: A PSED I Overview* (Hanover, Mass.: Now Publishers); Bregger, "Measuring Self-Employment."

8. M. Bitler, T. Moskowitz, and A. Vissing-Jorgensen, "Testing Agency Theory with Entrepreneur Effort and Wealth," *Journal of Finance* 60, no. 2 (2005): 539–76.

9. J. Pratt, "Homebased Business: The Hidden Economy" (paper prepared for the Office of Advocacy, U.S. Small Business Administration, contract no. SBAHQ-97-M-0862, 1999).

10. M. Van Gelderen, R. Thurik, and N. Bosma, "Success and Risk Factors in the Pre-Start-Up Phase," *Small Business Economics* 24 (2005): 365–380.

11. P. Reynolds and S. White, *The Entrepreneurial Process: Economic Growth, Men, Women, and Minorities* (Westport, Conn.: Greenwood, 2007).

12. Z. Acs, P. Arenius, M. Hay, and M. Minniti, *Global Entrepreneurship Monitor 2004 Executive Report* (Babson Park, Mass.: Babson College, 2004).

13. G. Haynes, "Wealth and Income: How Did Small Businesses Fare from 1989 to 1998?" (report for the U.S. Small Business Administration, contract no. SBAHQ-00-M-0502, 2001).

14. National Federation of Independent Businesses, *Small Business Policy Guide* (Washington, D.C.: National Federation of Independent Businesses, 2000).

15. Pratt, "Homebased Business."

16. Ibid.

17. http://coachville.com/tl/thomasleonard//karla/formsCD/334businessideas.pdf; http://www10.americanexpress.com/sif/cda/page/0,1641,15677,00.asp.

18. G. Hills and R. Singh, "Opportunity Recognition," in *Handbook of Entrepreneurial Dynamics,* ed. W. Gartner, K. Shaver, N. Carter, and P. Reynolds (Thousand Oaks, Calif.: Sage, 2004), 259–72.

19. A. Cooper, T. Folta, and C. Woo, "Initial Human and Financial Capital as Predictors of New Venture Performance," *Journal of Business Venturing* 9, no. 5 (1995): 371–95.

20. Hills and Singh "Opportunity Recognition."

21. Ibid.

22. R. Young and J. Francis, "Entrepreneurship and Innovation in Small Manufacturing Firms," *Social Science Quarterly* 72, no. 1 (1991): 149–62.

23. Hills and Singh, "Opportunity Recognition."

24. Ibid.

25. A. Cooper and W. Dunkelberg, "Entrepreneurship Research: Old Questions, New Answers and Methodological Issues," *American Journal of Small Business* 11, no. 3 (1987): 11–23.

26. Cooper and Dunkelberg, "Entrepreneurship Research."

27. "Evaluating New Business Ideas," http://smallbusiness.yahoo.com/r-article-a-1258-m-1-sc-12-evaluating_new_business_ideas-i.

28. Hills and Singh, "Opportunity Recognition."

29. Ibid.

30. W. Gartner, N. Carter, and P. Reynolds, "Business Start-Up Activities," in *Handbook of Entrepreneurial Dynamics,* ed. Gartner et al., 259–72.

31. J. Eckhardt, S. Shane, and F. Delmar, "Multistage Selection and the Financing of New Ventures," *Management Science* 52, no. 2 (2006): 220–32.

32. Reynolds and White, *Entrepreneurial Process.*

33. S. Parker and Y. Belghitar, "What Happens to Nascent Entrepreneurs? An Econometric Analysis of the PSED," *Small Business Economics* 27 (2006): 81–101; Van Gelderen, Thurik, and Bosma, "Success and Risk Factors."

34. Reynolds, *New Firm Creation.*

35. Reynolds and White, *Entrepreneurial Process.*

36. S. Shane and F. Delmar, "Planning for the Market: Business Planning before Marketing and the Continuation of Organizing Efforts," *Journal of Business Venturing* 19 (2004): 767–85.

37. Reynolds and White, *Entrepreneurial Process.*

38. F. Delmar and S. Shane, "Does Business Planning Facilitate the Development of New Ventures?" *Strategic Management Journal* 24, no. 12 (2003): 1165–85.

39. F. Delmar and S. Shane, "Legitimating First: Organizing Activities and the Survival of New Ventures," *Journal of Business Venturing* 19 (2004): 385–410.

40. J. Katz and W. Gartner, "Properties of Emerging Organizations," *Academy of Management Review* 13 (1988): 429–41.

41. Parker and Belghitar, "What Happens."

42. P. Reynolds, N. Carter, W. Gartner, and P. Greene, "The Prevalence of Nascent Entrepreneurs in the United States: Evidence from the Panel Study of Entrepreneurial Dynamics," *Small Business Economics* 23 (2004): 263–84.

43. Hills and Singh, "Opportunity Recognition."

44. Reynolds and White, *Entrepreneurial Process.*

45. Ibid.

46. Venture teams are very small. The data from the Panel Study of Entrepreneurial Dynamics reveals that only 26 percent of venture teams among a representative sample of start-ups are composed of more than two people. Factoring in the solo start-ups, this number means that only 13 percent of new ventures in the United States are founded and initially developed by a team of more than two people. (See H. Aldrich, N. Carter, and M. Ruef, "Teams," in *Handbook of Entrepreneurial Dynamics,* ed. Gartner et al., 259–72.)

47. Van Gelderen, Thurik, and Bosma, "Success and Risk Factors"; M. Ruef, H. Aldrich, and N. Carter, "The Structure of Founding Teams: Homophily, Strong Ties, and Isolation among U.S. Entrepreneurs," *American Sociological Review* 68 (2003): 195–222.

48. Aldrich, Carter, and Ruef, "Teams."

49. Ruef, Aldrich, and Carter, "Structure of Founding Teams"; Reynolds and White, *Entrepreneurial Process.*

50. Reynolds and White, *Entrepreneurial Process.*

Chapter 5. How Are New Businesses Financed?

1. M. Stouder and B. Kirchoff, "Funding the First Year of Business," in *Handbook of Entrepreneurial Dynamics,* ed. W. Gartner, K. Shaver, N. Carter, and P. Reynolds (Thousand Oaks, Calif.: Sage, 2004), 352–71; P. Reynolds, *Entrepreneurship in the United States* (Miami: Florida International University, 2005).

2. E. Hurst and A. Lusardi, "Liquidity Constraints, Household Wealth, and Entrepreneurship," *Journal of Political Economy* 112, no. 2 (2004): 319–47.

3. D. Blanchflower and A. Oswald, "What Makes an Entrepreneur?" *Journal of Labor Economics* 16, no. 1 (1998): 26–60.

4. P. Reynolds and S. White, *The Entrepreneurial Process: Economic Growth, Men, Women, and Minorities* (Westport, Conn.: Greenwood, 1997).

5. Reynolds and White, *Entrepreneurial Process.*

6. P. Kim, H. Aldrich, and L. Keister, "Access (Not) Denied: The Impact of Financial, Human, and Cultural Capital on Entrepreneurial Entry in the United States," *Small Business Economics* 27 (2006): 5–22.

7. Reynolds and White, *Entrepreneurial Process;* Stouder and Kirchoff, "Funding the First Year."

8. Hurst and Lusardi, "Liquidity Constraints."

9. T. Bates, "Self-Employment Entry across Industry Groups," *Journal of Business Venturing* 10 (1995): 143–56; R. Fairlie, "Self-Employment, Entrepreneurship, and the NLSY79," *Monthly Labor Review,* February 2005, 40–47; A. Henley, "Job Creation by the Self-Employed: The Role of Entrepreneurial and Financial Capital," *Small Business Economics* 25 (2005): 175–96; J. Butler and C. Herring, "Ethnicity and Entrepreneurship in America: Toward an Explanation of Racial and Ethnic Group Variations in Self-Employment," *Sociological Perspectives* 34, no. 1 (1991): 79–95; M. Taylor, "Earnings, Independence or Unemployment: Why Become Self-Employed?" *Oxford Bulletin of Economics and Statistics* 58, no. 2 (1996): 253–266.

10. A. Burke, F. Fitzroy, and M. Nolan, "When Less Is More: Distinguishing between Entrepreneurial Choice and Performance," *Oxford Bulletin of Economics and Statistics* 62, no. 5 (2000): 565–86; D. Evans and B. Jovanovic, "An Estimated Model of Entrepreneurial Choice under Liquidity Constraints," *Journal of Political Economy* 97 (1989): 808–27; D. Evans and L. Leighton, "Some Empirical Aspects of Entrepreneurship," *American Economic Review* 79, no. 3 (1989): 519–35; D. Holtz-Eakin, D. Joulfaian, and H. Rosen, "Sticking It Out: Entrepreneurial Survival and Liquidity Constraints," *Journal of Political Economy* 102 (1994): 53–75; D. Holtz-Eakin, D. Joulfaian, and H. Rosen, "Entrepreneurial Decisions and Liquidity Constraints," *RAND Journal of Economics* 25, no. 2 (1994): 334–47.

11. Hurst and Lusardi, "Liquidity Constraints."

12. N. Nicolaou, S. Shane, L. Cherkas, J. Hunkin, and T. Spector, "Is the Tendency to Engage in Self-Employment Genetic?" (working paper, Imperial College, 2006).

13. T. Lindh and H. Ohlsson, "Self-Employment and Windfall Gains: Evidence from the Swedish Lottery," *Economic Journal* 106 (1996): 1515–26.

14. Hurst and Lusardi, "Liquidity Constraints."

15. Stouder and Kirchoff, "Funding the First Year."

16. Ibid.

17. A. Berger and G. Udell, "The Economics of Small Business Finance: The Roles of Private Equity and Debt Markets in the Financial Growth Cycle," *Journal of Banking and Finance* 22 (1998): 613–73; R. Avery, R. Bostic, and K. Samolyk, "The Role of Personal Wealth in Small Business Finance," *Journal of Banking and Finance* 22 (1998): 1019–61; A. Hanley and S. Girma, "New Ventures and Their Credit Terms," *Small Business Economics* 26 (2006): 351–64.

18. Avery, Bostic, and Samolyk, "Role of Personal Wealth."

19. J. Eckhardt, S. Shane, and F. Delmar, "Multistage Selection and the Financing of New Ventures," *Management Science* 52, no. 2 (2006): 220–32.

20. Kim, Aldrich, and Keister, "Access (Not) Denied."

21. Eckhardt, Shane, and Delmar, "Multistage Selection."

22. Z. Fluck, D. Holtz-Eakin, and H. Rosen, "Where Does the Money Come From? The Financing of Small Entrepreneurial Enterprises" (Center for Policy Research Metropolitan Studies Program Discussion Papers, Syracuse University, no. 191, 1998); Eckhardt, Shane, and Delmar, "Multistage Selection"; R. Cole, "The Importance of Relationships to the Availability of Credit," *Journal of Banking and Finance* 22 (1998): 959–77.

23. Eckhardt, Shane, and Delmar, "Multistage Selection"; G. Cassar, "The Financing of Business Start-Ups," *Journal of Business Venturing* 19 (2004): 261–83.

24. National Federation of Independent Businesses, *Small Business Policy Guide* (Washington, D.C.: National Federation of Independent Businesses, 2000).

25. H. Van Auken and R. Carter, "Capital Acquisition in Small Firms," *Journal of Small Business Management* 27 (1989): 1–9.

26. Berger and Udell, "Economics of Small Business Finance."

27. Reynolds, *Entrepreneurship in the United States.*

28. Reynolds and White, *Entrepreneurial Process.*

29. Berger and Udell, "Economics of Small Business Finance."

30. M. Dollinger, *Entrepreneurship: Strategy and Resources* (Upper Saddle River, N.J.: Prentice Hall, 1999).

31. T. Bates, "Entrepreneur Human Capital Inputs and Small Business Longevity," *Review of Economics and Statistics* 72, no. 4 (1990): 551–59; Cassar, "Financing of Business Start-Ups."

32. Berger and Udell, "Economics of Small Business Finance."

33. Ibid.

34. Stouder and Kirchoff, "Funding the First Year."

35. Berger and Udell, "Economics of Small Business Finance."

36. "Creative Business Financing Options: Friends and Family," http://www

.startupnation.com/pages/articles/AT_Creative-Business-Financing-Options-Friends-Family.asp.

37. "The Myth of Free Government Money: A Perennial and Pernicious Scam," http://www.businessweek.com/smallbiz/0001/sa000111.htm.

38. "Deciding Who to Ask for Money," http://smallbusiness.aol.com/start/startup/article/_a/deciding-who-to-ask-for-money/20060319225809990001.

39. Stouder and Kirchoff, "Funding the First Year."

40. "The Myth of Free Government Money: A Perennial and Pernicious Scam," http://www.businessweek.com/smallbiz/0001/sa000111.htm.

41. "The Odds: Ever Wondered . . . ," http://www.funny2.com/odds.htm.

42. P. Auerswald and L. Branscomb, "Start-Ups and Spin-Offs: Collective Entrepreneurship between Invention and Innovation," in *The Emergence of Entrepreneurship Policy,* ed. D. Hart (Cambridge: Cambridge University Press, 2004).

43. G. Kawasaki, *The Art of the Start* (New York: Penguin Group, 2004).

44. "The Odds: Ever Wondered . . . ," http://www.funny2.com/odds.htm.

45. Berger and Udell, "Economics of Small Business Finance."

46. J. Lerner, "When Bureaucrats Meet Entrepreneurs: The Design of Effective Public Venture Capital Programs," in *Public Policy and the Economics of Entrepreneurship,* ed. D. Holtz-Eakin and H. Rosen (Cambridge: MIT Press, 2004).

47. Reynolds, *Entrepreneurship in the United States.*

48. Berger and Udell, "Economics of Small Business Finance."

49. Calculated from data contained in Reynolds, *Entrepreneurship in the United States.*

50. W. Bygrave, M. Hay, E. Ng, and P. Reynolds, "A Study of Informal Investing in Twenty-nine Nations Composing the Global Entrepreneurship Monitor," in *Frontiers of Entrepreneurship Research,* ed. W. Bygrave, C. Brush, P. Davidson, J. Fiet, P. Greene, R. Harrison, M. Lerner, G. Meyer, J. Sohl, and A. Zacharakis (Babson Park, Mass.: Babson College, 2002), 366–81; M. Maula, E. Autio, and P. Arenius, "What Drives Micro-Angel Investments?" *Small Business Economics* 25 (2005): 459–75.

51. G. Haynes and C. Ou, "A Profile of Owners and Investors of Privately Held Businesses in the United States, 1989–1998" (paper presented at the annual conference of Academy of Entrepreneurial and Financial Research, New York, April 25–26, 2002).

52. "Angel Investor Market Grows in the First Half of 2006," http://www.newswise.com/articles/view/523634/.

53. Reynolds, *Entrepreneurship in the United States.*

54. Bygrave et al., "Study of Informal Investing."

55. D. Amis and H. Stevenson, *Winning Angels: The Seven Fundamentals of Early Stage Investing* (London: Financial Times Prentice Hall, 2001).

56. Reynolds, *Entrepreneurship in the United States.*

57. Ibid.

58. Ibid.

Chapter 6. How Well Does the Typical Entrepreneur Do?

1. T. Stanley and W. Danko, *The Millionaire Next Door* (Atlanta: Longstreet, 1996).

2. D. Evans and L. Leighton, "Some Empirical Aspects of Entrepreneurship," *American Economic Review* 79, no. 3 (1989): 519–35; M. Taylor, "Survival of the Fittest? An Analysis of Self-Employment Duration in Britain," *Economic Journal* 109 (1999): C140–C155; M. Van Praag, "Business Survival and Success of Young Small Business Owners," *Small Business Economics* 21 (2003): 1–17.

3. B. Kirchhoff, *Entrepreneurship and Dynamic Capitalism: The Economics of Business Formation and Growth* (Westport, Conn.: Praeger, 1994); C. Brown, J. Hamilton, and J. Medoff, *Employers Large and Small* (Cambridge: Harvard University Press, 1990); R. McGuckin, and A. Nucci, "Survival Patterns for Small Businesses: Who Survives?" (*1991 Research Conference Report,* Document 7302 [Rev. 3–92], U.S. Department of the Treasury, Internal Revenue Service, Washington, D.C., 1992); B. Headd, "Business Success: Factors Leading to Surviving and Closing Successfully" (U.S. Census Center for Economic Studies Discussion Paper, 2000); R. Boden, "Analyses of Business Dissolution by Demographic Category of Ownership" (report for the U.S. Small Business Administration, contract no. SBA-HQ-00-M-0497, 2001); A. Nucci, "The Demography of Business Closings," *Small Business Economics* 12 (1999): 25–39.

4. "The Wonderland Economy," http://www.inc.com/magazine/19950515/2686.html (emphasis added).

5. B. Headd, "Redefining Business Success: Distinguishing between Closure and Failure," *Small Business Economics* 21 (2003): 51–61.

6. Office of Advocacy, *The Small Business Economy* (Washington, D.C.: U.S. Government Printing Office, 2005).

7. R. Fairlie and A. Robb, *Race, Families, and Business Success: A Comparison of African-American-, Asian- and White-Owned Businesses* (New York: Russell Sage Foundation, forthcoming).

8. M. Bitler, T. Moskowitz, and A. Vissing-Jorgensen, "Testing Agency Theory with Entrepreneur Effort and Wealth," *Journal of Finance* 60, no. 2 (2005): 539–76.

9. R. Uusitalo, *"Homo entreprenaurus?" Applied Economics* 33 (2001): 1631–38; D. Kawaguchi, "Compensating Wage Differentials among Self-Employed Workers: Evidence from Job Satisfaction Scores" (Discussion Paper no. 568, Institute of Social and Economic Research, Osaka University, 2002); B. Hamilton, "Does Entrepreneurship Pay? An Empirical Analysis of the Returns to Self-

Employment," *Journal of Political Economy* 108, no. 3 (2000): 604–31; R. Fairlie, "Does Business Ownership Provide a Source of Upward Mobility for Blacks and Hispanics," in *Public Policy and the Economics of Entrepreneurship,* ed. D. Holtz-Eakin and H. Rosen (Cambridge: MIT Press, 2004); R. Fairlie, "Self-Employment, Entrepreneurship, and the NLSY79," *Monthly Labor Review,* February 2005, 40–47.

10. Hamilton, "Does Entrepreneurship Pay?"

11. Kawaguchi, "Compensating Wage Differentials."

12. Hamilton, "Does Entrepreneurship Pay?"

13. W. Carrington, K. McCue, and B. Pierce, "The Role of Employer/Employee Interactions in Labor Market Cycles: Evidence from the Self-Employed," *Journal of Labor Economics* 14, no. 4 (1996): 571–602; I. Bernhardt, "Comparative Advantage in Self-Employment and Wage Work," *Canadian Journal of Economics* 27, no. 2 (1994): 273–89; P. Dolton and G. Makepeace, "Self-Employment among Graduates," *Bulletin of Economic Research* 42, no. 1 (1990): 35–53; Uusitalo, *"Homo entreprenaurus?";* Hamilton, "Does Entrepreneurship Pay?"; Fairlie, "Self-Employment"; Z. Lin, G. Picot, and J. Compton, "The Entry and Exit Dynamics of Self-Employment in Canada," *Small Business Economics* 15 (2000): 105–25.

14. D. Holtz-Eakin, H. Rosen, and R. Weathers, "Horatio Alger Meets the Mobility Tables," *Small Business Economics* 14 (2000): 243–74.

15. Bitler, Moskowitz, and Vissing-Jorgensen, "Testing Agency Theory."

16. Ibid.

17. Lin, Picot, and Compton, "Entry and Exit Dynamics"; Uusitalo, *"Homo entreprenaurus?";* D. Blanchflower, "Self-Employment: More May Not Be Better," *Swedish Economic Policy Review* 11, no. 2 (2004): 15–74; M. Puri and D. Robinson, "Who Are Entrepreneurs and Why Do They Behave That Way?" (working paper, Duke University, 2006).

18. Blanchflower, "Self-Employment: More May Not Be Better."

19. G. Arabsheibani, D. De Meza, J. Maloney, and B. Pearson, "And a Vision Appeared unto Them of Great Profit: Evidence of Self-Deception among the Self-Employed," *Economic Letters* 67 (2000): 35–41.

20. A. Cooper, C. Woo, and W. Dunkelberg, "Entrepreneurs' Perceived Chances for Success," *Journal of Business Venturing* 3 (1988): 97–108.

21. A. Henley, "Job Creation by the Self-Employed: The Role of Entrepreneurial and Financial Capital," *Small Business Economics* 25 (2005): 175–96.

22. B. Kirchhoff, *Entrepreneurship and Dynamic Capitalism* (Westport, Conn.: Praeger, 1994); H. Aldrich, *Organizations Evolving* (London: Sage, 1999); J. Duncan and D. Handler, "The Misunderstood Role of Small Business," *Business Economics* 29, no. 3 (1994): 7–12.

23. P. Reynolds and S. White, *The Entrepreneurial Process: Economic Growth, Men, Women, and Minorities* (Westport, Conn.: Greenwood, 1997).

24. Duncan and Handler, "Misunderstood Role."

25. National Federation of Independent Businesses, *Small Business Policy Guide* (Washington, D.C.: National Federation of Independent Businesses, 2000).

26. M. Gutter and T. Saleem, "Financial Vulnerability of Small Business Owners," *Financial Services Review* 14 (2005): 133–47.

27. V. Quadrini, "Entrepreneurship, Saving, and Social Mobility," *Review of Economic Dynamics* 3 (2000): 1–40; W. Gentry and R. Hubbard, "Entrepreneurship and Household Saving" (working paper, Columbia University, New York, 2005).

28. Gutter and Saleem, "Financial Vulnerability."

29. Quadrini, "Entrepreneurship, Saving, and Social Mobility"; Gentry and Hubbard, "Entrepreneurship and Household Saving."

30. Blanchflower, "Self-Employment: More May Not Be Better."

31. D. Blanchflower, "Self-Employment in OECD Countries," *Labour Economics* 7 (2000): 471–505; B. Frey and M. Benz, "Being Independent Is a Great Thing: Subjective Evaluations of Self-Employment and Hierarchy" (Working Paper no. 135, Institute for Empirical Research in Economics, Zurich, Switzerland, 2003); R. Finnie and C. Laporte, "Setting Up Shop: Self Employment among Canadian College and University Graduates," *Industrial Relations* 58, no. 1 (2003): 3–32; Blanchflower, "Self-Employment: More May Not Be Better."

32. Frey and Benz, "Being Independent"; Kawaguchi, "Compensating Wage Differentials."

33. National Federation of Independent Businesses, *Small Business Policy Guide*.

34. Frey and Benz, "Being Independent"; Blanchflower, "Self-Employment: More May Not Be Better."

Chapter 7. What Makes Some Entrepreneurs More Successful Than Others?

1. F. Delmar and S. Shane, "Legitimating First: Organizing Activities and the Survival of New Ventures," *Journal of Business Venturing* 19 (2004): 385–410; B. Schiller and P. Crewson, "Entrepreneurial Origins: A Longitudinal Study," *Economic Inquiry* 35, no. 3 (1997): 523–31; D. Evans and L. Leighton, "Some Empirical Aspects of Entrepreneurship," *American Economic Review* 79, no. 3 (1989): 519–35; P. Reynolds, "New Firms: Societal Contribution versus Survival Potential," *Journal of Business Venturing* 2 (1987): 231–46; J. Gimeno, T. Folta, A. Cooper, and C. Woo, "Survival of the Fittest? Entrepreneurial Human Capital and the Persistence of Underperforming Firms," *Administrative Science Quarterly* 42 (1997): 750–78; M. Hannan and J. Freeman, *Organizational Ecology* (Cambridge: Harvard University Press, 1989); G. Carroll and M. Hannan, "Density Dependence in the Evolution of Newspaper Organizations," *American Sociological Review* 54 (1989): 524–41; G. Carroll and J. Wade, "Density Dependence in Organizational Evolution of the American Brewing Industry from 1633 to 1988," *Acta*

Sociologica 34 (1991): 155–76; G. Carroll and J. Delacroix, "Organizational Mortality in the Newspaper Industries in Argentina and Ireland: An Ecological Approach," *Administrative Science Quarterly* 27 (1982): 169–98; G. Carroll and P. Huo, "Organizational Task and Institutional Environments in Ecological Perspective: Findings from the Local Newspaper Industry," *American Journal of Sociology* 91 (1986): 838–73; S. Olzak and E. West, "Ethnic Conflict and the Rise and Fall of Ethnic Newspapers," *American Sociological Review* 56 (1991): 458–74; T. Amburgey, T. Dacin, and D. Kelly, "Disruptive Selection and Population Segmentation: Interpopulation Competition as a Segregating Process," in *Evolutionary Dynamics of Organizations,* ed. J. Baum and J. Singh, 240–54 (New York: Oxford University Press, 1994); J. Freeman, G. Carroll, and M. Hannan, "The Liabilities of Newness: Age Dependence in Organizational Death Rates," *American Sociological Review* 48 (1983): 692–710; M. Hannan, "Social Change, Organizational Diversity and Individual Careers," in *Social Change and the Life Course,* ed. M. Riley (Newbury Park, Calif.: Sage, 1988); J. Wade, A. Swaminathan, and M. Saxon, "Normative and Resource Flow Consequences of Local Regulations in the American Brewing Industry, 1845–1918," *Administrative Science Quarterly* 43 (1998): 905–35; H. Haveman, "Between a Rock and a Hard Place: Organizational Change and Performance under Conditions of Fundamental Environmental Transformation," *Administrative Science Quarterly* 37 (1992): 48–75; J. Delacroix, A. Swaminathan, and M. Solt, "Density Dependence versus Population Dynamics: An Ecological Study of Failures in the California Wine Industry, 1941–1984," in *Ecological Models of Organization,* ed. G. Carroll, 53–68 (Oxford: Oxford University Press, 1989); W. Lehrman, "Diversity in Decline: Institutional and Organizational Failure in the American Life Insurance Industry," *Social Forces* 73 (1994): 605–36; W. Mitchell, "The Dynamics of Evolving Markets: The Effects of Business Sales and Age on Dissolutions and Divestitures," *Administrative Science Quarterly* 39 (1994): 575–602; M. Hannan, G. Carroll, E. Dundon, and J. Torres, "Organizational Evolution in a Multinational Context: Entries of Automobile Manufacturers in Belgium, Britain, France, Germany, and Italy," *American Sociological Review* 60 (1995): 509–28; W. Barnett, "The Dynamics of Competitive Intensity," *Administrative Science Quarterly* 42 (1997): 128–60; J. Mata and P. Portugal, "Life Duration of New Firms," *Journal of Industrial Economics* 42, no. 3 (1994): 227–43; T. Bates, "Entrepreneur Human Capital Inputs and Small Business Longevity," *Review of Economics and Statistics* 72, no. 4 (1990): 551–59.

2. Gimeno et al., "Survival of the Fittest?"; Schiller and Crewson, "Entrepreneurial Origins"; M. Taylor, "Self-Employment and Windfall Gains in Britain: Evidence from Panel Data," *Economica* 68 (2001): 539–65; G. Haynes, "Wealth and Income: How Did Small Businesses Fare from 1989 to 1998?" (report for the U.S. Small Business Administration, contract no. SBAHQ-00-M-0502, 2001); M. Gutter and T. Saleem, "Financial Vulnerability of Small Business Owners," *Financial*

Services Review 14 (2005): 133–47; A. Burke, F. Fitzroy, and M. Nolan, "When Less Is More: Distinguishing between Entrepreneurial Choice and Performance," *Oxford Bulletin of Economics and Statistics* 62, no. 5 (2000): 565–86; D. Williams, "Why Do Entrepreneurs Become Franchisees? An Empirical Examination of Organizational Choice," *Journal of Business Venturing* 14, no. 1 (1999): 103–24.

3. D. Audretsch, "New Firm Survival and the Technological Regime," *Review of Economics and Statistics* 73, no. 3 (1991): 441–50; B. Kirchhoff, *Entrepreneurship and Dynamic Capitalism: The Economics of Business Formation and Growth* (Westport, Conn.: Praeger, 1994); M. Taylor, "Earnings, Independence or Unemployment: Why Become Self-Employed?" *Oxford Bulletin of Economics and Statistics* 58, no. 2 (1996): 253–66; Taylor, "Self-Employment and Windfall Gains"; Gimeno et al., "Survival of the Fittest?"; Haynes, "Wealth and Income"; Gutter and Saleem, "Financial Vulnerability"; P. Reynolds and S. White, *The Entrepreneurial Process: Economic Growth, Men, Women, and Minorities* (Westport, Conn.: Greenwood, 1997); V. Schutgens and E. Wever, "Determinants of New Firm Success," *Papers in Regional Science* 79 (2000): 135–59; R. Cressy, "Pre-entrepreneurial Income, Cash-Flow Growth and Survival of Startup Businesses: Model and Tests on U.K. Data," *Small Business Economics* 8 (1996): 49–58; Reynolds, "New Firms"; P. Reynolds, "Autonomous Firm Dynamics and Economic Growth in the United States, 1986–1990," *Regional Studies* 28, no. 4 (1993): 429–42.

4. B. Headd, "Redefining Business Success: Distinguishing between Closure and Failure," *Small Business Economics* 21 (2003): 51–61; R. Boden, "Analyses of Business Dissolution by Demographic Category of Ownership" (report for the U.S. Small Business Administration, University of Toledo, 2000); H. Persson, "The Survival and Growth of New Establishments in Sweden, 1987–1995," *Small Business Economics* 23 (2004): 423–40; M. Van Praag, "Business Survival and Success of Young Small Business Owners," *Small Business Economics* 21 (2003): 1–17; Reynolds and White, *Entrepreneurial Process;* R. Cressy, "Pre-entrepreneurial Income."

5. Mata and Portugal, "Life Duration of New Firms"; T. Dunne, M. Roberts, and L. Samuelson, "Patterns of Firm Entry and Exit in U.S. Manufacturing Industries," *RAND Journal of Economics* 19, no. 4 (1988): 495–515; Audretsch, "New Firm Survival."

6. J. Eckhardt and S. Shane, "Creative Destruction or Creative Accumulation?" (working paper, University of Wisconsin, 2006).

7. Carroll and Huo, "Organizational Task and Institutional Environments"; Mata and Portugal, "Life Duration of New Firms"; D. Audretsch, "Innovation, Growth and Survival," *International Journal of Industrial Organization* 13 (1995): 441–57; J. Mata, P. Portugal, and P. Guimaraes, "The Survival of New Plants:

Start-Up Conditions and Post-Entry Evolution," *International Journal of Industrial Organization* 13 (1995): 459–81; Delacroix, Swaminathan, and Solt, "Density Dependence"; W. Barnett, "The Organizational Ecology of a Technological System," *Administrative Science Quarterly* 35 (1990): 31–60.

8. Audretsch, "New Firm Survival"; D. Audretsch and T. Mahmood, "New Firm Survival: New Results Using a Hazard Function," *Review of Economics and Statistics* 77, no. 1 (1995): 97–103.

9. Mata and Portugal, "Life Duration of New Firms"; Mata, Portugal, and Guimaraes, "Survival of New Plants."

10. Delacroix, Swaminathan, and Solt, "Density Dependence versus Population Dynamics"; Headd, "Redefining Business Success"; Persson, "Survival and Growth"; Gimeno et al., "Survival of the Fittest?"; Kirchhoff, *Entrepreneurship and Dynamic Capitalism;* Schutgens and Wever, "Determinants of New Firm Success"; Mata and Portugal, "Life Duration of New Firms"; Mata, Portugal, and Guimaraes, "Survival of New Plants"; Bates, "Entrepreneur Human Capital Inputs"; Reynolds and White, *Entrepreneurial Process;* T. Bates, "Self Employment Entry across Industry Groups," *Journal of Business Venturing* 10, no. 2 (1995): 143–56; Taylor, "Survival of the Fittest?"; Burke, Fitzroy, and Nolan, "When Less Is More"; Haynes, "Wealth and Income"; Gutter and Saleem, "Financial Vulnerability"; A. Alba-Ramirez, "Self-Employment in the Midst of Unemployment: The Case of Spain and the United States," *Applied Economics* 26 (1994): 189–204; G. Cassar, "The Financing of Business Start-Ups," *Journal of Business Venturing* 19 (2004): 261–83; M. Bitler, T. Moskowitz, and A. Vissing-Jorgensen, "Testing Agency Theory with Entrepreneur Effort and Wealth," *Journal of Finance* 60, no. 2 (2005): 539–76; I. Verheul and R. Thurik, "Start-Up Capital: Does Gender Matter?" *Small Business Economics* 16 (2001): 329–45; Freeman, Carroll, and Hannan, "Liabilities of Newness"; J. Bruderl and P. Preisendorfer, "Network Support and the Success of Newly Founded Businesses," *Small Business Economics* 10 (1998): 213–25; J. Bruderl, P. Preisendorfer, and R. Ziegler, "Survival Chances of Newly Founded Business Organizations," *American Sociological Review* 57 (1992): 227–302; J. Ranger-Moore, "Bigger May Be Better but Is Older Wiser? Age Dependence in Organizational Age and Size in the New York Life Insurance Industry," *American Sociological Review* 58 (1997): 901–20; D. Barron, E. West, and M. Hannan, "A Time to Grow and a Time to Die: Growth and Mortality of Credit Unions in New York City, 1914–1990," *American Sociological Review* 100 (1994): 381–421; J. Delacroix and A. Swaminathan, "Cosmetic, Speculative, and Adaptive Organizational Change in the Wine Industry," *Administrative Science Quarterly* 26 (1991): 631–61; J. Baum and S. Mezias, "Localized Competition and Organizational Failure in the Manhattan Hotel Industry, 1898–1990," *Administrative Science Quarterly* 42, no. 2 (1992): 304–38; W. Barnett and G. Carroll, "Competition and Mutualism among Early Telephone Companies," *Administrative Sci-

ence Quarterly 32, no. 3 (1987): 400–421; J. Baum, "Organizational Ecology," in *Handbook of Organizational Studies,* ed. S. Clegg, C. Hardy, and W. Nord, 77–114 (London: Sage, 1996); M. Fichman and D. Levinthal, "Honeymoons and the Liability of Adolescence: A New Perspective on Duration Dependence in Social and Organizational Relationships," *Academy of Management Review* 16, no. 2 (1991): 442–68; T. Bates, "A Comparison of Franchise and Independent Small Business Survival Rates," *Small Business Economics* 7 (1994): 1–12; T. Bates, "Financing Small Business Creation: The Case of Chinese and Korean Immigrant Entrepreneurs," *Journal of Business Venturing* 12, no. 2 (1997): 109–24; T. Bates and L. Sevron, "Viewing Self Employment as a Response to Lack of Suitable Opportunities for Wage Work," *National Journal of Sociology* 12, no. 2 (2000): 23–53; S. White and P. Reynolds, "Government Programs and High Growth New Firms," in *Frontiers of Entrepreneurship Research,* ed. P. Reynolds, S. Birley, J. Butler, W. Bygrave, P. Davidsson, W. Gartner, and P. McDougall, 661–35 (Babson Park, Mass.: Babson College, 1996); A. Cooper, W. Dunkelberg, and C. Woo, "Survival and Failure: A Longitudinal Study," in *Frontiers of Entrepreneurship Research,* ed. B. Kirchhoff, W. Long, W. McMullan, K. Vesper, and W. Wetzel, 225–237 (Babson Park, Mass.: Babson College, 1988).

11. R. Fairlie and A. Robb, *Race, Families, and Business Success: A Comparison of African-American-, Asian- and White-Owned Businesses* (New York: Russell Sage Foundation, forthcoming).

12. Boden, "Analyses of Business Dissolution"; Bruderl, Preisendorfer, and Ziegler, "Survival Chances"; Cressy, "Pre-entrepreneurial Income"; White and Reynolds, "Government Programs"; R. Avery, R. Bostic, and K. Samolyk, "The Role of Personal Wealth in Small Business Finance," *Journal of Banking and Finance* 22 (1998): 1019–61; Cassar, "Financing of Business Start-Ups."

13. Bates, "Survival Rates"; Bates, "Self Employment Entry"; N. Bosma, M. Van Praag, R. Thurik, and G. De Wit, "The Value of Human and Social Capital Investments for the Business Performance of Startups," *Small Business Economics* 23 (2004): 227–36; Burke, Fitzroy, and Nolan, "When Less Is More"; Bitler, Moskowitz, and Vissing-Jorgensen, "Testing Agency Theory"; Verheul and Thurik, "Start-Up Capital."

14. S. Shane and F. Delmar, "Planning for the Market: Business Planning before Marketing and the Continuation of Organizing Efforts," *Journal of Business Venturing* 19 (2004): 767–85.

15. Cooper, Dunkelberg, and Woo, "Survival and Failure"; Reynolds and White, *Entrepreneurial Process;* Schutgens and Wever, "Determinants of New Firm Success."

16. J. Eckhardt, S. Shane, and F. Delmar, "Multistage Selection and the Financing of New Ventures," *Management Science* 52, no. 2 (2006): 220–32; Delmar and Shane, "Legitimating First"; Reynolds and White, *Entrepreneurial Process;* W.

Dunkelberg, A. Cooper, C. Woo, and W. Denis, "New Firm Growth and Performance," in *Frontiers of Entrepreneurship Research,* ed. N. Churchill, J. Hornaday, B. Kirchhoff, O. Krasner, and K. Vesper, 307–21 (Babson Park, Mass.: Babson College, 1987); Schutgens and Wever, "Determinants of New Firm Success"; Shane and Delmar, "Planning for the Market"; F. Delmar and S. Shane, "Does Business Planning Facilitate the Development of New Ventures?" *Strategic Management Journal* 24, no. 12 (2003): 1165–85.

17. A. Cooper and W. Dunkelberg, "Entrepreneurship Research: Old Questions, New Answers and Methodological Issues," *American Journal of Small Business* 11, no. 3 (1987): 11–23; R. Young and J. Francis, "Entrepreneurship and Innovation in Small Manufacturing Firms," *Social Science Quarterly* 72, no. 1 (1991): 149–62; Shane and Delmar, "Planning for the Market."

18. A. Bhide, *The Origin and Evolution of New Businesses* (Oxford: Oxford University Press, 2000).

19. Reynolds and White, *Entrepreneurial Process;* Delmar and Shane, "Legitimating First."

20. Reynolds, "New Firms"; Reynolds and White, *Entrepreneurial Process;* Reynolds, "Autonomous Firm Dynamics"; Dunkelberg et al., "New Firm Growth and Performance."

21. T. Stearns, N. Carter, P. Reynolds, and M. Williams, "New Firm Survival: Industry, Strategy and Location," *Journal of Business Venturing* 10, no. 1 (1995): 23–42.

22. Gimeno et al., "Survival of the Fittest?"; Bruderl, Preisendorfer, and Ziegler, "Survival Chances"; Reynolds, "New Firms."

23. Shane and Delmar, "Planning for the Market."

24. R. Boden and A. Nucci, "On the Survival Prospects of Men's and Women's New Business Ventures," *Journal of Business Venturing* 15 (1998): 347–62; Bates, "Entrepreneur Human Capital Inputs"; Bates, "Survival Rates"; Bates, "Self Employment Entry"; Bates, "Financing Small Business Creation"; Bates and Sevron, "Viewing Self Employment"; Reynolds and White, *Entrepreneurial Process;* Burke, Fitzroy, and Nolan, "When Less Is More"; Bruderl and Preisendorfer, "Network Support"; Bruderl, Preisendorfer, and Ziegler, "Survival Chances"; G. Borjas and A. Bronnars, "Consumer Discrimination and Self Employment," *Journal of Political Economy* 97 (1989): 581–605; Evans and Leighton, "Empirical Aspects"; Schiller and Crewson, "Entrepreneurial Origins"; P. Robinson and E. Sexton, "The Effect of Education and Experience on Self-Employment Success," *Journal of Business Venturing* 9, no. 2 (1994): 141–56; C. Van Praag and J. Cramer, "The Roots of Entrepreneurship and Labour Demand: Individual Ability and Low Risk Aversion," *Economica* 68, no. 269 (2001): 45–62.

25. Fairlie and Robb, *Race, Families, and Business Success.*

26. Headd, "Redefining Business Success"; Bates, "Self Employment Entry";

Bates, "Entrepreneur Human Capital Inputs"; R. Fairlie, "Self-Employment, Entrepreneurship, and the NLSY79," *Monthly Labor Review* (February 2005): 40–47; Bosma et al., "Human and Social Capital Investments"; D. Holtz-Eakin, D. Joulfaian, and H. Rosen, "Sticking It Out: Entrepreneurial Survival and Liquidity Constraints," *Journal of Political Economy* 102 (1994): 53–75.

27. Boden and Nucci, "Survival Prospects"; Bruderl, Preisendorfer, and Ziegler, "Survival Chances"; Bruderl and Preisendorfer, "Network Support"; Taylor, "Survival of the Fittest?"; Robinson and Sexton, "Effect of Education"; Schiller and Crewson, "Entrepreneurial Origins"; Evans and Leighton, "Empirical Aspects."

28. Taylor, "Survival of the Fittest?"; Cooper, Dunkelberg, and Woo, "Survival and Failure"; Bates, "Entrepreneur Human Capital Inputs"; Bates, "Financing Small Business Creation"; Cressy, "Pre-entrepreneurial Income."

29. Bosma et al., "Human and Social Capital Investments"; Bruderl, Preisendorfer, and Ziegler, "Survival Chances"; Bruderl and Preisendorfer, "Network Support"; Delmar and Shane, "Legitimating First"; F. Delmar and S. Shane, "Does Experience Matter? The Effect of Founding Team Experience on the Survival and Sales of Newly Founded Ventures," *Strategic Organization* 4, no. 3 (2006): 215–47; Headd, "Redefining Business Success"; Cooper, Dunkelberg, and Woo, "Survival and Failure"; Gimeno et al., "Survival of the Fittest?"; Dunkelberg et al., "New Firm Growth and Performance."

30. Delmar and Shane, "Legitimating First"; Delmar and Shane, "Does Experience Matter?"; Taylor, "Survival of the Fittest?"; Bosma et al., "Human and Social Capital Investments"; Burke, Fitzroy, and Nolan, "When Less Is More"; P. Davidsson and B. Honig, "The Role of Social and Human Capital among Nascent Entrepreneurs," *Journal of Business Venturing* 18 (2003): 301–31.

31. Delmar and Shane, "Does Experience Matter?"

32. Cooper, Dunkelberg, and Woo, "Survival and Failure"; Gimeno et al., "Survival of the Fittest?"; Bosma et al., "Human and Social Capital Investments."

33. White and Reynolds, "Government Programs"; Cassar, "Financing of Business Start-Ups."

34. Evans and Leighton, "Empirical Aspects"; Schiller and Crewson, "Entrepreneurial Origins"; Taylor, "Survival of the Fittest?"

Chapter 8. Why Don't Women Start More Companies?

1. S. Clack and M. Weismantle, "Employment Status 2000: Census 2000 Brief," www.census.gov/prod/2003pubs/c2kbr-18.pdf; Office of Advocacy, "Women in Business: A Demographic Review of Women's Business Ownership" (working paper, U.S. Small Business Administration, 2003).

2. Clack and Weismantle, "Employment Status 2000"; Office of Advocacy, "Women in Business."

3. P. Reynolds, *New Firm Creation in the U.S.: A PSED I Overview* (Hanover, Mass.: Now Publishers, 2007).

4. Small Business Administration, *The Small Business Economy: A Report to the President* (Washington, D.C.: U.S. Government Printing Office, 2005).

5. D. Blanchflower, "Self-Employment in OECD Countries," *Labour Economics* 7 (2000): 471–505.

6. F. Delmar and P. Davidsson, "Where Do They Come From? Prevalence and Characteristics of Nascent Entrepreneurs," *Entrepreneurship and Regional Development* 12 (2000): 1–23.

7. H. Xu and M. Ruef, "The Myth of the Risk Tolerant Entrepreneur," *Strategic Organization* 2, no. 4 (2004): 331–55.

8. P. Reynolds, *Entrepreneurship in the United States* (Miami: Florida International University, 2005).

9. N. Carter and C. Brush, "Gender," in *Handbook of Entrepreneurial Dynamics,* ed. W. Gartner, K. Shaver, N. Carter, and P. Reynolds, 12–25 (Thousand Oaks, Calif.: Sage, 2004).

10. Ibid.

11. "Educational Attainment of the Population Twenty-five Years and Over by Sex: March 2002," http://www.census.gov/population/socdemo/gender/ppl-166/tab07.xls.

12. "Major Occupation Group of the Employed Civilian Population Sixteen Years and Over by Sex: March 2002," http://www.census.gov/population/socdemo/gender/ppl-166/tab11.xls.

13. Xu and Ruef, "Myth of the Risk Tolerant Entrepreneur."

14. P. Arenius and M. Minniti, "Perceptual Variables and Nascent Entrepreneurship," *Small Business Economics* 24 (2005): 233–47; Reynolds, *New Firm Creation;* A. Davis and H. Aldrich, "Work Participation History," in *Handbook of Entrepreneurial Dynamics,* ed. Gartner et al.

15. Delmar and Davidsson, "Where Do They Come From?"; Reynolds, *New Firm Creation.*

16. D. Blanchflower, "Self-Employment: More May Not Be Better," *Swedish Economic Policy Review* 11, no. 2 (2004): 15–74.

17. M. Kourilsky and W. Walstad, *The Entrepreneur in Youth* (Cheltenham, UK: Edward Elgar, forthcoming).

18. M. Minniti and P. Arenius, "Women in Entrepreneurship" (paper presented to the First Annual Global Entrepreneurship Symposium, New York, April 29, 2003).

19. M. Minniti, I. Allen, and N. Langowitz, *Global Entrepreneurship Monitor 2005 Report on Women and Entrepreneurship* (Babson Park, Mass.: Babson College, 2005).

20. R. Boden and A. Nucci, "On the Survival Prospects of Men's and Women's

New Business Ventures," *Journal of Business Venturing* 15 (1998): 347–62; N. Bosma, M. Van Praag, R. Thurik, and G. De Wit, "The Value of Human and Social Capital Investments for the Business Performance of Startups," *Small Business Economics* 23 (2004): 227–36; P. Reynolds and S. White, *The Entrepreneurial Process: Economic Growth, Men, Women, and Minorities* (Westport, Conn.: Greenwood, 1997).

21. Office of Advocacy, "Women in Business."

22. Ibid.

23. Ibid.

24. A. Robb and J. Wolken, "Firm, Owner, and Financing Characteristics: Differences between Male- and Female-Owned Small Businesses" (working paper, Federal Reserve Board of Governors, 2002).

25. R. Srinivasan, C. Woo, and A. Cooper, "Performance Determinants for Male and Female Entrepreneurs," in *Frontiers of Entrepreneurship Research,* ed. W. Bygrave, S. Birley, N. Churchill, E. Gatewood, F. Hoy, R. Keeley, and W. Wetzel, 43–56 (Babson Park, Mass.: Babson College, 1993).

26. R. Boden, "Analyses of Business Dissolution by Demographic Category of Ownership" (report for the U.S. Small Business Administration, University of Toledo, 2000); Srinivasan, Woo, and Cooper, "Performance Determinants."

27. I. De Bare, "Encouraging Women to be Entrepreneurs," *San Francisco Chronicle,* May 28, 2006, http://www.sfgate.com/cgi-bin/article.cgi?file=/c/a/2006/05/28/BUGR8J2JNO1.DTL.

28. G. Hundley, "Why Women Earn Less Than Men in Self-Employment," *Journal of Labor Research* 22, no. 4 (2001): 817–27.

29. Reynolds, *Entrepreneurship in the United States.*

30. Office of Advocacy, "Women in Business"; Robb and Wolken, "Firm, Owner, and Financing Characteristics"; Hundley, "Why Women Earn Less."

31. L. Edwards and E. Field-Hendrey, "Home-Based Work and Women's Labor Force Decisions," *Journal of Labor Economics* 20, no. 1 (2002): 170–200; R. Singh and L. Lucas, "Not Just Domestic Engineers: An Exploratory Study of Homemaker Entrepreneurs," *Entrepreneurship Theory and Practice,* January 2005, 79–90.

32. Robb and Wolken, "Firm, Owner, and Financing Characteristics."

33. R. Fairlie and A. Robb, *Race, Families, and Business Success: A Comparison of African-American-, Asian- and White-Owned Businesses* (New York: Russell Sage Foundation, forthcoming).

34. H. Buttner and D. Moore, "Women's Organizational Exodus to Entrepreneurship: Self-Reported Motivations and Correlates with Success," *Journal of Small Business Management* 26 (1997): 31–35.

35. B. Headd, "Redefining Business Success: Distinguishing between Closure and Failure," *Small Business Economics* 21 (2003): 51–61.

36. The differences in goals between men and women may also lead to differences in the number of hours that male and female entrepreneurs want to work. The average male entrepreneur works longer hours than the average female entrepreneur, which could account for some of the difference in performance of male and female entrepreneurs.

37. R. Boden, "Flexible Working Hours, Family Responsibilities, and Female Self-Employment," *American Journal of Economics and Sociology* 58, no. 11 (1999): 71–83; R. Boden, "Gender and Self-Employment Selection," *Journal of Socio-economics* 25, no. 6 (1996): 671–82; K. Lombard, "Female Self-Employment and the Demand for Flexible, Nonstandard Work Schedules," *Economic Inquiry* 39, no. 2 (2001): 214–37; Y. Georgellis and H. Wall, "Gender Differences in Self-Employment" (working paper no. 2002–019B, Federal Reserve Bank of St. Louis, 2004); R. Connelly, "Self-Employment and Finding Childcare," *Demography* 29, no. 1 (1992): 17–29; H. Presser and W. Baldwin, "Child Care as a Constraint on Employment: Prevalence, Correlates, and Bearing on the Work and Fertility Nexus," *American Journal of Sociology* 85, no. 5 (1980): 1202–13; K. Christensen, *Women and Home-Based Work* (New York: Henry Holt, 1988).

38. Minniti and Arenius, "Women in Entrepreneurship."

39. Boden, "Gender and Self-Employment Selection"; S. Birley, "Female Entrepreneurs: Are They Really Any Different?" *Journal of Small Business Management* 27, no. 1 (1989): 32–37.

40. Edwards and Field-Hendrey, "Home-Based Work."

Chapter 9. Why Is Black Entrepreneurship So Rare?

1. "A Tough Haul for Black Start-Ups," http://www.businessweek.com/magazine/content/02_41/c3803019.htm.

2. "As Traditional Black-Owned Retail and Service Businesses Decline, New More Ambitious Black Entrepreneurs Emerge," www.inc.com/magazine/19940601/2953.html.

3. "Black Entrepreneurs," www.ncpa.org/pd/affirm/pdaa/pdaa21.html.

4. "The Rise of the Black Entrepreneur: A New Force for Economic and Moral Leadership," www.acton.org/ppolicy/comment/article.php?id=137.

5. G. Haynes, "Wealth and Income: How Did Small Businesses Fare from 1989 to 1998?" (report for the U.S. Small Business Administration, contract no. SBAHQ-00-M-0502, 2001).

6. R. Fairlie, "The Absence of African-American Owned Businesses: An Analysis of the Dynamics of Self-Employment," *Journal of Labor Economics* 17, no. 1 (1999): 80–108; R. Fairlie, "Self-Employment, Entrepreneurship, and the NLSY79," *Monthly Labor Review,* February 2005, 40–47; R. Fairlie, "Recent Trends in Ethnic and Racial Business Ownership," *Small Business Economics* 23 (2004): 203–18.

7. Kourilsky and W. Walstad, *The Entrepreneur in Youth* (Cheltenham, UK: Edward Elgar, forthcoming).

8. P. Reynolds, *Entrepreneurship in the United States: The Future is Now* (New York: Springer, forthcoming).

9. "Blacks Make Gains in Business," http://www.timesdispatch.com/servlet/Satellite?pagename=RTD/MGArticle/RTD_BasicArticle&c=MGArticle&cid=1137836471973.

10. Fairlie, "Absence of African-American Owned Businesses."

11. "A Black Entrepreneur in Banking Gives Others a Break," www.businessweek.com:/smallbiz/news/date/9906/f990630.htm?scriptFramed.

12. R. Fairlie, "Does Business Ownership Provide a Source of Upward Mobility for Blacks and Hispanics," in *Public Policy and the Economics of Entrepreneurship*, ed. D. Holtz-Eakin and H. Rosen (Cambridge: MIT Press, 2004).

13. http://www.census.gov/population/socdemo/education/phct41/table3.xls.

14. Fairlie, "Absence of African-American Owned Businesses."

15. R. Fairlie and A. Robb, *Race, Families, and Business Success: A Comparison of African-American-, Asian- and White-Owned Businesses* (New York: Russell Sage Foundation, forthcoming).

16. P. Reynolds, *New Firm Creation in the U.S.: A PSED I Overview* (Hanover, Mass.: Now Publishers, 2007).

17. "Net Worth and Asset Ownership of Households: 1998 and 2000," http://www.census.gov/prod/2003pubs/p70-88.pdf.

18. Fairlie, "Absence of African-American Owned Businesses."

19. P. Reynolds, *New Firm Creation: The Future is Now* (New York: Springer, forthcoming).

20. Small Business Administration, *The Small Business Economy: A Report to the President* (Washington, D.C.: U.S. Government Printing Office, 2005).

21. Fairlie, "Absence of African-American Owned Businesses."

22. R. Fairlie and A. Robb, "Why Are Black-Owned Businesses Less Successful Than White-Owned Businesses? The Role of Families, Inheritances, and Business Human Capital" (working paper, University of California at Santa Cruz, 2003).

23. Ibid.

24. Small Business Administration, *The Small Business Economy: A Report to the President* (Washington, D.C.: U.S. Government Printing Office, 2005).

25. Fairlie and Robb, *Race, Families, and Business Success.*

26. Fairlie and Robb, "Why Are Black-Owned Businesses Less Successful?"

27. Ibid.

28. Ibid.

29. Ibid.

30. Ibid.

31. Ibid.

32. P. Reynolds, *Entrepreneurship in the United States (Miami: Florida International University, 2005)*.

33. K. Cavalluzzo and J. Wolken, "Small Business Loan Turndowns, Personal Wealth, and Discrimination," (working paper, Georgetown University, 2002).

34. Office of Advocacy, *Small Business Economy*.

35. Cavalluzzo and Wolken, "Small Business Loan Turndowns."

36. Fairlie and Robb, *Race, Families, and Business Success*.

Chapter 10. How Valuable Is the Average Start-Up?

1. D. Blanchflower, "Self-Employment: More May Not Be Better," *Swedish Economic Policy Review* 11, no. 2 (2004): 15–74; D. Bogenhold and U. Staber, "The Decline and Rise of Self-Employment," *Work, Employment and Society* 5, no. 2 (1991): 223–39.

2. "The Wonderland Economy," http://www.inc.com/magazine/19950515/2686.html.

3. P. Reynolds and S. White, *The Entrepreneurial Process: Economic Growth, Men, Women, and Minorities* (Westport, Conn.: Greenwood, 1997).

4. "States to Get Business Development Training," http://www.stateline.org/live/ViewPage.action?siteNodeId=136&languageId=1&contentId=14039.

5. "President Bush Addresses Small Business Week Conference," http://www.whitehouse.gov/news/releases/2006/04/20060413-2.html.

6. D. Blanchflower, "Self-Employment in OECD Countries," *Labour Economics* 7 (2000): 471–505; E. Hurst and A. Lusardi, "Liquidity Constraints, Household Wealth, and Entrepreneurship," *Journal of Political Economy* 112, no. 2 (2004): 319–47.

7. Blanchflower, "Self-Employment: More May Not Be Better"; Hurst and Lusardi, "Liquidity Constraints."

8. A. Mathur, "A Spatial Model of the Impact of State Bankruptcy Exemptions on Entrepreneurship" (report for the U.S. Small Business Administration, contract no. SBAHQ-03-M-0533, 2005); Y. Georgellis and H. Wall, "Entrepreneurship and the Policy Environment" (working paper no. 2002–019B, Federal Reserve Bank of St. Louis, 2004); W. Fan and M. White, "Personal Bankruptcy and the Level of Entrepreneurial Activity," *Journal of Law and Economics* 46 (2003): 543–67.

9. W. Gentry and G. Hubbard, "'Success Taxes,' Entrepreneurial Entry, and Innovation" (working paper, Columbia University, New York, 2004); D. Bruce and T. Gurley, "Taxes and Entrepreneurial Activity: An Empirical Investigation Using Longitudinal Tax Return Data" (report for the U.S. Small Business Administration, contract no. SBAHQ-04-M-0521, 2005); M. Robson and C. Wren, "Marginal and Average Tax Rates and the Incentive for Self-Employment," *Southern Eco-*

nomic Journal 65, no. 4 (1999): 757–73; D. Blau, "A Time Series Analysis of Self-Employment in the United States," *Journal of Political Economy* 95, no. 3 (1987): 445–65; R. Carroll, D. Holtz-Eakin, M. Rider, and H. Rosen, "Entrepreneurs, Income Taxes and Investment" (working paper no. 6374, National Bureau of Economic Research, 1998); R. Carroll, D. Holtz-Eakin, M. Rider, and H. Rosen, "Income Taxes and Entrepreneurs' Use of Labor," *Journal of labor Economics* 18, no. 2 (2000): 324–51; D. Holtz-Eakin and H. Rosen, "Economic Policy and the Start-Up, Survival, and Growth of Entrepreneurial Ventures" (report for the U.S. Small Business Administration, Syracuse University, 2001).

10. Blanchflower, "Self-Employment in OECD Countries"; Hurst and Lusardi, "Liquidity Constraints."

11. Bogenhold and Staber, "Decline and Rise."

12. D. Holtz-Eakin, "Public Policy toward Entrepreneurship," *Small Business Economics* 15 (2000): 283–91.

13. Bogenhold and Staber, "Decline and Rise."

14. Ibid.

15. Holtz-Eakin, "Public Policy."

16. T. Garrett, "Entrepreneurs Thrive in America," *Bridges,* spring 2005, www.stlouisfed.org/publications/br/2005/a/pages/2-article.html.

17. "The Wonderland Economy," http://www.inc.com/magazine/19950515/2686.html.

18. National Governors Association Center for Best Practices, *A Governor's Guide to Strengthening State Entrepreneurship Policy* (Washington, D.C.: National Governors Association, 2004).

19. Reynolds and White, *Entrepreneurial Process;* P. Reynolds and W. Maki, "Business Volatility and Economic Growth" (report for the U.S. Small Business Administration, contract no. SBA-4118-OA-89, 1990); P. Davidsson and M. Henrekson, "Determinants and Prevalence of Start-Ups and High-Growth Firms," *Small Business Economics* 19 (2002): 81–104.

20. D. Audretsch and Z. Acs, "New Firm Start-Ups, Technology, and Macroeconomic Fluctuations," *Small Business Economics* 6 (1994): 439–49; D. Grant, "The Political Economy of New Business Formation across the American States, 1970–1985," *Social Science Quarterly* 77, no. 1 (1996): 28–42; P. Reynolds, "Autonomous Firm Dynamics and Economic Growth in the United States, 1986–1990," *Regional Studies* 28, no. 4 (1994): 429–42; D. Keeble and S. Walker, "New Firms, Small Firms, and Dead Firms: Spatial Patterns in the United Kingdom," *Regional Studies* 28, no. 4 (1994): 411–27; J. Ritsila and H. Tervo, "Effects of Unemployment on New Firm Formation: Micro-Level Panel Data Evidence from Finland," *Small Business Economics* 10 (2002): 103–15; P. Reynolds, "Autonomous Firm Dynamics and Economic Growth in the United States, 1986–1990," *Regional Studies* 28, no. 4 (1993): 429–42; P. Davidsson, L. Lindmark, and C. Olafsson, "New Firm

Formation and Regional Development in Sweden," *Regional Studies* 28, no. 4 (1994): 347–58; Advanced Research Technologies, "The Innovation-Entrepreneurship Nexus" (report for the U.S. Small Business Administration, contract no. SBAHQ-03-M-00353, 2005); D. Audretsch and M. Fritsch, "Growth Regimes over Time and Space," *Regional Studies* 36, no. 2 (2002): 113–24; P. Reynolds, M. Hay, and S. Camp, *Global Entrepreneurship Monitor: 1999 Executive Report* (Kansas City, Mo.: Ewing Marion Kauffman Foundation, 1999); A. Zacharakis, W. Bygrave, and D. Shepherd, *Global Entrepreneurship Monitor: National Entrepreneurship Assessment, United States of America* (Kansas City, Mo.: Kauffman Center for Entrepreneurial Leadership, 2000); D. Birch, *Job Creation in America* (New York: Free Press, 1987); Reynolds and White, *Entrepreneurial Process;* B. Kirchhoff, *Entrepreneurship and Dynamic Capitalism: The Economics of Business Formation and Growth* (Westport, Conn.: Praeger, 1994); M. Carree, A. Van Stel, R. Thurik, and S. Wennekers, "Economic Development and Business Ownership: An Analysis Using Data of 23 OECD Countries in the Period 1976–1996," *Small Business Economics* 19 (2002): 271–90.

21. Z. Acs, P. Arenius, M. Hay, and M. Minniti, *Global Entrepreneurship Monitor 2004 Executive Report* (Babson Park, Mass.: Babson College, 2004).

22. Z. Acs and C. Armington, "Using Census BITS to Explore Entrepreneurship, Geography and Economic Growth" (report for the U.S. Small Business Administration, contract no. SBA-HQ-03-M0534, 2005).

23. J. Haltiwanger, J. Lane, and J. Speltzer, "Productivity Differences across Employers: The Roles of Employer Size, Age, and Human Capital," *American Economic Review Papers and Proceedings* 89, no. 2 (1999): 94–98.

24. Bogenhold and Staber, "Decline and Rise."

25. Blanchflower, "Self-Employment in OECD Countries."

26. Z. Acs, C. Armington, and A. Robb, "Measures of Job Flow Dynamics in the U.S. Economy" (discussion paper, U.S. Department of the Census, Center for Economic Studies, Upper Marlboro, Md., 1999); P. Reynolds, N. Carter, W. Gartner, and P. Greene, "The Prevalence of Nascent Entrepreneurs in the United States: Evidence from the Panel Study of Entrepreneurial Dynamics," *Small Business Economics* 23 (2004): 263–84.

27. "The Wonderland Economy," http://www.inc.com/magazine/19950515/2686.html.

28. Z. Acs and C. Armington, "Employment Growth and Entrepreneurial Activity in Cities," *Regional Studies* 38, no. 8 (2004): 911–27.

29. http://data.bls.gov/cgi-bin/surveymost.

30. S. Davis and J. Haltiwanger, "Gross Job Creation, Gross Job Destruction, and Employment Reallocation," *Quarterly Journal of Economics* 107 (1992): 819–62.

31. Z. Acs and C. Armington, *Entrepreneurship, Geography, and American Economic Growth* (Cambridge: Cambridge University Press).

32. Davis, Haltiwanger, and Schuh, *Job Creation and Destruction.*

33. A. Knaup, "Survival and Longevity in the Business Employment Dynamics Data," *Monthly Labor Review,* May 2005, 50–56; H. Persson, "The Survival and Growth of New Establishments in Sweden, 1987–1995," *Small Business Economics* 23 (2004): 423–40; J. Wagner, "The Post-Entry Performance of New Small Firms in German Manufacturing Industries," *Journal of Industrial Economics* 42, no. 2 (1994): 141–54; Kirchhoff, *Entrepreneurship and Dynamic Capitalism.*

34. Knaup, "Survival and Longevity."

35. Kirchhoff, *Entrepreneurship and Dynamic Capitalism;* Knaup, "Survival and Longevity"; Persson, "Survival and Growth"; Wagner, "Post-Entry Performance."

36. Reynolds and White, *Entrepreneurial Process.*

37. J. Wagner, "Firm Size and Job Quality: A Survey of the Evidence from Germany," *Small Business Economics* 9 (1997): 411–425.

38. National Federation of Independent Businesses, *Small Business Policy Guide* (Washington, D.C.: National Federation of Independent Businesses, 2000).

39. Reynolds and White, *Entrepreneurial Process.*

40. D. Bernstein, "Fringe Benefits and Small Businesses: Evidence from the Federal Reserve Board Small Business Survey," *Applied Economics* 34 (2002): 2063–67.

41. A. Wellington, "Health Insurance Coverage and Entrepreneurship," *Contemporary Economic Policy* 19, no. 4 (2001): 465–78; J. Gruber and J. Poterba, "Tax Incentives and the Decision to Purchase Health Insurance: Evidence from the Self-Employed," *Quarterly Journal of Economics* 109, no. 3 (1994): 701–33; A. Alba-Ramirez, "Self-Employment in the Midst of Unemployment: The Case of Spain and the United States," *Applied Economics* 26 (1994): 189–204.

42. Kaiser Family Foundation, "Employer Health Benefits," 1995, www.kff.org/insurance.

43. C. Armington and Z. Acs, "Job Creation and Persistence in Services and Manufacturing" (Discussion Papers on Entrepreneurship, Growth, and Public Policy, Max Planck Institute, no. 1604, 2003).

Conclusion

1. Venture Impact 2004, http://www.nvca.org/pdf/VentureImpact2004.pdf.

2. P. Gompers and J. Lerner, *The Money of Invention: How Venture Capital Creates New Wealth* (Boston: Harvard Business School, 2001).

3. Ibid.

Index